The Covenant of Grace

Samuel Petto

THE

GREAT MYSTERY

OF THE

COVENANT OF GRACE:

OR THE

DIFFERENCE

BETWEEN THE

Old and New Covenant
STATED AND EXPLAINED.

By SAMUEL PETTO,
LATE MINISTER OF THE GOSPEL AT SUDBURY IN SUFFOLK.

2020
Solid Ground Christian Books

SOLID GROUND CHRISTIAN BOOKS
1682 SW Pancoast Street
Port St Lucie FL 34987

(205) 587-4480

mike.sgcb@gmail.com
solid-ground-books.com

ISBN 978-1-59925-520-0

This edition published by
Tentmaker Publications
121 Hartshill Road
Stoke-on-Trent
Staffs. UK
ST4 7LU

© 2007

Previously published
Alexander Thomson, Aberdeen.
1820.

This edition has been retypeset with some of the language
and punctuation updated.

Original Publisher's Note

THE Publisher, having received many solicitations to undertake the republication of this Work, is happy to add the names of the following Ministers, entirely approving and recommending it, as a judicious and enlightened performance, well worthy the attention of Christians of every denomination.

Dr. M'Crie, Edinburgh.
Professor Paxton, Edinburgh.
Rev. George Moir, Edinburgh.
Dr. Pringle, Perth.
Rev. James Aird, Rattray.
—— Matthew Fraser, Dundee.
—— Adam Blair, South Ferry.
—— W. Ramage, Kirriemuir.
—— James Hay, Alyth.
—— Alex. Balfour, Lethendy.
—— David Waddell, Shiels.
—— Pat. Robertson, Craigdam.
—— J. Ronaldson, Auchmacoy.
—— John Bunyan, Whitehill.
—— James Millar, Huntly.

Dr. Kidd, Aberdeen.
Rev. A. Gunn, Wattan.
—— Niel Kennedy, Logie Elgin.
—— Hector Bethune, Alness.
—— Hugh Ross, Fearn.
—— Thos. Monro, Kiltearn.
—— John M'Donald, Thurso.
—— A. Stewart, Wick.
—— John Monro, Nigg.
—— Isaac Kitchin, Nairn.
—— David Anderson, Boghole.
—— Thomas Stark, Forres.
—— Simon Somerville, Elgin.
—— Robert Crawford, Elgin.

CONTENTS.

		Page
INTRODUCTION	Mark Jones	9
TO THE READER	Samuel Petto	29
TO THE READER	John Owen	41
CHAP. I.	Of a Covenant in general, and the distribution of the Covenant into that of works and of grace,	47
CHAP. II.	Of the oneness of the Covenant with Jesus Christ and us,	59
CHAP. III.	Of Christ as the sum of the Covenant,	71
CHAP. IV.	Of the date of Covenant Mercies,	79
CHAP. V.	General inferences from the whole,	83
CHAP. VI.	Of the Old and New Covenant, what they are, and how distinct,	93
CHAP. VII.	Of the nature of the Mount Sinai Covenant,	113
CHAP. VIII.	Of the Sinai Covenant, whether ceased or continuing,	153
CHAP. IX.	Of the good that was in the Sinai Covenant,	165
CHAP. X.	Of the differences between the Old and New Covenant, and the excellency of the latter above the former,	169
CHAP. XI.	Of the time of first coming into Covenant,	211
CHAP. XII.	Of the evidences of interest in the New Covenant,	227
CHAP. XIII.	Of the use of Absolute Promises,	235
CHAP. XIV.	Of those that are called Conditional Promises,	243

INTRODUCTION.

If John Owen is the forgotten man of English theology,[1] it may rightly be said that Samuel Petto is the unknown man of English theology.[2] However, with the timely re-publication of this book by Tentmaker coupled with the recent resurgence of interest in Puritanism,[3] Petto's name will, it is hoped, become more familiar to those wanting to understand the theological context of the seventeenth century. Indeed, several of his writings, which will be introduced below, deal with some of the principal theological controversies in the seventeenth century; controversies that will now be better understood now that his excellent work, *The Great Mystery of the Covenant of Grace* or *The Difference Between the Old and New Covenant Stated and Explained*, has been made more accessible to students of English Puritanism.

Tentmaker has done the church a real service in making available Petto's work on the covenants, especially for the

---

[1] There has, however, been a recent renaissance of interest in Owen during the last ten years which is correcting this fact first suggested by Carl Trueman.

[2] There is, to my knowledge, no secondary literature devoted specifically to Petto. However, scholars of the seventeenth century occasionally refer to Petto in passing. See Richard L. Greaves. "John Bunyan and Covenant Thought in the Seventeenth Century," *Church History* 36 (June 1967), 152, 162; Ivan Bunn, *A Trial of Witches: A Seventeenth-Century Witchcraft Prosecution* (Routledge, 1997), 184; Ian Bostridge, *Witchcraft and Its Transformations, c. 1650 - c. 1750* (OUP, 2003), 28; Geoffrey F. Nuttall, *The Holy Spirit in Puritan Faith and Experience* (Univ. of Chicago Press, 1992), 12.

[3] There is a great deal of debate over what the term "Puritanism" means and who is a "Puritan". In this essay I am using it in its broadest sense, thus including Protestants both inside and outside the Church of England. Petto, then, is in some sense both a Puritan, by virtue of his theology, and a nonconformist.

contemporary reader who will no doubt be pleased with its accessibility. Unfortunately, there are few modern reprints of Puritan works devoted specifically to the doctrine of the covenant.[4] Thankfully, however, we now have Petto to look to as we read this work commended by Owen who declares Petto to be a "Worthy Author" who has labored "unto good success"; and, for my own part, I agree with Owen's assessment.

In this introductory essay I would like to (1) give a brief biographical sketch of Petto; (2) review his other writings; and (3) introduce you to his very important work on the covenants.

BIOGRAPHY

Samuel Petto (c.1624–1711) was among the ejected ministers with the passing of the Act of Uniformity (1662). He matriculated from St Catharine's College, Cambridge, on 19 March 1645 and graduated MA in 1648. That same year he became "Preacher of the Gospel" of Sandcroft in Suffolk. All that we know of his family life is that his wife's name was Mary and they baptized their son Samuel at South Elmham St Cross on 27 April 1654. Mary, unfortunately, died sometime in 1655.

While still preaching at Sandcroft, as a Congregationalist minister, Petto mentioned in a letter, dated 17 August 1658, that many in Suffolk were either opposed to or had reservations about infant baptism. It is not surprising, therefore, that two of his works defended the practice of infant baptism at a time when the paedobaptism was being criticized by Baptist theologians such as Nehemiah Coxe, John Tombes, and Thomas Grantham.

In 1660 Petto was ejected from Sandcroft. He moved to the area of Norfolk and continued his gospel ministry. Despite the political change and attitude towards the nonconformists,

---

[4] Those feeling particularly ambitious might wish to consult Owen's recently translated work *Theologoumena Pantodapa*. See John Owen, *Biblical Theology*, trans. Stephen P. Westcott (PA: Soli Deo Gloria Publications, 1994).

Petto preached to a crowd of over 300 at Gillingham. During this time Petto was able to finish his various writing projects. With the passing of the Conventicle Act (1664) and Five Mile Act (1665), Petto, on May 1672, was forced to be licensed a congregational teacher at his own house at Wortwell. Two years later he began his long ministry in Sudbury, Suffolk.

At this time in Sudbury there was no settled minister in the town. Typically, services took place in conventicles; the teaching being contingent upon men like Petto who risked imprisonment because of their continued nonconformity. Many in Sudbury hoped to petition parliament to provide proper maintenance for Petto. Stephen Wright remarks, "... in 1684 local tories alleged that the former mayor John Catesby had so favoured dissenters, that 'Mr Petto the Nonconformist preacher in the barn' had been unmolested there for ten years, only once having been brought before the quarter sessions, and then not punished."[5] The petition to help support nonconformist ministers like Petto ultimately failed however. This was not Petto's only problem. On 1677, in a letter to Increase Mather, Petto speaks of his daughter, born to his second wife Martha, who has "become a prodigal".[6] Less than a year later, however, the "prodigal" had returned.

Petto's correspondence with Mather gives us important clues into the value of the ever-growing list of printed works, especially to ministers who faced particular challenges due to the rise of heretical groups (i.e Socinians, Quakers, etc.). For example, in a letter written sometime in 1672, Petto writes: "I cannot but thank you for the particulars contained in your letter; for which I have nothing to return . . . . but the Transactions of ye last year. . . . . The Discourse of Mr. Boyle concerning the Origine and Vertue of Gems is not yet printed off: when it is, you shall not faile, God permitting, of

---

[5] Stephen Wright, 'Petto, Samuel (c.1624–1711)', *Oxford Dictionary of National Biography*, Oxford University Press, 2004 [http://www.oxforddnb.com/view/article/22067, accessed 5 May 2007].

[6] 'Letters of Samuel Petto', Collections of the Massachusetts Historical Society, 4th ser., 8 (1868), 341.

having a Copy of it sent you by ye first ship y^t shall goe for y^r parts after its publication."[7] Similarly, in 1677, Petto writes: "I also intend to send with it [his letter], Dr Owen of the reason of faith";[8] and again in 1678, "I have herewith sent you three books *Christianismus Christianandus,* and M^r Ny's paper, of a question which is much debated here, . . . also Mr Troughton of Divine Providence, ... if I knew what other such bookes would be acceptable to you, I would send them."[9]

In 1690 Petto's second wife, Martha, had bore him twelve children. References to Petto in recent contemporary literature focus on Petto's polemics against the rising practice of witchcraft in the late 1600s. His opposition to witchcraft was evident in his 1693 publication of *A Faithful Narrative.* During his remaining years Petto remained in Sudbury where he continued to gain the esteem of the dissenters. In 1711 Petto died in Sudbury and was buried in on 21 September in the churchyard of All Saints.

LITERATURE REVIEW

Petto's *Works* cover various issues that arose in his Pastoral context. They are, therefore, varied, covering topics such as witchcraft, eschatology, pneumatology, paedobaptism, and covenant theology. Besides his lengthy work on the place of the covenant at Sinai in relation to the covenant of grace, Petto defended the Reformed practice of infant baptism in his work, *Infant Baptism of Christ's Appointment* (London, 1687), aware that "many books have been already written by others on this subject".[10] In this work Petto positively

---

[7] Massachusetts Historical Society, Proceedings, 1st Series, xvi. 248

[8] *Ibid.,* 431.

[9] *Ibid.,* 343.

[10] Samuel Petto, *Infant baptism of Christ's appointment, or A discovery of infants interest in the covenant with Abraham: shewing who are the spiritual seed and who the fleshly seed. Together, with the improvement of covenant interest by parents and children* (London, 1687), A2.

develops his argument along covenantal lines arguing for the inclusion of infants in the new covenant church based upon the continuity of the covenant of grace, especially the administration of the Abrahamic covenant which, in substance, remained determinative for the new covenant church. The work demonstrates, among other things, that Petto's arguments were principally fueled by exegetical considerations; texts from Scripture abound as Petto develops his case for the inclusion of the seed of believers into the covenant community known as the church.

The title of Petto's second work on infant baptism, titled *Infant-baptism vindicated from the exceptions of Mr. Thomas Grantham* (London, 1687), shows that Baptist polemics were very much alive in the seventeenth century. This work is a short reply (18 pages) to Thomas Grantham, who for many years was the principal minister among the general Baptists. Petto refers to Grantham's exceptions as "Presumption, and no proof". In this reply Petto lays out Grantham's objections to his previous work and then seeks to answer them not by restating his arguments from his first work, but clarifying them against, what Petto perceives to be, gross misunderstandings.

Catechetical training became something of a norm among Christian, particularly Calvinistic, families in seventeenth-century England. Given Petto's pastoral context where some doubted the legitimacy of infant baptism, it is not surprising that Petto wrote *A short scriptural catechisme for little children* (London, 1672). This goal of this catechism, in the form of questions and answers, with scriptural proofs, is to confirm to children their blessed state in the covenant of grace while at the same time urging them to lay hold of the promises held out to them.

Besides infant baptism, the doctrine of the Holy Spirit was of crucial importance to Petto. His work *The Voice of the Spirit* (London, 1654) represents his earliest – and perhaps most intriguing – work. The structure of the work falls under several questions. First, what is the witnessing work of the Spirit? Second, how does the Spirit witness to a soul in adoption?

Third, who are capable of attaining the witnessings of the Spirit? Fourth, how may a soul know its enjoyment of them? And finally, by what means may a soul attain them? As in his other works, there is a deep experiential theology bound up in a desire to present a pneumatology based on exegesis that mitigates against the view that the work of the Spirit can be understood apart from special revelation. In this work Petto is aware that if we emphasize the word without the Sprit we will dry up, if we emphasize the Spirit without the word we will blow up, but if we emphasize both we will grow up, thus echoing Owen who commented "[h]e that would utterly separate the Spirit from the word" may as well burn his Bible.[11] Appended to this work is *Roses from Sharon or Sweet Experiences reached out by Christ to some of his beloved ones in this wilderness* (London, 1654). This work is especially important in terms of the understanding seventeenth-century conversion narratives. The narratives are the spiritual experiences of his Christian friends with the intention of showing the nature of God's dealings with his saints. What we learn is that the Christian experience is one of deep intimacy between the believer and Christ; a relationship best expressed in the Song of Solomon between Christ and the church.

The Puritans excelled in many areas. However, eschatology was not one of them. Petto's work, *Revelation Unveiled* (London, 1693) is no exception to this trend. Petto is aware that many have failed in their understanding of the book of Revelation, especially with regards to date-setting. But, nevertheless, his exposition proceeds; often running into the same errors of his contemporaries.[12] In typical Puritan

---

[11] *The Works of John Owen.* 24 vols. (London: Johnstone and Hunter, 1850-5), 3:192. Hereafter cited *Works* 1, pp.

[12] For example, Goodwin took the year 1666 as the expiration of popery. This date is arrived at by looking at "666" as the time of the beast's ending. This is added to the "1000" years in Rev. 20. The expiration date is, therefore, 1666 years after Christ. Further, based on Rev. 13:5 the 42 months of the beast's rule is equivalent 1260 days (cf. Rev. 12:6). Goodwin then subtracts 1260 from 1666 and

fashion, the conversion of the Jews plays an important role in Petto's eschatology. This work, like his work on the covenants, is fairly representative of seventeenth-century Puritan theology; and for that reason it is helpful, for it helps us to understand not just the theology of the Puritans, but also the political climate in which they lived and how they understood, what Baxter called, "this incredible age" in light of the historical unfolding of events in the book of Revelation.

When Petto is mentioned in recent secondary literature, it is almost always in reference to his work *A Faithful Narrative* (London, 1693). The full title gives us an important clue into what Petto's goal is in this work. It reads, *A Faithful Narrative of the Wonderful and Extraordinary Fits Which Mr. Tho. Spatchet (Late of Dunwich and Cookly) Was Under by Witchcraft, or, A Mysterious Providence in His Even Unparallel'd Fits With an Account of His First Falling into, Behaviour Under, and (in Part) Deliverance Out of Them : Wherein Are Several Remarkable Instances of the Gracious Effects of Fervent Prayer*. This book was printed many years after Petto had witnessed Spatchet's, among others, extraordinary fits; fits that, according to Petto, were of such a nature that one could not understand them as a purely natural phenomena. The phenomena was, of course, disturbing to Petto who wrote the work in the hope of "awakening some to seek freedom from the dominion of Satan" who has power over both body and soul. Again, the value in this work shows that belief in demon possession was very much alive in the seventeenth century and the only cure for it is Christ, who sets sinners free from Satan's bondage.

The Great Mystery of the Covenant of Grace or The Difference Between the Old and New Covenant Stated and Explained

The history of Reformed covenant theology has not always been well understood.[13] Richard Greaves refers to Petto, as

---

comes to 406 A.D. Hence, Pope Innocent, who assumed the papacy in 401, begins the rise of the beast (see *Works*, 3:73ff.).

[13] See John Von Rohr, *The Covenant of Grace in Puritan Thought* (Atlanta: Scholars Press, 1986), 1-36.

well as Owen, Goodwin, and Ussher, as "strict Calvinists" who belong to one of three different groups in the covenant tradition.[14] Greaves mistakenly posits a tension between the Calvin-Perkins-Ames tradition, which supposedly distinguished itself by promulgating an unconditional character to the covenant of grace, and the Zwingli-Bullinger-Tyndale tradition, which is characterized by the conditional nature of the covenant of grace. Greaves is wrong to place these two groups in tension with one another. The truth is that both "groups" understood the covenant of grace as having conditions; namely, faith and obedience. However, because the faith and obedience that is required in the covenant of grace is the "gift of God" it may also be said that the covenant of grace is some sense unconditional.[15] These nuances have often been missing in twentieth-century historiography.

Another problematic descriptive-historical study is Ernest Kevan's influential work, *The Grace of Law*, where he distinguishes between those who viewed Sinai as a works covenant and those who viewed it as properly belonging to the covenant of grace.[16] The issue is, however, more complex than Kevan would have us believe, for there are a number of different ways in which the covenant at Sinai was viewed in relation to the covenant of grace.[17] Fortunately, we are now

---

[14] Richard Greaves. "John Bunyan and Covenant Thought in the Seventeenth Century," *Church History* 36 (June 1967), p. 152.

[15] For example, Owen writes: "I do not say the covenant of grace is absolutely without conditions, if by conditions we intend the duties of obedience which God requireth of us in and by virtue of that covenant; but this I say, the principal promises thereof are not in the first place *remunerative* of our obedience in the covenant, but *efficaciously assumptive* of us in the covenant, and establishing or confirming the covenant." *Works* 23:68-9.

[16] Kevan, Ernest Frederick, *The Grace of Law; A Study in Puritan Theology* (Grand Rapids: Baker Book House, 1965), 113-116.

[17] For example, see: Mark W. Karlberg, *Covenant Theology in Reformed Perspective: Collected Essays and Book Reviews in Historical, Biblical, and Systematic Theology* (Eugene, Or: Wipf and Stock, 2000), 17-57.

able to re-evaluate this much misunderstood issue in light of the re-publication (no pun intended) of Petto's work.[18] How then does Petto fit into this stream of thought regarding the Mosaic covenant as it pertains to the history of redemption? It is hoped that in the foregoing we will show how Petto's work is representative of many seventeenth-century Puritans. Indeed, the list of ministers who approved of the work speaks volumes about both the quality and the relative orthodoxy of the work in its seventeenth-century theological context.

The reader of Petto's work will no doubt have a particular interest in how Sinai relates to the covenant of grace. However, the first five chapters are principally concerned with an exposition of the covenant of grace in an attempt to lay the foundation for the rest of the work that deals with Sinai's role in the history of redemption.

Petto's exposition of the covenant of grace is fairly typical of Reformed theology. As a result, his law-gospel antithesis represents a Reformed approach, against a Lutheran one, to the covenants, especially the Abrahamic.[19] That is to say, under the rubric of the covenant of grace, with both Eden and Sinai in mind, Petto places a significant emphasis on the third use of the law (*tertius usus legis*) while, at the same time, not omitting second use (*usus elenchticus* or *pedagogicus*), the favorite use of the Lutherans.

---

[18] The position set out by Petto sees Sinai as a *republication* or *revival* of the covenant of works. Similarly, Owen argues that the covenant at Sinai "*revived*, declared, and expressed *all the commands of* [the covenant of works] *in the decalogue*" (emphasis mine). *Works*, 23:77.

[19] A good example of the different application of the law-gospel antithesis is seen in comparing Bullinger (Reformed) with Luther (Lutheran) on Gen. 17. Luther's law-gospel hermeneutic forces him into a form of Dispensationalism, where Gen. 17 is a covenant of law for the Jew only, in *opposition* to the New Covenant. In contrast, Bullinger and the Reformed understood Gen. 17 to be a covenant for the church for all ages, consistent with the coming of Christ, and therefore part of the covenant of grace.

Axiomatic for Petto is the necessary demarcation of God's covenants with man into the covenants of works (*foedus operum*) and grace (*foedus naturae*). This distinction is laid out in chapter one and forms the basis for understanding Sinai in relation to the covenant of grace. What is interesting about Petto's exposition is that he, unlike Owen, posits two, not three covenants. By the mid-seventeenth century, the covenant of redemption (*pactum salutis*) was understood as a pre-temporal agreement between the Father and the Son that formed the basis of the temporal covenant of grace. Though Petto does not make this distinction, he clearly speaks of the pre-temporality of the covenant of grace in chapters two and four.[20]

In agreement with Reformed covenant theologians, Petto sees the covenant of grace inaugurated with the *protoevangelium* (Gen. 3:15) and renewed and applied to the patriarchs. This covenant is made with Jesus Christ "on the behalf of men" and so is "made with us in Christ".[21] The antithesis between works and grace is not, however, forced by Petto so as to leave no room for works in the covenant of grace and grace in the covenant of works. At this point, his language here is perhaps confusing and he fails to make the explicit distinction in the covenant of works between salvific grace (not present) and condescending grace (present); though he does hint at the idea.[22] But, as one moves through the work, specifically after chapter five, Petto becomes clearer on the works element in the covenant of grace.

---

[20] Elements of the covenant of redemption can be traced back to Calvin, particularly instructive is his exegesis of John 17. Certainly, it was given explicit attention by Cocceius, Witsius, and Owen. Turretin, however, spoke only of the covenants of grace and works, but he also has a pre-temporal aspect to his exposition of the covenant of grace. I am aware that Owen had a fourfold covenant schema, but Sinai was a revival of the covenant of works, so it is possible to argue that his schema was threefold as well.

[21] Petto, *The difference between* ... 56.

[22] *Ibid.* Cf. Owen, *Works* 6:471-2; 23:68; 19:337; 23:116.

The goal of the covenant of grace, in Owen, for example, is to bring sinners into union with Jesus Christ.²³ Petto, similarly, argues that the salvation of the elect is based upon their union with Christ the head who appropriates to his seed the promises and blessings associated with the covenant, albeit to a lesser degree than he receives himself. Like in Goodwin's theology, the doctrines of adoption and union with Christ are central to Petto's theology. By virtue of union with Christ, believers are secure in their surety who is the foundation and substance of the covenant, the reality of all the types and shadows; indeed, he is the "excellence, marrow, and sweetness ... the covenant of the people".²⁴

As mentioned above, Petto differentiates between the pre-temporality (Isa. 42:1-8) and the temporality (Gen. 3:15) of the covenant of grace. Even though he refers to Owen, he does not use Owen's distinction of the *foedus gratiae* and *pactum salutis*. One area in which work needs to be done is the Holy Spirit's role in the *pactum salutis*. Much attention has been given to the role of the Father and the Son, but few, including Petto, have given prominence to the Spirit's role in redemption, particularly the pretemporal "counsel of peace" (Zech. 6:13).²⁵

To understand the covenant, it is best to compare the covenant of works, made with Adam, with the covenant of grace, made with Christ on behalf of his people, and to compare Sinai with the new covenant. The former comparison has been set out by Petto as "do this and live" (works) versus "live and do this" (grace); the latter comparison now occupies his attention, to which we now turn.²⁶

---

²³ *Works* 21:146-150; 3:516.

²⁴ Petto, 76.

²⁵ For a brief summary of the role of the Spirit in the *pactum salutis* in Johannes Cocceius' theology, see: Willem Van Asselt, *The Federal Theology of Johannes Cocceius (1603-1669)*. Studies in the history of Christian thought, v. 100 (Leiden: Brill, 2001), 233-36.

²⁶ On page 111 Petto writes of the "Live and do this" principle, an outworking of his law-gospel hermeneutic: "Christians ought to perform all duty, in conformity to Jesus Christ, in the way to salvation, but not in the least as that which justifies or saves."

Obedience to the law in its three parts – moral, civil, and ceremonial – requires obedience as a condition of the covenant at Sinai. Because Sinai, called the 'old covenant' by Petto (and others) is understood in covenantal terms, temporal mercies are promised to Israel upon condition of their perfect obedience. The new covenant is better than the old on account of four things. First, the law is inscribed on the hearts of men in the new (Heb. 8:10), whereas in the old it was infrequent due to the powerful external obligations. Second, in the new covenant, God communes more intimately with his people. Third, whereas in the old the Israelites had "some dark, typical, shadowy representations of God and Jesus Christ; under the new, they shall have those that are more clear …"[27] Fourth, forgiveness in the old was typical, but in the new it is real. In setting out these differences, Petto asks the important question "Whether this better covenant be distinct from that at mount Sinai? Are they two covenants, or but one?"[28]

Petto answers that the "new or better covenant is distinct from that at mount Sinai. It is usually said, that they are two administrations or dispensations of the same covenant: I think, they are not merely one and the same covenant, diversely administered, but they are two covenants."[29] While some scholars have pressed many unwarranted tensions between Reformed covenant theologians, it is undeniable that the Reformed were not all agreed on whether Sinai belonged to the covenant of grace. On the one hand, Calvin and Bullinger, in the sixteenth century, argue that the covenant made at Sinai was part of the covenant of grace but it was administered legally and served a pedagogical function. Turretin, writing in the seventeenth century, echoes similar thoughts to those of Calvin and Bullinger: "It pleased God to administer *the covenant of grace* in this period [from Moses to Christ] under a rigid legal economy – both on account of

---

[27] *Ibid.*, 100.
[28] *Ibid.*, 102.
[29] *Ibid.*, 103.

the condition of the people still in infancy and on account of the putting off of the advent of Christ and the satisfaction to be rendered by him" (emphasis mine).[30] However, Petto falls in line with the likes of Thomas Boston and John Owen who viewed Sinai as a different covenant altogether.

Petto cautiously proceeds to argue that though Sinai does not belong to the covenant of grace, it still "had a special relation to the covenant of grace."[31] Moreover, "the elect were saved in one and the same way, for substance and essence, in all ages, *viz.* by grace through a Mediator, by faith in him."[32] By maintaining the unity of the covenant of grace in all ages, Petto, as well as Owen and Boston, have a great deal in common with their sixteenth-century forefathers, Calvin and Bullinger. Their insistence upon demarcating between Sinai and the new covenant is based on exegetical considerations; that is to say, the force of Hebrews 8:6ff. and 2 Corinthians 3:6ff. leave the likes of Petto and Owen no choice but to separate the old and the new.

And it is nothing but exegetical considerations that forces Petto to press on in his argument. For example, the new covenant and Sinai are "contradistinguished, and so must be two distinct covenants; else the opposition were groundless – Jer. xxxi. 31, 32."[33] His references to the book of Hebrews, where Owen labored most, abound; for in it several passages leave no room for doubt that Sinai is distinct from the new covenant.[34] The value in Petto's exegetical work is found in his attempt to maintain the unity of the covenant of grace while at the same time being sensitive to the various passages in Scripture that posit a sharp distinction between the old and new covenants. It is an attempt that, for my own part, is largely successful.

---

[30] Francis Turretin, *Institutes of Elenctic Theology*, trans. George Musgrace Giger and edition James T. Dennison, Jr., vol. 2 (Phillipsburg, 1992-97), 227.

[31] Petto, 103.

[32] *Ibid.*

[33] *Ibid.*, 106.

[34] The texts for Petto are: Heb. 7:18; 8:7, 13; 10:9;

The dangers of antinomianism and legalism are not far from Petto's mind at this point in his work. He speaks of a "sinful mixing of these two covenants"[35] whereupon the works of believers are not to be joined with Christ's works as a means of procuring salvation. Notwithstanding this however, Petto rejects the charge of antinomianism.[36] We shall turn to the place of the law in the Christian life below.

In chapter seven, Petto turns to the specific nature of the old covenant. One of the chief strengths in Petto's work is the way in which he often summarizes his intended purpose in each chapter. Regarding the covenant at Sinai, he writes, "[i]n general, it was a covenant of works, as to be fulfilled by Jesus Christ, but not so to Israel. Or, it was the covenant of grace as to its legal condition to be performed by Jesus Christ, represented under a conditional administration of it to Israel."[37] This "knotty" question is developed both positively and affirmatively.

Negatively, he answers in four propositions. *First*, "[t]he Sinai law was not given as a covenant of works to Israel. It was designed to be a covenant of works, as to be accomplished by Jesus Christ…"[38] *Second*, "the Sinai law was not a mixed covenant for eternal life to Israel."[39] *Third*, "the Sinai law was not only a covenant for temporal mercies, as the land of Canaan, and such like, but did in some further way belong to the covenant of grace, and had the great concernment thereof, even our eternal salvation, as its principal aim and end."[40] And finally fourth, "That the Sinai law is not merely a gradually different administration of the covenant of grace to Israel, from that with us in the new and better covenant."[41]

Affirmatively, Petto gives two propositions. *First*, "the Sinai covenant was a covenant of works, as to be fulfilled by Jesus

---

[35] *Ibid.*, 110.
[36] *Ibid.*, 111. Cf. 141.
[37] *Ibid.*, 113.
[38] *Ibid.*, 113.
[39] *Ibid.*, 118.
[40] *Ibid.*, 120.

Christ, represented under an imperfect administration of the covenant of grace to Israel."[42] And *second*, "[t]hat the Sinai covenant, under a typical servile administration of the covenant of grace, promised temporal mercies to Israel, upon the condition of their obedience."[43] In developing these two propositions, Petto brings out the rich Christology of both the old and new covenants coupled with a definite pastoral sensitivity to those now living under the new covenant.

Antinomianism, a term referred to those who abrogated the necessity of the moral law in the new covenant, was alive and well in the seventeenth century. While Tobias Crisp has been mistakenly identified as an antinomian, it still had its proponents in the likes of John Saltmarsh, Vavasor Powell, and Walter Cradock.[44] Petto's work helps to understand the covenantal response to antinomianism, a response from someone firmly entrenched in the camp that separates Sinai from the covenant of grace. He affirms that the moral law, contained in the Sinai dispensation, "is still obligatory" because it is a "perfect rule of righteousness" and, therefore, is perpetual. However, if it is understood as a covenant or testament, it does not continue since Christ perfectly satisfied and fulfilled the moral law given at Sinai and so satisfied the threats, which were poured out on him, inherent in the old covenant.[45]

In chapter nine, Petto is concerned to show what excellence there was in the "worse covenant".[46] This covenant separated Israel from the pagan nations with a stamp of righteousness, not always realized, upon them. Moreover, the law given to Israel

---

[41] *Ibid.*, 123.

[42] *Ibid.*, 125.

[43] *Ibid.*, 139.

[44] Greaves, *op. cit.*, 152, makes this mistake. However, for evidence exonerating Crisp from this charge, see: Karlberg, *op. cit.*, 31; John Rippon, *A Brief Memoir of the Life and Writings of John Gill* (London: J. Bennett, 1838), 67; C. H. Spurgeon, *The Sword and The Trowel* (London: Passmore and Alabaster, 1887), 123-4.

[45] Petto, 153-158. Here, Petto acknowledges that both the ceremonial and judicial laws are, for the most, part, abrogated.

[46] *Ibid.*, 165.

served a fivefold function. First, it acted pedagogical tool to bring the Israelites to Christ. Second, it restrained them from sin. Third, it acted as a directory to Israel for the worship of God. Fourth, it was a model for civil and ecclesiastical government. And finally, the law gave a typical representation of the "glorious mysteries appertaining to the covenant of grace".[47]

The excellencies of the old covenant only serve to highlight the even greater excellencies of the new. Petto has already spoken of the "better promises", but sees the need now to look at further evidences of the superiority of the new. The glory of the new is the finished work of Jesus Christ, acting as surety for his people, that satisfies the Father's wrath so that he is now lovingly disposed towards his people, now full of absolute promises as opposed to conditional ones under the old. Petto goes to great lengths to uphold the gracious character of the new covenant. For example, "obedience, though evangelical, is no such condition of the new covenant, as there was of the old unto Israel."[48] The manner in which Petto deals with the problem of the moral law in relation to the free grace of the new covenant is particularly helpful, perhaps even more so than Owen who sometimes leaves the his readers confused about the requirements for "new obedience" in the new covenant.[49]

Another benefit of Petto's treatise is his exposition of justification by faith alone in light of his covenant theology. As in the case of Owen, *sola fide* is only intelligible in the broader theological context of a thoroughgoing covenant theology. That is to say, apart from a healthy Reformed understanding of the covenants of grace and works, the doctrine by which the church stands or falls would be unintelligible. Petto is no exception to this trend.[50] Along with

---

[47] *Ibid.*, 166-8.

[48] *Ibid.*, 183. Perhaps Petto's best summary statement on the place of the law, not as a condition but as a fruit, of the Christian life can be found on page 167.

[49] See Owen's *Greater Catechism* in *Works* 1:482.

[50] See Petto, 193-202.

Petto's exposition of justification in light of the covenant is the doctrine of adoption, a doctrine that pervades the thought of his contemporary Thomas Goodwin.[51] The doctrine of adoption, whereby believers can refer to God now as *Abba*, Father, is peculiar to the new covenant Christian. While the doctrine of justification has received greater attention historically, it is true to say that many Reformed theologians understood adoption as the greatest blessing in the new covenant.[52] Adoption, however, is not as central in this work as one might expect it to be, especially given that union with Christ – that which gives Christians the right to call God their Father – is so central to Petto's discussion in the early chapters.

As Petto comes to a close in the remaining chapters he deals with issues that reflect a more pastoral emphasis. Of course, all that has preceded is in some sense pastoral, but Petto, in typical Puritan fashion, looks at the practicality of covenant theology; it is experiential theology at its finest. Chapter eleven, then, is taken up with dealing with the issue of when believers actually partake of the covenant blessings and the difference between those who are visible members of the covenant and others are really under the covenant.[53] We now live in a time when the historical distinction between the visible and invisible church is under attack. Petto's work is timely in that respect insofar as it defends this distinction within the larger context of the covenant. Those who are part of the visible *and* invisible church are in union with Jesus Christ; they partake of the blessings of the covenant by union through faith, "not one moment of time before."[54]

The doctrine of assurance, understood by Petto as a soul knowing it has an interest in the new covenant, is dealt with

---

[51] See Thomas Goodwin, *An Exposition on the Epistle to the Ephesians* (London, 1681), 96.

[52] See James Buchanan, *The Doctrine of Justification; An Outline of Its History in the Church and of Its Exposition from Scripture* (Baker Book House, 1955), 262-63.

[53] Petto, 210.

[54] *Ibid.*, 212. Cf. 217-219, 221.

in chapter twelve in some detail.[55] Petto's doctrine of assurance has a definite twofold aspect understood both subjectively and objectively. The centrality of faith in Christ is evident in his discussion, for it is through faith that one can "have a clear knowledge of its actual interest in the new and better covenant".[56] Faith looks to (1) the free promises of God in Jesus Christ to sinners;[57] (2) Jesus Christ alone;[58] (3) the free grace and faithfulness of God in his covenant;[59] (4) the victory of the righteous seed of the woman (Gen. 3:15) over the devil;[60] and (5) itself, as received freely by Christ, to withstand the spiritual assaults of this present evil age.[61]

Petto closes out his work with two chapters on absolute and conditional promises. Absolute promises are of great value to the humbled heart in revealing the wonders of divine grace, the superiority of the new covenant over the old, and revealing the glories of Christ. Conditional promises hold out to unbelievers the privileges of being in Christ under the new covenant (*e.g.* Matt. 11:28). While conditional blessings can refer to those outside of the covenant, they also speak to those in the covenant who must persevere to the end by laying hold to the promises. Petto summarizes his thought well in these words: "It is a gross mistake to think, that if there be no condition to be performed by us, then we need not take any care, or trouble ourselves about the matter. For we must know, there are divine commands putting upon the use of

---

[55] For a good summary of the doctrine of assurance in the sixteenth and seventeenth centuries, see: Joel R. Beeke, *The Quest for Full Assurance: The Legacy of Calvin and His Successors* (Edinburgh: Banner of Truth, 1999), passim; Michael S. Horton, "Thomas Goodwin and the puritan doctrine of assurance: continuity and discontinuity in the reformed tradition, 1600-1680." Ph.D. diss., Wycliffe Hall, Oxford, & Coventry University, 1995.

[56] Petto, 227.
[57] *Ibid.*, 228.
[58] *Ibid.*, 230.
[59] *Ibid.*, 231.
[60] *Ibid.*, 232.
[61] *Ibid.*, 233.

means in order to the execution of absolute promises; and those are called conditional promises ..."[62]

CONCLUSION

In conclusion, let me offer a word about the style of this work. Whereas Owen, for example, and Goodwin less so, requires the highest concentration due to his Latinized English, Petto is fortunately very readable. There are places in this work that border on obscurity due to the arrangement of his arguments, but overall the modern reader will have little difficulty understanding Petto's argument, especially now with the reprint of this work by Tentmaker where care has been taken to modernize it without substantial changes.

The rewards are to be reaped from a careful study of this work. I would suggest keeping a Bible and pencil close by since Petto is constantly making reference to the Scriptures without giving the quotation of the passage cited. But more importantly, I would suggest keeping your heart firmly fixed upon the Lord Jesus Christ as he reveals to you, by his Spirit, *the great mystery of the covenant of grace.*

---

[62] *Ibid.*, 248.

To The Reader.

IT is a matter of the highest concern unto the souls of men to have a special acquaintance with the Covenant of Grace, the great charter which all spiritual and eternal blessings are holden by; and the way and means wherein they have their conveyance, or are derived to them.

There are many useful treatises already extant on this subject; but still there are some weighty points referring to it, as with Jesus Christ, and especially concerning the old mount Sinai covenant, and also the new,—which have need of farther clearing, for the unfolding of many scriptures, the establishing the faith, and promoting the comfort, of Christians. If it might be the fruit of my present undertaking to contribute any thing this way, or to give light into those glorious mysteries, so as God might be honoured thereby, I should have my aim.

In order to the further opening of some matters insisted on in this treatise, I shall add that which follows.

As the covenant of works was made with the first Adam, and all his seed in him, promising preservation in life, upon the condition of *man's own perfect obedience to the will of God,* Gen. ii. 17.; so, the covenant of grace was made with Jesus Christ (not merely as God, but as to be incarnate, or designed to be a Mediator), as a second Adam, and with a gospel seed in him; promising all spiritual blessings, even eternal life and salvation, upon the condition or consideration of his undergoing the curse, and yielding perfect obedience to the law on their behalf, Isa. liii. 10, 11. Rom. v. 6 to the end.

In this large sense, it comprises that between the Father and the Son for our redemption, which was full of grace, and did flow from the *free favour of God to poor sinners,* 2 Tim. i. 9. Tit. i. 2., as well as that to or with us, *viz.* the new covenant, for the application of what is promised thereupon, which some speak of as if it only were the covenant of grace. Thus its constitution was from eternity, Tit. i. 2., though its revelation was in time to Adam, Abraham, David, &c. Gen. iii. 15.; xii.; &c.

Now, that being the condition of the covenant of grace, that the righteousness of the law should be performed, or all the demands of it, as to duty and penalty, answered by Jesus Christ; hence it was necessary that there should be some means for his coming actually under our very obligation. To that end, the Lord, in infinite wisdom, made a revival or repetition of the covenant of works, as to the substance of it, (with a new intent,) in the covenant at mount Sinai (which did run upon *Do and live,* Gal. iii. 10, 12.): Not that Israel should have eternal life, by their own doing; but that Jesus Christ should be born under the very law that we were obliged by, Gal. iv. 4. Not merely to make a valuable satisfaction by something in lieu of it (for his taking our nature, and making intercession or other works of his, being of infinite merit and value, might have served the turn, without his sufferings); but, as the word, Gen. ii. 17., required to undergo the very curse, and to fulfil the very righteousness of it, in our stead, which he did accordingly; and in this especially our redemption consists—Gal. iii. 12.; iv. 4, 5.

The fulfilling the old, and confirming the new covenant, are the immediate effects of his death. He stood therein as *the Mediator, not of the old, but of the new testament,* Heb. ix. 15. Therefore, he died, not merely to procure a new covenant, or that God might, with honour, deal with men upon new terms; but to make good the terms or conditions of the new.

The mount Sinai covenant (with reference to the matter of it) may be said to express the legal condition of the covenant of grace, as to be fulfilled by Jesus Christ; even as the new covenant holds forth the blessings promised unto us, that condition being performed by him. These are matters so distinct, as I hope none will take offence, that I (as I have explained myself) speak of the old and new as two distinct covenants, when compared each with other, as Gal. iv. 24. Heb. viii. 8.

Seeing I do not assert that at Sinai to be a covenant of works for eternal life to Israel, upon their obedience to it, as some would have it, rather its reference is wholly to that of grace, though it be not the whole of it. Neither do I assert two covenants of grace, or ways of salvation, for substance distinct.—But, whereas it is usually judged that the old is one and the same with the new, differing from it only in some circumstances and accidents, as rigorous exaction of duty, by fear, terror, &c. I on the other hand think, that spiritual blessings were dispensed out by the covenant with Abraham; and, though Israel's obedience to the moral law was on another account, a fruit of holiness and sanctification; yet, as the same obedience had relation to the mount Sinai covenant, so it ushered in only temporals to them: Even as a child owes obedience to his father by a natural obligation, but if a father should promise an estate upon some acts of the same obedience, then they would be clothed with a double respect, or have a double use: so here.

The mount Sinai covenant being thus opened, many scriptures will be explained; and it will be discovered what those works of the law are, which we are so often denied to have justification by, *viz.* All works performed by ourselves as the least of a righteousness unto justification (or which comes to the same), as a condition giving right and title to salvation—Acts xv. 1. Rom. ix. 30, 31, 32. Phil. iii. 9. It is only the obedience of Jesus Christ to the law that avails to these ends. The apostle industriously proves, that men have not such eternal mercies by their own works, moral or ceremonial, either without or in conjunction with Jesus Christ, Rom. iii. 20, and ix. 3. Gal. iii. 11, 21. Gal. v. 4. The seeking to be justified or saved thereby is opposite unto true sanctification; whence discourses thereof are often interwoven in the epistle to the Romans and Galatians. It is true, the very works of the law of Moses are most particularly opposed, because the controversy of that day with the Jews and Judaizing professors of Christianity was concerning these; yet, if men give any other works the same place and office, by acting upon a legal ground, they become as works of the law; and the apostle's arguments are equally forcible against them.

For, he thus reasons, That cannot be a justifying righteousness in our present fallen estate, 1. which is not perfect, for the least sin is enough to condemn, Rom. iii. 20. Gal. iii. 10.; nor, 2. which is our own, of our own working out, Rom. x. 3, 5.; nor, 3. which leaves any place for boasting, Eph. ii. 9; Rom. iv. 2.; nor, 4. which is opposite unto grace, Rom. iv. 4. And upon these accounts, all evangelical works are excluded out of justification; for they are imperfect, they are our own subjectively. They would leave room for some boasting, if acceptance to life were upon these, seeing it should be by our giving unto God: Also, the way were opposite to grace; for, if the condition were never so small, yet, being performed, the reward might be claimed upon our act; and so would be of debt, not of gospel-grace, Rom. iv. 4. The works of Abraham and David, after conversion, are excluded out of justification, ver. 2, 3, 6., which argues, that although evangelical obedience kept in its due place, does not derogate from the grace of God, yet it does, and is opposite to it, if introduced into justification. So that gospel-grace does not consist in a bare abatement of the rigour of the law, nor in making a bargain with us (for the sake of Christ) to accept of our faith, repentance, and sincere obedience, instead of that which is perfect; but it stands, in excusing us from a personal performance of that righteousness which is the condition of life, and admitting Jesus Christ to answer the law in our stead: for, the grand difference between the law and the gospel is, the one justifies by our own, the other by another's righteousness. If man himself be the doer for life, that is the righteousness of the law, which says, Rom. x. 5., *the man that doth them shall live in them.* In opposition to it, that of the gospel is called *the righteousness of faith,* ver. 6., and *of God,* ver. 3., because it is to be sought out of ourselves, in another, in the free promise; and that which we are the subjects of is to be disclaimed here, Phil. iii. 9. Rom. x. 3. The asserting it to be by any of our personal performances, gives them the very place of works in the covenant of works, which is anti-evangelical; and introduces some merits, as well as perfect works would have done. The being enabled by grace to them does not hinder meriting, any more than (as one says) my furnishing a man with my tools to work with, hinders his deserving a reward. All ability that Adam had in innocence was from the favour of God; and what he was to do was duty. Faith itself is not the least of that righteousness—it is an act of obedience; but as such, it is not said to justify, nor as it works by love, although it does so work, Gal. v. 6.; nor as a condition of life (as I have elsewhere manifested), but only as a means for the applying Christ and his righteousness; much less can any works of ours be a part thereof. The new creature avails to being crucified to the world, Gal. vi. 14, 15., *i.e.* as a means; but it is not said that it avails to justification.

To justify, is to declare a person to be righteous; the true God cannot pass a false sentence. Therefore, we cannot have justification, without having a righteousness. This cannot consist in any act of ours, as faith, repentance, or obedience, as is already manifested; therefore, it must be of another's working out, the very righteousness of Jesus Christ, Rom. v. 18, 19. 1 Cor. i. 30. And if his obedience (being to the law) may be called a legal righteousness, yet, as the same is applied by faith, it is to us an evangelical righteousness. All the question, then, is, whether evangelical works are not of the same use in justification, that faith is of? Have they not the same place and office there, that faith has? I answer negatively, they have not; for often we read of the righteousness of faith, never of the righteousness of love in that business. We are said to be justified by faith, not (in the same sense) to be justified by love or works.

It is true, there is a necessity of evangelical works to testify our faith, obedience, and thankfulness to God; but they are required, not as conditions, but as effects and declarations of our justification. Things are said to be done, when they are manifested, as, Rom. iii. 7. and iv. 15.; a tree is known by the fruits. And thus, not only open acts, but those that are secret (when regular), have an aptitude to evidence faith; and that a person is justified, even when they are not actually seen. Paul speaks of being justified before God, by receiving or applying the righteousness of Jesus Christ in the free promise, this is only by faith. James speaks of being justified by manifesting to a man's self or others that it is applied; this is by evangelical works, and not by faith only. Thus, by offering up Isaac, the person of Abraham was declaratively justified, as it did show his faith to be true, ver. 18., (Gen. xxii. 12.); and not his working, but his believing, is said to be imputed to righteousness, Jam. ii. 23. If this be justification in the sense of Paul, yet it is by faith (and he was called the friend of God) there is justification declared by works; as God acted kindly towards him, so he acted in a friendly way towards God. He is a vain man that contents himself with a faith that stands in a bare assent to some propositions of truth, without the power of them upon his heart, ver. 14, 9, 20.

That is a dead faith which does not profit, is not attended with salvation, which remains without works, ver. 17, 20, 26.; therefore, it is not the same true faith which any are justified by, but another thing. That unfruitful faith which is blamed here, certainly was as far from justifying them as it was from saving them, and so is not the faith which Paul insists upon; for, by that, men were justified, and that in order before works; for they cannot be performed in an instant, though they certainly follow. But the justification and faith which they are put upon, and called to declare by works, these are of a gospel stamp.

The Lord Jesus having fully performed the law, as the condition of the new testament, hence it becomes absolute to us. If improperly a duty, a way, or means to the enjoyment of some blessings of it, be called a condition, I contend not. But a condition, properly, is more than a *causa sine qua non,* it is a cause that has a moral efficiency in it; for, the fulfilling of it is that which gives right, and upon which a man has a title to what is promised, and without it none; and so it is a moral efficient cause of the enjoyment of the good promised in a covenant. Faith and repentance are great duties; but nothing performed by us can be such a cause or condition in the new covenant. There is absoluteness, 1. In the form of the new covenant. 2. In the actual admission into it. 3. In the freedom of those under it from the curse of the old, and in their participation of the blessings of the new.

1. Wherever the form of the new testament is given forth, it is an absolute way, *I will, and ye shall,* Heb. x. 16, 17. Heb. viii. 8, to the end. He insists upon it that now, Jer. xxxi. 31, 32., was made good; and this purposely to draw off the Hebrews from the old covenant, which they did too much take up in, and to put them upon looking unto the new.—Other scriptures may discover what is our duty before and after being actually interested in the blessings of it; but the nature of the covenant is most

fully expressed here in these texts, which speak of the great matters or promises contained in it, of the Mediator and subjects of it. The tenor thereof must be fetched from these places where the covenant is purposely insisted upon, rather than from others, where only one promise is named, and it not so much as mentioned. And here it is not called a purpose or prophesy, but a covenant, or rather testament, and is so absolutely held forth, as God undertakes all. He promises as well that they shall be his people, as that he will be their God. He promises not only that he will remember their sins and iniquities no more, but also that he will write his laws in their hearts, *i.e.* give a frame of faith and new obedience. These are as absolutely promised here, as any other matters; and, therefore, believing and obeying cannot properly be causes or conditions, but are fruits and effects of the covenant, by its being accomplished upon them. Their duty is necessarily implied, yet, as it stands here in the covenant, the design of it plainly is, to express the work of God, what he will do for them, how he will furnish and capacitate them to discharge it towards him.

2. The actual admission of all that Jesus Christ stood for, into the new covenant, or the bringing them under it, is absolutely determined. He had an absolute assurance that his undertaking should take effect on all those that he designed therein, Isa. liii. 10, 11. He shall see his seed, all that he travailed* for; and therefore they must be effectually brought into covenant with him. There was no condition that his obedience had dependence upon, or upon which it was to be accepted for such souls, otherwise not. He did not suffer at any such uncertainty, but for those which were assuredly to become the heirs of promise. Indeed, the making covenant with us, is challenged by the Lord as his work, Isa. liii. 3 and lxi. 8: *I will make or cut an everlasting*

---

* travelled *[orig.]*

covenant with you, so Jer. xxxi. 31, 32; Jer. xxii. 40; Ezek. xvi. 8; Heb. viii. 10. God has undertaken to bring under the promise, and make an application of it. Attendance upon means is duty; but it is not said that men do make the covenant with God, or bring themselves into it, by an act of theirs, but God makes it with them; they do but *take hold of God's covenant,* Isa. lvi. 4, 6. The will of God is not determined by any act of man. When God will work, who shall let him? what he undertakes, shall be absolutely accomplished. Hence, as those under the old covenant who were to be redeemed, are represented under the name of Israel; so also are those under the new, to whom all is to be applied—the same are the subjects of both.

3. Those that are actually in covenant, have an absolute freedom from the curse of the old, and a like promise of the blessings of the new. Jesus Christ has not only suspended; but redeemed us from the curse of the law, being *made a curse for us,* Gal. iii. 13. Hence we are said not to be under the law, and to be dead to it, Rom. vi. 14 and vii. 4; Gal. ii. 19. Christians, then, have not only a conditional freedom from the curse of the law in this life, but such as is absolute; and if they should believe themselves to be under it, they should believe a lie, Rom. viii. 1. Yet divine threats are of great use, not only to the unregenerate, but even to believers, to strike them into a filial fear, so as to deter them from sin, which has such punishment annexed to it, and this when they see themselves secured from it; even as an ingenuous child will be afraid upon hearing his father threaten another for a fault, and will beware of committing it. The non-elect are formally under the curse of the law and vindictive justice. The elect, before conversion, are not only materially under it, but the law's sentence of condemnation is against them. Believers are so freed from it, as their sicknesses, death, &c. are but materially the same mentioned in the curse, and turned into blessings to them.

Also, all the promises of the new covenant are absolute to all that are under it, Heb. viii. 6; &c. No act of ours induces an obligation upon God to vouchsafe salvation to us. That great blessing of the covenant, justification, is by faith; not said to be by it as a condition; and the same may be said of other blessings thereof. Yet I deny not but, figuratively, that may be ascribed to faith, which belongs to Jesus Christ alone. The absoluteness of the covenant is not attended with any such consequence, as that then man is at liberty, but God is not; for, such as are yet out of covenant, or want a personal interest in the blessings of it, even all men are under a divine law, and an obligation to obedience, else they could not be charged with sin, as they are, Rom. iii. 23 and v. 12. Where there is no law, there is no transgression, seeing sin is the transgression of the law, 1 John iii. 4. So, then, the obligation unto duty does not arise merely from entering or coming into covenant; and that is so far from taking off the tie, that it superadds strength to it; but no man is at liberty, whether he be in or out of covenant. As to the way of the Lord's entering into covenant with men, it is thus:

He, by his spirit, in the gospel reveals, and gives Jesus Christ (for he is the first saving gift), and all the promises are vouchsafed in and with him, Col. ii. 6. 1 John v. 12. Rom. viii. 32; Eph. iii. 6; 2 Cor. i. 30; 2 Pet. i. 4. The same new covenant, or testament, has various effects. As the spirit works effectually by the promise of it upon the souls of men, so it is a covenant of life and grace to them: it is by the new testament that the Lord says to any souls, live, and that the first grace is wrought in them—Ezek. xvi. 8 and xxxvi. 26; Heb. viii. 10; 2 Cor. iii. 6. As the Lord, by giving and promulgating the promises, obliges or puts himself under engagements to make them good to men, so it is a covenant to or with them; because they obtain personal interest therein, so as to have a ground to claim many privileges thereof. Thus often the covenant was renewed with Abraham, after his being in it.

As by the same covenant, or promise, the Lord obliges himself to all acts of communion, and expressions of love, and kindness suitable to, or that can be expected in, a conjugal relation; so it is a marriage covenant with them: the same instant they are enabled to consent by faith (Heb. viii. 10; John i. 12) to receive and enjoy the blessings promised; as a necessary fruit and effect of the covenant. It is promised therein that they shall be his people, they shall resign up themselves to the Lord. He has undertaken that one (*i.e.* one by one) shall say, *I am the Lord's,* Isa. xliv. 3, 5. A consent is promised by the Lord, as well as any other matter. So that our engaging ourselves to God (or covenanting with him) is not constitutive of the covenant of grace, but executive, namely, that which is produced in the execution of it, and may often be repeated or renewed by distinct engagings. God, dealing with men as reasonable creatures, that act out of judgment and their own choice, urges duty (as believing, repenting, &c.) by arguments from the advantage of coming up to it, *All that believe shall be saved;* and the danger of neglecting it, such shall be damned, as Mark xvi. 16; Rom. x. 9; Rev. iii. 20. Such general propositions do not express the full tenor of the covenant, but only are means towards the execution of it; for, the invitations extend to all nations, Mat. xxviii. 19; Mark xvi. 15 (since the death of Christ, not before, Psalm cxlvii. 19, 20); whereas the covenant is only with the *Israel* of God, Heb. viii. 8.

I shall add no more at present to this; but that my design in all is, the right stating evangelical duty, and the asserting the doctrine of free grace, which, as it is the most Christ-exalting, so it is the most sin-mortifying, soul-humbling and abasing, and self-emptying doctrine. It is not the law of works, but of faith, that excludes boasting—Col. i. 18, 19; Rom. vi. 1.14; Tit. ii. 11, 12; Rom. iii. 27.

READER, the following treatise has been divers years prepared, and not one leaf added to it since October, 1672, which I mention for a special reason. My desire is, that all which I have said for clearing up of the mind and will of God in this great matter, may be weighed in the balance of the sanctuary, and received as it holds weight there. And that thy sharing in the blessings of the everlasting covenant may be promoted hereby, shall be the prayer of him who is,

Thy Servant in the work
of the Gospel,
S. PETTO.

Mon. 4. *day* 20. 1673.

CHRISTIAN READER,

THE ensuing discourse contains a sober endeavour for the declaration and true stating of the nature and difference of the two covenants of works and of grace. A subject this is, which, by reason of the weight and use of it in the whole business of religious obedience, has been attempted by many; and wherein, by reason of the difficulty of it, in conjunction with their own prejudices, not a few have miscarried. Neither do I know of any who have yet handled it with that fullness and perspicuity, as to shut up the way unto the diligence of others in the investigation and declaration of the truth, or to render labour in the same kind either useless or superfluous. The stores of heavenly wisdom, grace, and truth, which are treasured up in the divine revelations concerning God's covenants, are far from being fully exhausted or drawn forth by the labours of any in this kind, although very many have already brought to light excellent and useful instructions, in the mind of God, and the duty of them who do believe. But the thing itself is so excellent, the mystery of it so great, the declaration of it in the scripture so extensive and diffused throughout the whole body of it, from the first to the last, as also in its concernment unto the whole course of our faith and obedience, that there is a sufficient ground whereon to justify a renewed search into the mind of God therein, as revealed in his word. There is no doubt but the greatest product of divine grace, goodness, and condescension, next unto the sending of the only Son of God to take our nature on him, with the direct effect and consequence thereof, is this of his entering into covenant with the children of men; nor has any thing a greater tendency unto the advancement of his own glory. God might have dealt with mankind in a way of sovereignty or mere dominion, as he does with the remainder of the creatures here below; but then it must be acknowledged that, in such a way of rule and procedure, there would not have been that evident demonstration of the divine excellencies, his goodness, righteousness, and faithfulness, as ensues upon the supposition of his condescension to take mankind into covenant with himself. And thence it is that he never did, nor ever would, treat with any of that race any otherwise, or on any other terms. Wherefore, when the first covenant was broken by the entrance of sin, God had no other relation unto mankind, but that of a supreme Ruler and Judge, to reward them according to the penalty threatened, and established in the covenant. But, as for any advantage in a way of love, peace, and goodness, there was none remaining, until he had made and established a new covenant to that end and purpose. And this fully discovers how great a concern there is of the glory of God in the covenant which he made with us and proposes unto us, seeing he never declared or intimated any other way of gracious or acceptable intercourse in him; and the effects of it do issue in eternity. Moreover, this dispensation of God in making a covenant with our first parents, was the greatest evidence of the pre-eminence of that nature wherewith in time we were endowed, and only demonstration of our being capable to be brought unto eternal enjoyment of him; for, God herein, admitting us into an intercourse with him, by a declared rule of his own goodness and faithfulness, manifested that we were capable of eternal rewards, which he proposed unto us in himself. And these things make the investigation of the true nature of the covenant with God, first made with Adam, and the terms whereby it was made, both necessary and profitable; for, although that covenant is ceased, by the entrance of sin, as to any spiritual or eternal advantage unto us, yet is it, as revealed, still instructive in the wisdom and goodness of God, as also in the excellence of that state and condition in which we were created, with the honour that God put upon our nature, whence directions unto due apprehensions of God, and ourselves, may be taken or derived. But, as to the new covenant, which is in and with us in Christ, and so is comprehensive of the whole work of his mediation, it is the only instrument of our present relation unto God; of his communicating of himself in a way of grace, love, and mercy unto us; of our fixing faith, trust, and affiance on him, and yielding obedience unto him; as also of the bringing of our souls unto the eternal enjoyment of him. The knowledge hereof, therefore, is necessary to everyone who thinks it necessary for him to endeavour an acquaintance with God or Christ, the present state or future condition of his soul. It is, therefore, doubtless a labour worthy of acceptance in any whom God has given light unto in this mystery of his wisdom and grace, and ability for the declaration thereof, to endeavour the direction and instruction of others in the truth and doctrine hereof, wherein all our faith, obedience, present comfort, and future happiness, do depend. But yet further, besides these two solemn stated covenants, the one suited unto the preservation of the state of integrity wherein we were created,—and the other to the renovation of the image of God in us, through Jesus Christ, which we had lost by sin,—there is mention in the scripture of sundry particular intervening covenants that God made with his church, or single persons, at several seasons. Now, whereas they did all partake of the nature of a divine covenant in general, so were they emanations from, and particular expressions or limitations of, one or other of the two solemn covenants mentioned; for, a covenant of another kind absolutely, or more covenants, God never made with mankind. But yet, under the old testament, while the wisdom of God was to be hid in its own mysteries, and not clearly brought forth to light, there was such a mixed dispensation, revealing, for certain ends, the notion, sense, and power of the first covenant, and preparative for the introduction of the full revelation and declaration of the latter by Jesus Christ, who was in all things to have the pre-eminence; as that it is not easy to discern and distinguish what belongs unto the one in them, and what to the other, or from whether of them they are to be denominated. Here, therefore, is a blessed field of sacred truth, wherein humble, sober, and judicious persons may exercise themselves, to the great benefit and advantage of the church of God. To state, I say, aright the nature of a divine covenant in general, with its essential properties, which must be in every one that is so, to manifest the true difference that is between the first and second covenant which God has made with us, in themselves, and their nature, with their different effects and ends, to declare what properties, doctrines, and ends of the first covenant, or covenant of works,—with what of the nature, power, and efficacy of the second covenant, or the covenant of grace, God brought in and declared in that dispensation under the old testament, wherein there was a mixture of both, though one only established in power, to manifest what there was of Christ in the law, and how the whole power and sanction of the first covenant was through the law conferred upon Christ, and in him fulfilled and ended, is a work deserving the most diligent travail of those who are called unto the teaching of the mysteries of the gospel. And in these things, with sundry other of an alike importance, has this worthy author laboured, if I am not much mistaken, unto good success. And, as his design is to extricate things which seem perplexed, to give light into the whole doctrine of the covenants, by declaring the proper order and method of the things contained in them, with their respect one unto another; that the grace of God, in the covenant of grace, may be exalted, and his faithfulness, with his holiness, in the covenant of works, both in and by Jesus Christ, the end of the one, and the life of the other. So the reader will find, I hope, that satisfaction in these great and deep enquiries, which he will have occasion to return praise and thanks to God for.

JOHN OWEN.

THE
GREAT MYSTERY
OF THE
COVENANT OF GRACE.

CHAPTER I.

Of a Covenant in general, and the distribution of the Covenant into that of Works and of Grace.

THE all-wise God, that he might magnify his loving kindness towards miserable man, in guaranteeing him fellowship and communion with himself, in all ages had this admirable contrivance of dealing with him, not in the way of prerogative, but in the way of covenant. When man was in a state of innocence, there was a covenant of works, wherein he put himself under engagements to him to continue him in life, if he kept his standing, and remained obedient; and also man being in a fallen state, he chooses still to converse with him in the way of a covenant, not as made with the first Adam, but with Jesus Christ, as a second Adam, and with all his seed in him.

There are many scriptures which give clear intimations of such a federal transaction between God the Father, and Jesus Christ, the Son, in order to the recovery and everlasting salvation of sinners; even where we do not find the very notion or name of it. Thus Isa. liii. 10-12., there is a mutual agreement, something to be undergone by Jesus Christ, he is to *make his soul an offering for sin;* something promised to him thereupon, *he shall see his seed.*—So Isa. xlii. 6. Here are the parties covenanting, the Father and the Son; not men, but I the Lord, who cannot err in my appointments, who am faithful and able, even the Almighty God, I, have called thee, *i.e.* Jesus Christ, and will give thee, the speech is turned and directed to him, thee, who art my only beloved Son. Here is the Father's designation and sealing of him (John vi. 27.) to the mediatorial employment, promising him much upon his undertaking it, and his acceptation of this office and voluntary submission to the will of the Father in it—*so I come to do thy will,* &c., Heb. v. 4, 5. Psal. xl. 7, 8. John x. 17, 18. and these together amount to or make up a covenant between them; for what more can be necessary thereunto? Here we have the matters or things promised, *viz.* all that conduce to the compassing the great end of salvation. Was man under alienation from God? Behold it is promised, I will give for a covenant; no way imaginable whereby this wide breach could be made up but by a covenant; and that of works being broken, man would not be trusted any more, and therefore now Jesus Christ as a surety undertakes all necessary for the ending and making up the difference, and the retaking and restoring his seed into divine favour again for ever; so as he is even the covenant of the people, all the condition of life on their part to be performed is found in him. Yea, he has undertaken the removal of all obstacles and impediments within, that would hinder their attainment of covenant mercy; he is given for *a light to the Gentiles,* he takes away the inward blindness that is found with them. No sinfulness or unworthiness may be a discouragement, for behold all is in a way of free grace, *(I will give thee);* Christ himself, the fountain of all, is freely given, and the Father is upon the highest determination and resolution for bringing all to effect—*I will give thee*———.

So there are many promises made to Jesus Christ of assistances and all requisites to the management of this great work. *I will hold thy hand, i.e.* will assist and be thy helper, as Isa. xli. 13.; and many promises of success, and of his being victorious over all his enemies, and having the heathen for his inheritance, &c. Psal. ii, 8, 9. Zech. ix. 10. Psal. lxxii. 8. Dan. vii. 14. upon his obedience; all which plainly argue a covenant between the Father and the Son. It is implied also in the ascribing to him the working out of redemption, for unto that is requisite an agreement between parties. The Father promises, that upon the payment of such a price by his Son, such souls shall be ransomed and set free; Jesus Christ consents, pays it, and thus becomes a Redeemer: this amounts to a covenant.

But in order to the further clearing of this matter, I shall consider a covenant in general, and then its distribution into that of works and that of grace; the interest of Jesus Christ in the latter, and also the date of it.

The word (covenant) in Hebrew ברית, *Berith,* is taken either (properly) for a mutual contract or agreement between, two parties, and is differenced from a law which is without obligation on the lawgiver or commander, and from a single promise, which is without stipulation from him to whom it is made. Covenant may be thus taken, when applied to the whole covenant of grace between the Father and the Son, for therein was stipulation.

Or covenant is taken (figuratively) in scripture, either for a bare divine promise, as Gen. ix. 9, 10., that was with every living creature, many of which were incapable of contracting with God, or of making, any stipulation. So covenant is taken for a bare sign or seal of it, Gen. xvii. 10., also for a part, as the moral law, which was but a part of the old covenant, is called the covenant, Exod. xxxiv. 28. Deut. ix. 9, 11. 15. Thus covenant and promise may be used promiscuously, a part for the whole, Rom. iv. 13. Gal. iii. 17, 18, 19.; and thus figuratively Jesus Christ himself is called the covenant, Isa. xlii. 6.

The covenant of God on the behalf of man is two-fold, and is thus distinguished:—

I. The covenant of works, with the first Adam and his seed.
  II. The covenant of grace—
    1st, With Jesus Christ, the second Adam, for all his, from eternity.
    2nd, With his, in and with him in time, considered,
      1st, in its legal condition, typical manifestation, and servile temporary administration at mount Sinai.
      2nd, Evangelical disposition as to matter and form, *viz.* Spiritual promises, free and lasting dispensation, and all this considered,
        1st, in its primary revelation, and renewing with the Fathers, as Abraham, David, &c. before the incarnation of Jesus Christ, Gal. iii. 14, 16, 17., under the old testament, when the Messiah was promised, and privileges in him.
        2nd, Ratification, consummation, or perfection, after the incarnation of Christ under the new covenant or testament, Heb. viii. and ix., wherein the Mediator is exhibited, and privileges coming and to be applied absolutely by him, more clearly enumerated.

Or thus:—

The covenant of God on the behalf of men is two-fold, and is thus distinguished:—
  I. The covenant of works, with the first Adam, and his seed in him.
  II. The covenant of grace,
    1st, in its constitution with Jesus Christ, the second Adam, and his seed in him, from eternity, consisting of promises and agreements for their (*i.e.* his seed's) recovery from a state of sin and death to a state of righteousness and life, in and by him.
    2nd, Declaration and manifestation, as with us, in and with Christ in time; and thus it is considered,

1st, in its more private dispensation whilst the church was domestic, or in families; as to its,
    1st, Primary revelation and promulgation to Adam, Gen. iii. 15.
    2nd, After secondary renewing execution and application to the patriarchs, Abraham, &c. Gen. xii. xv. And
2nd, More public dispensation, when the church became congregational.
    1st, As to its legal condition and administration in the mount Sinai covenant, Exod. xix. and xx.
    2nd, Evangelical disposition, *viz.* absolute promises and unchangeable administration in the new covenant; Heb. viii. 8-10, 12.

The first part of this division is *generis in species, viz.* into covenant of works and of grace.

The second part, *viz.* the division or distribution of the covenant of grace is three-fold.
1. *Accidentis in subjecta, viz.* with Christ as principal, and with us in him.
2. *Effecti in suas causas,* and that extrinsical and intrinsical, *viz.* legal condition, evangelical disposition.
3. *Accidentis in accidentia, viz.* primary revelation, ratification.

1. There was a law or covenant of works made with the first Adam and his seed, before the fall; in that state man was to seek eternal life in the way of his own obedience. Then God was upon those terms with man (Do and live) for that divine threatening of death. Gen. ii. 17: *In the day thou eatest thereof thou shalt surely die,* does strongly imply a promise of enjoying life if he were obsequious; else he might have said, if I eat or eat not, it is all one, yet I am liable to death.

Doubtless, as the threatened death was intended purposely to deter from eating, so the hope of life was also a persuasive to this forbearance.

Yea the tree of life confirms this: man was made an exile out of paradise, Gen. iii. 22. *Lest he put forth his hand, and take also of the tree of life, and eat, and live for ever.* Such an act of banishment would have been needless for prevention, if it had never been intended for such an end to establish man in life, in case he had kept his standing. Some divine law or covenant, therefore, there must be this way. Some may doubt whether this was a covenant of works, because here is only a threatening of death upon eating the forbidden fruit, Gen. ii 17., upon disobedience to that one positive law or command, and perfect obedience unto all moral commands, not so much as mentioned, nor death threatened to the want of it.

I answer, Man, in his first creation, was under a natural obligation to an universal compliance with the will of God. Eccles. vii. 29. *God hath made man upright;* this rectitude of nature imports an exact conformity to the divine will; it is opposed here to all those inventions, evil devices, new tricks, vain and crooked counsels, which were the inlets to all iniquity. He was created in the image of God, (Gen. i. 27.) which did not consist merely in the faculties of the soul, as understanding, will, &c. but in gifts of illumination, righteousness, and holiness, Coloss. iii. 10. Eph. iv. 24. There was an inscription of the divine law upon Adam's heart, yea even the Gentiles by nature show the work of the law written in their hearts, Rom. ii. 14, 15.; although this is exceedingly defaced and obliterated by the fall of man, yet, not wholly razed out or extinguished.

Now there being such original righteousness, a law of nature that obliged man (as soon as created) to all moral obedience, it was needless for the Lord (in entering into covenant with him) to make a repetition of that law without, which was antecedaneously written in lively characters, with a deep impression as a law within.

All, therefore, that was necessary unto the making or forming of it into a covenant of works was, the addition of some positive law or command, as a test or trial of obedience to the whole, and this we find in that supervenient command of not eating of the tree of knowledge, Gen. ii. 17., under the highest penalty of death itself, in case of disobedience. This is the more evident, because this positive precept was of such a nature, and so entwisted with the other, as Adam could not fall by transgressing of it in eating of the forbidden fruit, without a violation or breaking of all the moral commandments, and involving himself in all sin and iniquity thereby. Christ himself is giving the sum of the law in these two, of due love to God and our neighbour, Mat. xxii. 37-39. Now, the trial of love is by keeping his commandments, John xiv. 21, 24.; and by eating that fruit Adam transgressed his command, Gen. ii. 17., and gave an evident proof of his want of love to God and to his neighbour also, thereby murdering not only himself, but all his posterity with him.

Yea, though it seemed a small and indifferent thing in itself; yet there was the sum of all sin, in that first transgression, which the apostle comprises in three things, 1 John ii. 16. *All that is in the world, the lust of the flesh, the lust of the eyes, and the pride of life.* And Gen. iii. 6. *The woman saw the tree was good for food;* in this pleasing of a carnal appetite was the lust of the flesh; *and pleasant to the eyes*—here is the seeking to satisfy undue desires, *the lust of the eyes,* and *to be desired to make one wise,* or, as the serpent suggested, verse 5. *to be as Gods;* this is ambition, or *pride if life.*

It might be manifested, how all or most of the commandments were broken by this act. Here was infidelity, not believing the word of God and seeking to deify himself, against the first commandment; Adam's preferring the voice of his wife, yea of the serpent, before the word of God, against the second; a conferring with God's enemy about his word (a part of his name) without due zeal for his glory, against the third; a not resting from his own work, against the fourth; Eve out of her place in eating without her husband's advice and consent, against the fifth; a running under a divine threatening of death to many thousands, yea millions of men, against the sixth; a giving way to an inordinate sensual appetite in eating the forbidden fruit, against the seventh; a taking what was not his own, being reserved by God, against the eighth; a receiving a false accusation against God, Gen. iii. 5., against the ninth; discontent with the state and condition God had placed him in, aspiring to be higher than he saw it meet, against the tenth commandment. And thus there was an universal disobedience in Adam's eating the forbidden fruit, (there is the seed of all sin in original sin), and therefore such an exact obedience to the moral or natural, as well as, to the positive law, was required there, as rendered it a law or covenant of works.

But man cannot now obtain happiness and salvation by his own doing, according to that, for it is said to be, Ephes. ii. 9. *Not of works, lest any man should boast.* So that Jesus Christ is not given for the renewing that old covenant of works with us again, as the way to eternal life, though the matter of it is drawn into the covenant of grace, to be performed by him for us, as may be further manifested afterwards.

2. There is a covenant of grace provided for the recovery of some, by Jesus Christ, from a state of sin and death unto a state of righteousness and eternal life. All that conduces to salvation is of grace, Ephes. ii. 8. *By grace ye are saved.* Rom. xi. 6. *If by grace, then it is no more of works, otherwise grace is no more grace: But if it be of works, then it is no more grace, otherwise work is no more work.* The way of salvation

THE COVENANT OF GRACE 55

is here ascribed unto grace; the holy Spirit gives us both the terms of the distinction, by making grace and works such opposite terms, as one excludes the other; that, therefore, made with the first Adam was a covenant of works, that for restoration by Jesus Christ is a covenant of grace— see verses 26-28. Rom. vi. 14. The accepting of Jesus Christ in our stead, to be our second Adam, was as by covenant, so of mere grace, as well as what is promised to us through him, they together make up but one covenant of grace.

Some call the former a covenant of amity or friendship, because God and man were in perfect amity, and a covenant of nature, because natural integrity did capacitate to perform it; but these do not so fully express the nature of it, seeing the promised life therein was to be by working.

Some call the latter a covenant of faith; and there is indeed an opposition between the law of faith and the law of works, in the matter of justification, Rom. iii. 27, 28. That particular privilege of the covenant, *viz.* justification, is by faith, and not by the works of the law; but in a distribution, these are not the most distinct members of the whole covenant, seeing faith is but a particular blessing and fruit of it, hence that cannot be expressive of the whole nature thereof: that is not the opposite condition, or does not take the place that works had in that covenant with the first Adam; it is rather what was done or suffered by Jesus Christ that supplied this, Isa. liii. 10. It is, therefore, improper, especially unless by faith be meant the righteousness of Jesus Christ applied thereby, rather than that particular grace for application.

And note, that in the epistles to the Romans and Galatians, justification is said to be by faith, in opposition only to works, not to Jesus Christ, or free grace. If we should give faith the place that was given by the false prophets unto works, we should be culpable, and egregiously cross the mind of the apostle in this matter, as well as they did. Some grace in that covenant with the first Adam does no more make it coincident with, or deny that in and with Christ to be a covenant of grace, than some works, (*viz.* evangelical) in that with Christ, do deny that with the first Adam to be a covenant of works; or than some faith in God, required in the covenant of works (*viz.* the believing that word, Gen. ii. 17.) does deny that which they call the covenant of faith to be so.

It must, therefore, be said, it was not gospel grace, or faith in a Mediator, that was found in the covenant of works, and so as properly as this may be denominated of works, so may the other be called a covenant of grace, especially seeing the gospel is called the word of grace, Acts xiv. 3. xx. 32.

As to the several parts following in the distribution of this covenant of grace, some of them carry evidence with them, as what is said of primary revelation, renovation, consummation, &c. the other will be further cleared in the sequel; yet thus much I would say here, for the clearing of them.

That the covenant of grace was made with Jesus Christ, that text witness, Isa. xlii. 6., for the Father is contracting with him, indeed all the covenant of the people is first with him; he not only removes obstacles that would hinder their fruition of federal blessings, as an interested friend (whose name is not in a covenant) may do among men; but he is the great covenanter, (a covenant of the people): the promises are primarily made to him on the behalf of men, and he makes the first claim to all, as his own right, his own due, by a grant or covenant, under the hand and seal of the Father, to himself.—This will be proved in the next question.

That also the covenant is made with us in Christ is no less evident. Believers are of the seed of Abraham and David, and of the house of spiritual Israel, to whom the promises run; they may lay claim to them in their head, Gal. iii. 9, 14, 29. Rom. xi. 27. Ezek. xx. 37. Jer. xxxi. 31. Heb. viii. 8.

If any doubt of the second distinction, into legal and evangelical, let them know, I am far from thinking that the mount Sinai dispensation was a covenant of works to Israel, as if the design and intendment of God therein had been to afford eternal life to Israel upon their own doing; but yet it is called the law, Rom. x. 5. Gal. iii. 10, 13, 17., even in way of opposition to the promise, verse 12., yea, verse 8., God preached before the gospel to Abraham.

Here the covenant with Abraham is expressly called gospel, and that in contradistinction from the very Sinai dispensation, which is called the law; undeniably he speaks of the law, not as given to Adam before the fall, (for then man himself must have been the door for life, and not another for him), but as given at mount Sinai, four hundred and thirty years after that promise to faithful Abraham, verse 17.

So that the covenant of grace is rightly distinguished by legal and evangelical, for the holy Spirit here gives us both parts of the distinction, speaking expressly of that at mount Sinai as one member of it; yea, he makes these so opposite, as he says, verse 12. *and the law is not of faith,* and so is not the covenant of grace; but yet the Sinai law appertains and refers to it, *viz.* as holding forth the condition thereof to be fulfilled by Jesus Christ.

CHAPTER II.

Of the oneness of the Covenant with Jesus Christ and us.

THE covenant of grace was made or established, not only with us, but jointly with Jesus Christ, and us in him, so as both are within one and the same covenant; for the great transactions with Jesus, yea, even the giving and sending of him, and his accepting the office of a Redeemer, and undertaking for us, these are all of grace, as well as what is promised to us through him; therefore the covenant of grace must take in all that conduces (otherwise than by a mere decree) to our restoration and eternal salvation. And in Isa. xlii. 6., the Father is contracting with the Son, *I will give thee for a covenant of the people;* therefore that with the Son and with the people belong to one and the same covenant.

Indeed, as that which partakes of the nature, or is a part, is put for the whole, so that with the people alone, even here, bears the name of a covenant, as being within the grand contract with Jesus Christ, as a branch and parcel thereof; yet both together make up that one covenant of grace, as appears thus:—

1. There is no scripture evidence for making these two covenants, one of suretyship or redemption with Jesus Christ, and another of grace and reconciliation made with us. That distinction, which some use, is improper, for the parts of it are coincident, seeing that as with Jesus Christ was out of mere grace also, John iii. 16. And it is promised that Jesus Christ should be given for a covenant; therefore it is of grace that we are redeemed by him, 2 Tim. i. 9. There was grace before the world was, and that must be

in the covenant as with Jesus Christ; which was for the reconciling the world unto the Father, 2 Cor. v. 18, 19. Coloss. i. 20, 21.

It is true, Christ only is our surety and Redeemer, not we in our own persons; yea he is our head, our Lord, and King, and on that account of his standing in those different capacities, he hath some peculiar precepts and promises appropriated to him, which are not afforded to us in the same manner or degree; yet this hinders not the oneness of the covenant with him and us. As it is promised unto Abraham that in him all the families of the earth should be blessed, that he should be a Father of many nations, Gen. xii. 3. and xvii. 4., which promises are of a higher nature than are made to us, (for every believer is not the Father of many nations), yet we are within the same covenant that was made with Abraham, Rom. iv. 11-13. Gal. iii.

As in covenants between princes, some articles may be concerning prerogatives or royalties, that are peculiar to them in their public capacities, which the people share not in, but in them, as striking sail, &c.; other grants may concern the people in their private capacities, as merchants, mariners, &c. yet prince and people within the same contract. So doubtless there may be diverse grants to Jesus Christ, in his public capacity, in the office of a Mediator, other promises made to his seed; yet king and subjects, head and members, are within one and the same covenant, as the principal debtor and the surety within the same obligation, Gal. iv. 4, 5.

Indeed the same covenant of grace may be distinguished, as it is made with Jesus Christ, and as with us; yet not to intimate two distinct and complete covenants, but two subjects of the same covenant. As with Jesus Christ, it had its constitution from eternity, before we had a being; as with us, it hath its application in time, after we exist. I had rather, therefore, distinguish one and the same covenant of grace into these two parts;—

1. For redemption and reconciliation; this as with Jesus Christ for us, Gal. iii. 13. Tit. i. 2.

2. For application; this as with us in him, Heb. viii. 10.

From eternity Jesus Christ was a Mediator, undertaking the covenant; but in time is executing and interceding for our participation of it.

2. The covenant of grace was made with Jesus Christ as a public person, a second Adam; and, therefore, with all his seed in him; the covenant of works being violated, Jesus Christ was appointed as the means for restoration and recovery. He was our David, king of saints, Isa. liii. 3. Luke i. 32., and so represented many subjects; he was a common parent, having a great spiritual seed, Isa. liii. 10. The first Adam was a figure of him that was to come, Rom. v. 14., *i.e.* of Jesus Christ, and wherein it is specified; as the first, standing for his seed, derived unto them sin and misery, death and condemnation; so the second, standing for and representing his seed, derives unto them righteousness, justification, and eternal life, verse 15 to the end, 1 Cor. xv. 45, 47.

Thus they are compared together, and Jesus Christ, the second, preferred before the first.

If the first Adam had never fallen, it is not imaginable that he should have enjoyed life by one covenant, and his posterity by another; their life would have been by keeping, as their death, was by breaking, one and the same law of works; so, Jesus Christ, the second Adam, and all his spiritual seed, enjoy justification and life by one and the same covenant of grace. *We are quickened together with him,* Coloss. ii. 13. *i.e.* as our common person standing in our stead.

3. All in the covenant as with us is undertaken for and promised in the covenant, as between the Father and the Son, and so together make up but one covenant. For, his being *the covenant of the people* implies, that all promised to, or to be performed by, the people, it is secured in the

contract with Jesus Christ. Whatsoever was requisite unto our restoration, redemption, and reconciliation, he agreed to work it out, Isa. liii. 10.; there were the same objects and end in that as with him, and that as with us, 1 Pet. i. 18, 19. 1 Cor. vi. 20.

Yea, all necessaries also for application are in the covenant as with him. Is justification and the giving of a new heart promised to us? Jer: xxxi. 31.; the same is promised to Jesus Christ, Isa. liii. 11. *By his knowledge (i.e.* by the knowledge of him) *shall my righteous servant (i.e.* Jesus Christ) *justify many*—and *he shall see his seed, and be a light to the Gentiles,* Isa. xlii. 6., which implies newness of heart, and having God for their God.

4. All blessings afforded in a covenant way to us were primarily granted to Jesus Christ, and therefore the covenant is jointly with him and us; as Mr. R. observes, Christ is first justified and acquitted from the guilt of sin, and then we, Isa. liii. 11. Christ first sanctified and filled with the spirit, and then we, Isa. xlii. 1.; he first glorified, and then we, Heb. i. 2. Rom. viii. 17. Jesus Christ is our great feofee in trust; he hath all the riches of grace and glory granted to, and vested in him, to our use and benefit; both have them by the same covenant.

Indeed he takes precedence, he excels in dignity and power, he is the first-born among many brethren, Rom. viii. 29.; the first-born from the dead, Coloss. i. 18, 19. All fullness dwelling in him; all is firstly granted into his hands, and, in the second place, to us. If we would obtain any spiritual gifts, any graces, any comforts, any glory, we must be beholden to him, borrow all from his store, receive all from his hand. The divine spirit is from him, John xvi. 7, 8.; all grace from him, Rom. xvi. 20, 24. 1 Cor. xvi. 23.; repentance from him, Acts v. 31. *He is exalted to give repentance and the forgiveness of sins;* faith itself from him, Heb. xii. 2.; which argue that all flow from the same covenant. The name of Jesus Christ is in the covenant—

THE COVENANT OF GRACE 63

he is the principal party there, to whom all the promises are primarily made, on our behalf.

5. Union with Jesus Christ is the only way to promised blessings, and, therefore, the covenant is made jointly with him and us, 2 Cor. i. 20.; not only some, but *all the promises of God in him are yea, and in him amen;* twice in him. None of the promises are made immediately to us, but all invariable, unchangeable, in their making, and in their performance or accomplishment—yet it is in him.

I might argue also from Jesus Christ his receiving the same signs with us, baptism and the supper: and why were they applied to him, if he were under one covenant, and we under another?

6. All the ancient covenant expressures run jointly to Jesus Christ, and also to believers, which are his seed. The promises to Adam, Abraham, David, &c. were not so many distinct covenants of grace; they were but various gradual discoveries of the some covenant, according to the variety of occasions in the several ages, every new one being for some new end, and bringing with it a further degree of manifestation—and all run to Jesus Christ and us.

7. That gracious promise revealed to Adam primarily runs unto Jesus Christ, as to the blessed seed, and then to us, in him. Wretched man having eaten of the forbidden fruit, what could he expect every moment but the execution of that dreadful sentence, Gen. ii. 17. *In the day thou eatest, dying thou shalt die.*

O what inexpressible astonishment must needs seize upon his guilty soul on this account, there being no contrivance by any creature wisdom, no way open, either for the escaping the stroke of divine wrath, or for standing under it; for how should a feeble creature bear up, or avoid being crushed under the weight of an omnipotent arm?

Now, behold, in the cool of the day, when the shadows of the evening were coming, upon undone fallen man, then was the first dawning of a day of grace: says God, Gen.

iii. 15. *I will put enmity between thee and the woman, and between thy seed and her seed; it shall bruise thy head,* &c. The bowels of divine compassion did so tenderly roll towards him, that he could not pass one day, without some intimation of his love, and revealing his gracious intendments towards him.

Indeed this was immediately spoken, not to Adam as a promise, but to the serpent as a threatening, yet was uttered that Adam might over-hear and spell out something of a promise in it. But Jesus Christ is primarily this seed of the woman which bruises the serpent's head; for it is he that stands conqueror over all the enemies of salvation; sin, Satan, death, and hell, he procures their utter overthrow; destroys the works of the devil, 1 John iii. 8.; vanquishes and overcomes him, Revel. xii. 9. Christ is chiefly intended by it. Believers are victorious only in and by Jesus Christ, they overcome by the blood of the Lamb, and so the promise is jointly to him and them.

Many matters in this first discovery of the covenant did lie dark, and were hidden, it not discovering distinctly what seed of the woman it should be, nor the way or means to this or that; he should be God as well as man, and how this should be brought about; which were afterwards revealed.

2. The covenant with Abraham was jointly with Jesus Christ and us. There was a gracious promise (which faith might hang upon) as early as the days of Adam; this was a promise of a blessed seed to be given for man, but the covenant with man concerning it seems to be dated, not from Adam, but from Abraham, Gal. iii. because the Lord was pleased to deal with Abraham in a more familiar way than with others before him, putting himself under covenant engagements to him, Gen. xii. 3. *In thee shall all the families of the earth be blessed,* and Gen. xvii.

They must needs be at a great loss about the seed of the woman, of whose posterity it should come, and it was the chief additional excellence of this federal expressure to assure Abraham that the Messiah should come of his seed, according to the flesh—Gen. xxii. 18. *In thy seed shall all the nations of the earth be blessed;* and thus that which was more general in the former to Adam, is here more particular, for it is restrained to this family, and it was an advantage to know the family which he should come of. There were other promises made to him, as concerning the land of Canaan, and that the Lord would be his God, Gen. xvii. 7. The latter was hinted before, and to another person, Gen. ix. 26. *Blessed be the Lord God of Shem.* It is observed by some, that Shem was the first man in all the scripture that had this honour. It is not expressly said, that he was the God of Adam, or of Noah, but the God of Shem. Now this becomes more general, he will be the God of Abraham and his seed.

And this seed expressly is Christ, Gal. iii. 16. Now to Abraham and his seed were the promises made, he says not unto seeds, as of many, but as of one, and to thy seed, which is Christ. So verse 19., whether it be taken for Christ mystical, or as a public person, yet Christ is first that seed, and it is as clear as the sun, that not only Christ, but believers also, are the seed, in the same Abrahamic covenant, Gal. iii. 7, 26., especially verse 29. *and if ye be Christ's, then are ye Abraham's seed, and heirs, according to the promise.* What can be more evident? Believers are also of the seed, and so the covenant with Abraham runs jointly to Jesus Christ and them.

3. The covenant made with David runs jointly to Jesus Christ and us; Psal. lxxxix. 20, 28, 29. *I have found my servant David; my covenant shall stand with him.* Abraham was not a king, but David was, and the covenant was made with him in that capacity, as the great additional excellence thereof; and it typically holds forth Jesus Christ in his exaltation to regal dignity. Herein are some things applicable only to Jesus Christ, as verse 27., and often

he is called the Son of David; and it is promised; Ezek. xxxiv. 24, 25. *I the Lord will be their God, and my servant David a prince among them.* This was long after David was dead, and, therefore, must refer to Jesus Christ. And also this covenant with David extended to that seed which would break statutes, and sin against the Lord, Psal. lxxxix. 30-32., which cannot refer to Jesus Christ, but to us; and thus that covenant expressure did run jointly to Jesus Christ and to us.

4. The new covenant runs jointly to Jesus Christ and to us; for he died as Mediator, not of the old but of the new testament, Heb. ix. 15., which he could not have done, if he had not been under it.

As an additional excellence of the new, Jesus Christ is mentioned, not as undertaking, but as actually exhibited, or come; and his being the Mediator, and the new covenant itself whereof he is the Mediator, are distinct things, yet both within the covenant of grace. Indeed, whatever promises there are, for application of blessings to us in Christ, are included in the new covenant, that extends to all matters of his ministration, as already in that office: but the promises are all first made to Jesus Christ, and to us in him.

Corollary 1. Hence the covenant of grace is very extensive; it takes in all the promises made to Jesus Christ and to us; yea, all the ancient promises of a blessed seed to come did belong to that covenant, in lieu of which we have a Mediator actually exhibited, and also the new covenant. It may be questioned by some, whether all the promises still in force in the book of God do belong to the covenant of grace, because so few are enumerated, where it is mentioned, as with us—Gen. xii. and xvii.; Heb. viii. 10-12.

But seeing all are made and fulfilled in Christ, hence they must all flow as living streams from that fountain. The covenant of grace with Jesus Christ, that is the great charter that we hold all our privileges by; and all the promises do some way or other appertain to that.

Some promises are constitutive of the covenant, as those between the Father and the Son concerning a seed; others are executive, or referring to the execution and application of it, Isa. liii. 10, 11. Heb. viii. 10-12.

Some are principal, and concerning the end, eternal life, Heb. viii.; ix. 15. Gal. iii. 8, 9, 18. Others less principal, concerning the means—internal, the spirit and faith; or, external, as ordinances.

Not only spiritual, but even promises of temporal blessings, as of succour and relief in particular cases and conditions, in outward straits and distresses, yet these belong to the covenant of grace. Psal. cv. 39-41. *He spread a cloud for a covering,* here is protection; *a fire to give light by night,* that intimates direction; *he brought quails, and satisfied them with the bread of heaven,* here is gracious provision; *he opened the rock, and the waters gushed out,* this speaks miraculous refreshment and consolation. And whence was all this care over them? verse 42. *For he remembered his holy covenant, and Abraham his servant.* All these then were to be deemed covenant mercies. Where had the Lord particularly promised any such extraordinary reliefs to Abraham or his seed? O he witnessed himself to be their God, and promised the land of Canaan, and that implies all mercy and means necessary for them in the pursuance of the call to it. So that all protections, preservations, provisions, all for the sustaining, upholding, and succouring of the people of God, yea even their lowest mercies, have a tincture of covenant love to put quickness into them. So, returns of prayers in a day of outward affliction are in remembrance of his covenant, Psal. cvi. 44, 45. 2 Kings xiii. 22, 23.

Yea, observe, in some places where the covenant is mentioned, there are promises added (and so belong to it) which in other repetitions of it are left out, as Jer. xxxii. 38-40. Oneness of heart and way, and his fear in their hearts, are promised in the covenant, yet are omitted in the recital thereof, Jer. xxxi. 31-35.; and the word covenant is omitted, and yet many promises thereof are mentioned, Ezek. xxxvi. 25. to the end, as appears by the identity of some with those expressly in it elsewhere. So that we are not to confine the covenant of grace to those mentioned in the new covenant; all the promises to us are some way comprised in it.

Corollary 2. Hence there is infallible certainty in, and grounded consolation issuing from, the covenant of grace, seeing it is made jointly with Jesus Christ and us.

All the promises are his right, as well as ours, and so can never fail. Is Jesus Christ the seed of the woman, who hath assurance of being victorious over the serpent? Gen. iii. 15.

So are believers; yea they are of the seed of Abraham and David, interested in the same promises, Gal. iii. 19, 21.

If any thing be a condition of the covenant of grace, it must be so, of the promises to Jesus Christ, as well as of those to us, that taking in all, and being jointly with both and principally with him and with us but in him, as his seed: and so faith cannot be it, for the promises were not made to Jesus Christ upon condition of our believing, but upon what he himself should do and suffer; rather therein he hath a promise, assurance that we shall believe, Isa. liii. 10. *he shall see his seed.* It would highly derogate from the honour of the Lord Jesus to say, that the efficacy and effect of all his undertaking had dependence upon any act of ours, as that of believing.

It is by the efficiency of the word of the new testament that faith is given, Rom. x. 14-17. Acts xiii. 47, 48.

Yea, the gift of faith is promised in that, of writing his law in their hearts, Heb. viii. 10., and therefore by its obligation; for it is a contradiction to speak of a promise without obligation for performance unto the persons to whom it is made; and what matter is it whether it be upon an obligation to the sinners themselves, or to another, (to

Jesus Christ), their feofee in trust for them; it is by the new covenant which is made to them, and that of grace is jointly with Christ and them.

Believers are not only the objects for or concerning whom he promises to Jesus Christ that he will do them good, (as brute or inanimate creatures are improperly said to be in covenant with him), but the subjects to whom he promises special blessings in Christ, so as the promises are directed to and may be claimed by them; Jesus Christ hath an interest therein, they are his right, as well as theirs, and this is no damage, but an advantage, as giving assurance that they will be made good to a title, Jer. xxx. 20, 21. *if you can break my covenant of the day, and my covenant of the night, then may also my covenant be broken with David my servant.* Long before the prophesying of Jeremiah, David had been in the dust, and yet the covenant with him holds still: and it being made with Jesus Christ, who is our David, hence the order of nature, the intercourse and revolutions of night and day, might as readily fail, as any promises made to him be disannulled, or go unaccomplished; yea, he will sue them out for us, when, by reason of inward cloudings and darkness (even about an interest in them) we cannot lay any claim unto them ourselves. He should be a loser, if they should not be fulfilled; he should lose his right, as well as we ours, Christ and we having a joint interest therein. Had Christ assurance of being victorious over the serpent, we also have assurance of standing conquerors over him in Christ, by the same promise, and that under the same notion of the seed of the woman. So that this is a bottom of everlasting consolation, that Jesus Christ and we are within one and the same covenant.

CHAPTER III.

Of Christ, as the sum of the Covenant.

THE covenant of grace runs primarily to Jesus Christ, and to us in him, so as he not only makes it with, but even is, the covenant of the people, Isa. xlii, 6. It will be necessary to enquire, what interest Jesus Christ has, or how and in what place and office he stands, in reference to the covenant.

1. Jesus Christ is the very foundation which the evangelical covenant is built upon, as he is our life, Coloss. iii. 3; 1 John v. 20., the cause of it; so he the covenant, *i.e.* the very basis of it, as 1 Cor. iii. 11. *For other foundation can no man lay than that is laid, which is Jesus Christ.* The covenant of works was founded upon something in man, his con-created ability, and natural strength; all the obedience of the first Adam, (if he had stood), and the fruits thereof, would have been resulting from the sufficiency of his own power and free will; and he failing, all the fabric fell.

But the Lord has established another glorious covenant, and this is built upon what is firmer, and of greater strength, even Jesus Christ; this stone that is laid in Zion is a tried stone; Isa. xxvi. 16. *A sure foundation.* Now the structure of our salvation will never fall, because it has such a sure ground work, able to bear up the weight and stress of all that is laid upon it; no other can be laid. He is the only foundation of all the promises, of all the graces, of all the obedience, of all the peace, of all the comfort, of all the glory, that is promised. That with Abraham before his incarnation was *confirmed of God in Christ,* Gal. iii. 17. He was the Mediator of Abraham's covenant, and, therefore, that had in it the same for substance with the new.

Indeed, Jesus Christ is the foundation of all the blessings and special privileges in the covenant, as with us. If the Lord be a God to any, it is in Christ; if their iniquities be forgiven, it is in the blood of Christ; if the divine law be written in their hearts, it is by the finger of the spirit of Christ; thus he lies at the bottom of all, and so is the covenant of the people.

2. Jesus Christ makes way for our enjoyment of all federal blessings, by standing in manifold relations to the covenant.

As he stands between God and us as a middle person, to make reconciliation, so he is the Mediator of the covenant, Heb. ix. 15. There was a wide breach that we could never have made up; indeed, such a variance as there was no possibility of our approaching to God to enter upon a treaty of peace, much less to procure our own reconciliation; sin raised such an enmity, as the Lord would have been a consuming fire to us, if we had come near to him; now the Lord Jesus interposed, and took up this case, undertook to compose and put an end to this difference. There were iniquities in the way to hinder our fruition of promised mercies, but he took an effectual course for the removal of these. He is the Mediator of the new testament; for what end? *for the redemption of the transgressions that were under the first testament.* Satisfaction was made by him to divine justice to the full; he answered all the demands of the righteous law, and so wrought out reconciliation for us.

As he undertook for the parties at variance, so he was the surety of the covenant, Heb. vii. 22. Jesus made a surety of a better testament. The Lord would not take our bond for that great debt which we had contracted, and were never able to pay. It was now with us as with a poor man under an arrest for a vast sum, unless there can be procured an able sufficient man to enter bond with him, he must to prison, without hope of being released any more: so the law of the righteous God arrested us, for infinite breaches thereof; it exacted a great and yet most just debt at our hand, which we (being already bankrupts) were never able to answer: it required a debt of infinite suffering, the just due of our sin, which, if laid upon us, would sink us for ever; for *the wages if sin is death.* The Lord demanded a debt of perfect obedience, universal righteousness unto life, which we were never able to yield; and now unless one able and sufficient will undertake and be bound for us, there is no possibility of escaping the prison of hell, the chains of infernal darkness, the everlasting wrath of the omnipotent God. Under this misery we must have lain, without hope of recovery: this was our state upon the fall of our first parents, and in this strait and distress, one not of our procuring, but of his own grace offering it, even Jesus Christ stepped in, and became a surety for us to pay our ransom, to answer our debt to the utmost farthing; he put his name into our obligation, *was made under the law, to redeem those that were under the law,* Gal. iv. 4.

He became God's witness to us, to free us from all doubts about the fulfilling of the covenant to us; he undertook and promised that he *would lose nothing that was given him,* John vi. 39., *but would raise it up at the last day, i.e.* to everlasting salvation; for others shall be raised up also unto condemnation, but these unto eternal glory.

As he ratified and confirmed all, so he was the testator of the covenant. Heb. ix. 16, 17. *Where there is a testament, there must also of necessity be the death of the testator, for a testament is of force after men be dead.* Nothing less than death itself was threatened upon the first transgression, Gen. ii. 17.; that must be endured if ever sinners be recovered into a fruition of eternal life. And now behold the matchless love of Jesus Christ; says he, I will die in their stead, to save them from eternal death, and thus he turned it into a testament, a new testament, sealing it with his own blood.

As he acts for our obtainment of the blessings promised, so he is the messenger of the covenant. Mal. iii. 1. *The messenger of the covenant, whom ye delight in, behold he shall come.*

We should have been without a knowledge of this grace, altogether strangers to it, and unacquainted with it, if he had not revealed it to us, and so we should not have made out after all, but come short of those spiritual blessings of the covenant; but now Jesus Christ himself travails* with these blessed tidings—he makes a report of all the federal transactions between the Father and him in order to our salvation, he opens all those soul-ravishing mysteries, and all those precious promises, indeed the way to our participation of those blessed privileges, and so he is the messenger of the covenant.

As he seeks to satisfy us of the reality of God in all those federal transactions, so he is the witness of the covenant. Isa. lv. 4. *Behold I have given him for a witness of the people.* When poor souls hear the tidings of covenant love in the heart of God towards them, they are ready to suspect it is too good news to be true; are apt to be incredulous here, are hardly persuaded to believe the truth thereof, at least as to themselves: now Jesus Christ condescends so far, as to take upon him the office of a witness, to assure of the truth of all; now he is in heaven, he does not throw up that office, he continues still in this work, and sends down news from heaven thereof, Revel. i. 5. and iii. 14. He is the faithful witness still; as if he should say, I lay in the bosom of the Father, I have seen all transactions, all passages, I know how the heart of God stands towards this covenant work; if my word may have any credit with you, I testify (says Jesus

---

* travelleth *[orig]*.

Christ) that the Father is real herein, and the work is done, the covenant is struck, ratified and sealed with my blood.

When souls are full of jealousies concerning the willingness of God to give entertainment to them, and admittance into covenant grace, and to deal with them in a covenant way, though they cannot peep into heaven and look into the bosom of the Father, and read all things there, yet Jesus Christ stooped so low as to take upon him the office of a faithful witness, to give assurance thereof.

As he is our spiritual head and the blessed seed, so he is a party contracting in the covenant. He is the chief seed of Abraham and of David, Gal. iii., to whom the promises are made, verse 19. Mat. xv. 22. All is assured to him, as well as to us; and his standing on our side, as a party with us in the same covenant, as it is an honour, so it is a comfort to us, in that it gives assurance of its accomplishment to a title; for the Lord will not fail his only Son, Jesus Christ, of any thing which he has promised to him; and he being a party, it were an injury to him if any thing were unfulfilled.

As he is the substance of the covenant, so he is said to be the covenant of the people; and well may he bear this name, he standing in all these relations to it.

3. Jesus Christ was the principal promise of the covenant; this denominates him the covenant, his being really the chief part of it, or thing first promised in it, and all other things for his sake. Thus he primarily was the seed of the woman, that was promised to break the serpent's head, Gen. iii. 15. Heb. ii. 14. 1 John iii. 8. He is that seed of Abraham, in whom all the nations are blessed, Gen. xxii. 18. Gal. iii. 16. He is the royal seed of David, to be enthroned, of whose kingdom there shall be no end, Luke i. 32, 33.

Indeed, this is a grand privilege of gospel times, that what was of old the great thing under promise to come, *viz.* a blessed seed, a Messiah, is now turned into a performance, and he now stands actually a Mediator, instead thereof. All the prophecies were of him. Acts x. 43. *To him give all the prophets witness.* Of the scriptures he says, John v. 39. *They are they which testify of me;* as if they said nothing else but Christ, Christ: and thus he is the covenant.

4. Jesus Christ is really to us all that which, under any ancient covenant, was typically represented unto men; and so he is substantially the covenant of the people. As Dr. Sibbs* observes, Christ is all to us which was held forth of old; either in personal types, he is the second Adam, the true Isaac, Joseph, Joshua, Solomon, Melchizedek; or, in real types, he is the true brazen serpent that cures sin-stung souls, which, by an eye of faith, are looking to him, John iii. 14, 15. He is the true manna, bread of life, to all those that believingly feed upon him, John vi. 31, 33, 35. He is the true sacrifice, the paschal lamb; our hearts being sprinkled with his blood, the destroying angel shall pass over us. He is our true tabernacle, true altar, and true ark, all typified by these, is really fulfilled in him.

5. Jesus Christ is the excellence, marrow, and sweetness, indeed the sum and substance of all that is under promise, and so he is the covenant of the people; indeed he is the very storehouse where the promises are treasured up. All mercies from the Father must have their conveyance to us through the hands of his Son. Jesus Christ is the very quintessence, the chief in, the very life of all the mercies themselves, and all come with him— Rom. viii. 32. *How shall he not with him also freely give us all things.* It is Christ that puts fullness into other things, and adds sweetness to them; they are embittered, and as nothing, if without him. The promises, though full in themselves, yet are empty to us, unless taken with Christ; all privileges empty, all enjoyments empty, unless taken

---

* Sibbes.

with him; hence he is said to be *all in all,* Col. iii. 11. He is all in all graces, all in all peace, in all promises, in all comforts, in all glory.

6. Jesus Christ does all that is necessary for the procurement of all federal blessings, and so he is the covenant of the people. As he is the resurrection, *i.e.* the cause of it, John xi. 25., so he is the cause and procurer of all federal blessings. Not only shall he make a covenant with the people, but be a covenant of the people, *i.e.* all that is required, in a federal way, from the people, that Jesus Christ shall be to them. If the Father demands it of them, they must not present him with any duties or performances of their own for acceptation unto life, but with Jesus Christ; he is their covenant, to perform all for them, which they are obliged to, in order to that end. Says the Lord, I will not enter into covenant, or deal in an immediate way with them, as with the first Adam, but I will take a surer course, I will give thee for that end; you shall undertake all the matters therein: even for thy seed, I will look to thee for the performance thereof: and thus he is the covenant of the people.

All that is promised to Jesus Christ, or to us, it is upon his obedience, Isa. liii. 10-12.

Not by the obedience of everyone for himself, but *by the obedience of one, i.e.* of Jesus Christ, *many are made righteous,* Rom. v. 19. Justification of life and remission of sins are procured by him, verse 18. Rom. iii. 24. And so reconciliation, or promised peace, Isa. liii. 5. *The chastisement of our peace was upon him.* We must for ever have stood at enmity, if he had not stepped in for the procurement of our peace; hence *he is our peace,* Ephes. ii. 14. Not only the author and procurer, but even the sum of it. So the promise of propriety in, and communion with God, has its procurement, and takes effect only upon the obedience of Jesus Christ. All are afar off from God, under the greatest estrangement, till made nigh by the blood of Jesus Christ, Ephes. ii. 12, 13. The promise of the communication of sanctifying grace, of giving the law into the heart, is from him, Isa. liii. 10. 1 Cor. i. 30. Indeed, the promise of salvation and eternal life takes effect from him; his death was for this end, Heb. ix. 15. *That they which are called might receive the promise if the eternal inheritance.* And thus he is for a covenant of the people.

CHAP. IV.

Of the Date of Covenant Mercies.

IF it be inquired, when the covenant of grace was made between God the Father, and Jesus Christ the Son? it must be answered—it was from eternity, it was an eternal covenant. Indeed, the actual giving him for a covenant was not till his incarnation: it is mentioned as a future thing, he was promised before, but given then; whence Isa. xlii. 1-3, &c. is applied to him when he had taken our nature, Mat. xii. 17, 18, &c.

Also the first revelation of it was, Gen. iii. 15.—in the promise of his becoming the seed of the woman to bruise the serpent's head. That argues a fore-agreement or consent, to grapple with the serpent, but does not give the first date to the covenant; so as the first declaration of the covenant of grace was there, but the constitution, or making of it, was before all time, even from *eternity.* This appears, for,

1. There were mutual operations, or actings, of the will of God the Father, and Son, from eternity, concerning the restoration of lapsed man, which amount to a covenant; for what more is requisite thereunto! It is revealed, that such a compact was between them, Isa. liii. 10-12. xlii. 1-8. God *worketh all things after the counsel of his own will,* Ephes. i. 11. Therefore, so great a transaction was not without it; and the will of God is eternal, for he does not begin to will or nill that which he did not before. According to their distinct personality, the will of the Father was, that the Son should, in fullness of time, take our nature, do and suffer all necessary to the restitution

and recovery of the elect. The will of the Son echoed back and answered to that of the Father, accepting the office; and this distinct acting, or new habitude (as Dr. Owen calls it) of will in the Father and Son toward each other, is beyond a bare decree that the thing should be, and so it is an eternal covenant.

2. The designation of Jesus Christ to, and his undertaking of the Mediatorial office, (which amount to a covenant or agreement), was before all time. For, Eph. i. 4. *He hath chosen us in him, i.e.* in Christ. And when? *Before the foundation of the world.* He is, though not the cause, yet the medium or means for the execution of election: that did not run upon an uncertain means, and, therefore, there was an agreement concerning it from eternity. Indeed, as to his mediatorial employment, he is said to pre-exist all creatures. Prov. viii. 23. *I was set up* (or anointed, *i.e.* to be king, priest, and prophet), *from everlasting, or ever the earth was,* verse 24 to 31.

3. Many did believe, (Heb. xi.) and so salvation was obtained, in the times of the old testament, by Jesus Christ, through a covenant of grace. To say that they were saved by virtue of a mere decree, were to assert that their salvation was obtained one way, ours another, and would render the covenant superfluous, vain, and needless, if some were saved without it; and it is against Rev. xiii. 8., which says, he was *a lamb slain from the foundation of the world.* Their partaking of the fruits and benefits of his death (before it actually was) could be no other way but upon assurance that Jesus Christ would, in due time, take our nature, and suffer death: this assurance could arise from nothing but a covenant, wherein Jesus Christ promised to do it, and the Father trusted the Son for a due performance of it. This covenant then was before his incarnation, and so must be made with him personally considered, or as the second person in the Trinity, and consequently from eternity; for no acts between them as

THE COVENANT OF GRACE

God but are eternal. The Father and the Son, as so, do not begin to act towards each other what they did not before; there was, therefore, an eternal covenant.

4. There were some reciprocal or federal actions of the Father giving souls, and the Son's receiving of them, antecedaneous to faith, John xvii. 2, 6, 12. *That he should give eternal life to as many as thou hast given him.* This deed of gift is for the same end that the covenant of grace serves to, *viz.* that they might enjoy eternal life—John vi. 37. *All that the Father giveth me shall come to me, i.e.* shall believe, verse 35.; this free giving is first, and believing after, and therefore seems to be eternal. This donation is an act of the divine will, granting of persons to Jesus Christ that they might be ransomed or redeemed: right to receive and take them is relative to it, and, therefore, (I think), differs from election. For the reason of that stands not in such a grant, but in a distinct act of the same will, *viz.* in divine love, with separation, severing some to salvation, with a refusing of others. This giving, then, is a federal act from all eternity.

5. Some federal matters are declared to be from eternity. Tit. i. 2. *In hope of eternal life, which God, that cannot lie, promised*—When? *before the world began.* And we are saved and called, not only according to his purpose, but grace, which was given us in Christ, 2 Tim. i. 9. But when? *Before the world began.* All promises of eternal life, and all such grace, belong to the covenant of grace, and these were then made or given, not to us in our own persons, (for we had no existence so early), but in Jesus Christ. As it would sound harsh to interpret the word promised thus, decreed to promise, so it were as absurd to render either text from the beginning of the world, the word being πρo, *ante,* before, not since. I ask, is it to be rendered so as to election, or Jesus Christ, Ephes. i. 4. 1 Pet. i. 20.? If not, let us own this truth, that, in the covenant of grace, eternal life was promised, and grace given in Jesus Christ from all eternity.

CHAPTER V.

General Inferences from the whole.

COROLLARY 1. Hence we may behold infinite condescension, that the eternal God will deal or treat with us in a familiar covenant way. What an honour is this? By his prerogative and sovereignty, he could have commanded all duty from us, without promising any thing to us: but behold the Lord has put himself under everlasting engagements to his people, that, upon the account of his faithfulness, they may expect (through Christ) all mercy needful in all estates and conditions. When they are under great sufferings, (as Israel of old), this covenant may be of encouraging use—Exod. ii. 23, 24. *God remembered his covenant, and had respect to them.* When under temptation, to think that divine wrath and displeasure will go out against them, it is of succouring use, Isa. liv. 9, 10. As readily might the waters of Noah return, and as easily might the mountains depart, as the covenant of his peace be removed. When under pressing wants, it is of relieving use—2 Chron. vi. 42. *Remember the mercies of David, thy servant.* When looking death in the face, it may be of comforting use—2 Sam. xxiii. 5. *Although my house be not so with God, yet he hath made with me an everlasting covenant.* These were the last words of David, verse 1. So that this unchangeable covenant may make a dying man lift up his head with rejoicing. His house was not duly ordered towards God, and yet he could bear up with this against all his failings, unworthiness, undeservings.

Corollary 2. Hence there are transcendent excellencies in the covenant of grace, far above what are found in the covenant of works. For, here the Father is promising unto the Son, that he should be a covenant of the people; the, excellence of this might be evinced from its properties—it is a free, gracious, holy, well-regulated, sure, and an everlasting covenant, 2 Tim. i. 9. Luke i. 72. 2 Sam. xxiii. 5. Isa. lv. 3. These things being largely handled by others, I do but touch upon them.

Also the vast difference between those covenants of works and of grace clear this. The covenant of works was made with the first Adam, and with all his seed in him, without a mediator, requiring perfect personal obedience, by his natural concreated power, with free will to stand or fall, implicitly promising life, upon keeping, and threatening death, and a forfeiture of all, upon breaking of it, Gen. ii. 17. It speaks nothing of remission of sin, upon the deepest sorrow and repentance: if Adam could have wept day and night, and even tears of blood, yet that promised nothing, not the least mercy or favour after its violation, nothing but death to be expected from it; which speaks the misery of all who are in a natural condition, and not come under a better covenant.

But the covenant of grace is made with Jesus Christ, the second Adam, and with all his seed in him, as their Mediator, to make reconciliation, and work out a righteousness for them, so as now the promise is sure to all the seed, 1 Tim. ii. 5; Rom. iv. 16.

The Father is covenanting with Jesus Christ, as a more glorious head than the first Adam, promising to give him to be a covenant of the people, to stand on their side: this must argue a pacification in that he who was God (the person offended) would be a God-man, a Redeemer, so as he and the people make but one party in this covenant; yea, he wrought out that righteousness which is unto justification of life, Rom. v. 18, 19.

In handling the subject of the covenant, the clearest way is, to compare the covenant of works with the first Adam, and the covenant of grace with Jesus Christ, the second Adam, together; so the two Adams are paralleled, Rom. v. And also to compare the old covenant at mount Sinai, with the new covenant, as Jer. xxxi. 31, 32. The jumbling of these together has occasioned darkness in many matters; these differences being rightly stated, in a secondary way any of them might be compared, with less danger of miscarrying.

Corollary 3. Hence it is rich grace and special favour to be in the number of the people that were covenanted for, between the Father and the Son; seeing none are freed from the sentence of death and condemnation, or saved, but in the way of a covenant of grace, Ephes. ii. 8. 2 Tim. i. 9.—The being under that is not a privilege that betides all; it reaches some, and not others: for there is no covenant expressure that extends now to all mankind, without exception; that Gen. iii. 15. implies, that some are the seed of the serpent, and others are the seed of the woman; all the world are not the seed of Abraham or David, nor the house of Israel and Judah, with whom the new covenant is made, Jer. xxxi. 31. The Father's act of donation was not of all, without exception.—John xvii. 9. *I pray not for the world, but for them which thou hast given me.* The antithesis, or opposition, does strongly prove, that some are of the world, and these are not given unto Jesus Christ, nor prayed for by him. It would sound harsh to say, either that he covenanted with the Father to die for and redeem some that were never given him, or that he would not intercede and pray for some that he did redeem; and the giving act was absolute, not upon the condition of our believing; for, John vi. 37. *All that the Father giveth me shall come to me.* All them that were given shall certainly believe, and so shall be saved, Mark xvi. 16.; and, therefore, some were never given to him. Impetration and application are of equal latitude and extent, Rom. v. 10. From reconciliation, which is by the death of his son, the apostle argues unto salvation, with a much more. All those, therefore, that it was purchased for, shall certainly have it applied to them, and be reconciled in their own persons.

In the great charter, the covenant as between the Father and the Son, an effectual application of federal blessings is absolutely promised.—Isa. liii. 10, 11. *He shall see his seed, and he shall see of the travail of his soul, and be satisfied, and he shall justify many.* How many shalls are here, and on this account, because he shall bear their iniquities. All then whose iniquities he did bear, he shall convert and justify. He has the highest assurance that he should enjoy the very seed which he travailed for. It was not a mere conditional satisfaction that he made: upon his death, all matters became absolute; the very persons were appointed, and an unalterable determination of the Father concerning their conversion, which cannot reach unto all men without exception, for, then all should certainly be saved. So, Isa. xlii. 6, 7, it is not only promised that he should be a covenant of the people, (the Jews), but also a light of the Gentiles; which imports a removing of spiritual blindness, by affording special illuminations: not only will he be redemption to the Gentiles, but a light for the applying of it to all that he has redeemed. Indeed, he will bring them from the prison, from their spiritual thraldom and bondage to sin and Satan, which denote effectual vocation, Acts xiii. 47, 48; xxvi. 18. So that an effectual application of covenant grace unto conversion is absolutely necessary to be vouchsafed unto all those whom Christ did undertake for: yet you see here that the accomplishment hereof is by ways and means of his appointment, and the Lord does not mock or delude men in the general invitations and calls of the gospel, any more than he mocked Pharaoh, when he (by Moses) commanded him to let Israel go, and yet declared that he would *harden his heart, that he should not let the people go,* Exod. iv. 21, 23. The Lord, by his will of precept, commands all, wherever the gospel comes, to believe; and all which do believe shall

The Covenant of Grace

certainly be saved, Mark xvi. 16.; and, therefore, he does not mock. The dispensation of the gospel is the means which he sanctifies and blesses to that end, for the working or begetting of faith. If any will neglect, abuse, and misimprove, or *make light of it,* Mat. xxii. 5., and treat spitefully the messengers that are sent with these blessed tidings, or if they will attend more to their worldly matters, their farms and oxen, they sinning against the means of grace, it is putting a slight upon the grace and salvation tendered in the means, and thus leaves them inexcusable, and will expose the sinners to just condemnation. They had power to forbear such acts of sin against God, by means, though they had not power to render it effectual; and who (either preacher or hearer) knows that he is not of that number which Jesus Christ covenanted for, and will make it effectual to? However, the Lord is not bound to abate of his demand of duty, because of man's impotency, and (sinfully contracted) disability to obey.

All, therefore, ought to give utmost attention to the general call of the gospel, as a matter of the highest concernment to their souls for eternity; and the neglecting thereof is a despising of Jesus Christ, and his benefits— Luke x. 16., and then no wonder if the *wrath of God abideth on them.*

Corollary 4. Hence there were glorious transactions in order to the salvation of the elect, long before their believing. Though the actual application of federal blessings to them is not one moment of time before the gift of faith, yet, before that, there are glorious advantages arising from the covenant, as between the Father and the Son, on their behalf.

Virtually and *ex fædere* all conducing unto happiness was secured for them from eternity; then there was not only a passing such an act as they cannot eventually be damned, (which is so far from proving an actual justification as that), a mere decree of election would have been sufficient unto this, seeing that must certainly have its execution; but by a federal act, so early was the undertaking of Jesus Christ on their behalf; then was the covenant made between the Father and the Son, which had all blessedness in the womb of it, Tit. i. 2. Indeed he had not actually our sin upon him, nor was so justified before his incarnation, Isa. l. 7, 8. For, his coming in the flesh had been vain and unnecessary, if he had been actually discharged before.

And this may show, that our justification does not every way run parallel to his; for believers under the old testament were actually justified before Jesus Christ was so; but so early, the elect did, in some special way, belong unto God, being federally made over by him to Jesus Christ, for gracious ends, John xvii. 6. *Thine they were, and thou gavest them unto me.*

And this was a great business, for he was appointed to be their representative, and to pay their ransom money; so as when he did it, they were virtually deemed as justified, sanctified and glorified there, not in their own persons, but in him—Eph. ii. 5, 6. *Hath quickened us, together with Christ, and hath raised us up together, and made us sit together in heavenly places, in Christ Jesus.*

Carol. 5. Hence, there was some love in the bosom of God towards the elect, from all eternity. Sending Christ himself (who is given for a covenant, and is the sum of it), is the fruit and effect of it. John iii. 16. *God so loved the world, that he gave his only begotten Son.* And if the covenant was from everlasting, then that divine love, which is the fountain and first spring from whence it flows, must needs be so early also.

God does actually love the elect before they are regenerate, or can actually believe, with a love of benevolence, or good will, though not with a love of complacency and delight. He bears love to their persons, though not to their qualities and actions, nor to their state

The Covenant of Grace

and condition. God owns them, not only with electing but with redeeming love. Rom. v. 8. *God commended his love towards us, in that, while we were yet sinners, Christ died for us.* This extols his love, and makes it surmount all others, that he gave his Son to die for them, whilst they were in a state of sin and misery. There was some federal love, so far as to give them unto Jesus Christ to be redeemed by him, John vi. 37, 39. so as to own them as the persons which should share in covenant grace afterwards, when others were left out. The love of God, is an unchangeable and eternal act of his will, ever one and the same, admits of no increase or decrease in him; he does not begin to love any person that he hated before— he *changeth not,* Mal. iii. 6. But to help our weak understandings, according to his acting towards us, and to the change that is made in us, and as we partake of his benefits, so he is said to let it out to us. 1 John iii. 1. *Behold what manner of love the Father hath bestowed on us, that we should be called the sons of God.* Thus the Lord loves not his creatures equally, or all alike, but some more than others, the regenerate more than the unregenerate, and those most who share most in the effects of it, both for this life, and that which is to come. From eternity, although God had not a love of approbation to the state of the elect unconverted, yet he had a love of commiseration unto their persons—Psal. ciii. 17. *But the mercy of the Lord* (which has miserable creatures as the proper objects of it) *is from everlasting to everlasting upon them that fear him,* &c. Before the foundations of the earth were laid, he considered them as possibly miserable, and was a God of mercy. Then he had such a love of benevolence to them as certainly issues in a love of beneficence or soul-enriching bounty. Eph. ii. 4, 5. *But God, who is rich in mercy, for his great love wherewith he loved us, even when we were dead in sins, hath quickened us, together with Christ,* &c. Here the first operations of divine grace, the recovery of a soul out of a dead state unto spiritual life, the first quickenings of a soul from the death of sin are made the issues of divine favour, they spring from mercy and rich mercy, from love and great love.

Corollary 6. Hence, the covenant of grace, as made with Jesus Christ, had the precedence, was before the covenant of works; that was first, this after. For, though there was a divine decree concerning the creation and the covenant of works to be in time, yet that was not actually made so early, because Adam (who was to be the head of it) was not then existing, had not a being for it to be made with. Whereas, Jesus Christ (who was the head of the covenant of grace) was not only really existing, but undertaking, from eternity. The covenant of grace (without any incongruity) may be asserted, in its constitution and making, to be first, or before the covenant of works, though in its execution and application it comes after, and presupposes the breaking of it. As a healing balsam may be prepared before the wound is made, and a salve before there be a sore, although the applying thereof be afterward; so the covenant of grace was made from eternity, not actually with us in our own persons, but with Jesus Christ for us, as our great feofee in trust, though we then were unborn, and had not a being.

Corollary 7. Hence the whole contrivance of the covenant of grace must be ascribed to God alone, seeing it was from all eternity. No creature was then existing, to have any hand or stroke therein; there was none to counsel, advise, or persuade this way. It was conceived in the heart and bosom of God, and none but he had to do in the concluding of it, and so he is alone to be magnified and extolled therein. A Christian, as one transported, may cry out on this account, as Isa. xxv. 1. *O Lord I will exalt thee, for thou hast done wonderful things; thy counsels of old are faithfulness and truth.* Now, there is no room for our boasting, nothing to be ascribed to ourselves; God alone is to be admired in covenant grace, seeing it was working towards us from all eternity—2 Tim. i. 9. it is said to be, *not according to our works*. The eternity of our mercy is exclusive of our duty, as any cause of his affording of it. This puts a glory upon covenant grace and love, that it is ancient, before the world began.

Corollary 8. Hence there is stability in covenant mercies, seeing that compact, which gives assurance thereof, was from an eternity. Says he, Psal. xxv. 6. *Remember, O Lord, thy tender mercies and thy loving kindnesses.* Why? *For they have been ever of old.* The ancientness thereof is a good argument to urge for the obtainment of them. We may have hope to receive what the Lord was so early determined, to give out—2 Tim. ii. 19. *The foundation of God standeth sure.* The apostacy of eminent professors is a great temptation unto many sincere Christians: they are apt to say, if such glistering, shining stars fall, good Lord how shall we stand? But to help against it, he tells us, the foundation that is steadfast, firm, unmoveable, it stands sure, by the covenant of grace they are granted to Jesus Christ from all eternity, 2 Tim. i. 9. Such eternal acts of God are firm and stable, abiding for ever, will secure against defection or falling away; Satan shall never utterly prevail against them; grace shall never utterly be overthrown or extinguished. *Having this seal, the Lord knoweth them that are his.* He has set his mark upon them, and, wherever they be, he can distinguish them from the world; as he knows them by number, so also by mark or seal, and when he makes up his jewels, not one of them which are his shall be wanting.

Carol. 9. Hence there is a bottom of consolation for all that are within the covenant of grace, in that it was established from all eternity. O how may it fill them with comfort, that their salvation stands by an eternal act of God, that cannot be repealed, altered, or changed; by a covenant act, wherein the faithfulness of God is engaged for the affording of it, even by the Father's gift. How often does Jesus Christ mention them as given to him, John vi. 37, 39., xvii. 2, 9, 12., as if he delighted, and gloried in, or boasted of, this giving act. How may this secure them against all fears of everlasting miscarrying, that they are given to Jesus Christ from all eternity! For he will never forfeit his Father's gifts, nor displease him so as he should withdraw them from him: they will be gifts, without repentance. This eternal act will never he recalled, which may make for their everlasting consolation.

CHAPTER VI.

*Of the Old and New Covenant
—what they are, and how distinct.*

HAVING cleared the covenant of grace as to the transactions between the Father and the Son from eternity, and as to the first revelations of its grace to the patriarchs, as Abraham, and David, &c. before the incarnation, wherein the great thing promised was that blessed Seed, so as all blessings were to be expected only in him: we come now to consider—

I. That dispensation which held forth the way and means whereby Jesus Christ came under our obligation, and, by answering of it, confirmed the covenant of grace; and this is contained in the old covenant, made at mount Sinai.

II. That dispensation, whereby the special blessings and privileges (which are the issue of his obedience), are imparted to us, and this is the new covenant.

The apostle compares these together, in diverse chapters in the epistle to the Hebrews, and says of Jesus Christ, Heb. viii. 6. *He obtained a more excellent ministry, by how much also he is the Mediator of a better covenant;* which implies that there is another testament, *viz.* that at mount Sinai, when they came out of Egypt, verse 9., which the Aaronic priesthood appertained to, that is worse; but it is the excellence of Jesus Christ that his ministration is conversant about a better testament; that has the pre-eminence on this account, as being established upon better promises. And the opposition is not laid between the covenant of works, as with the first Adam, and the new covenant, but between that at Sinai and the new. The word for covenant is διαθηκη, testament; it notes a disposition or declaration, by way of will or promise, and may be the act of one or more. Indeed, the Hebrew word *berith* is used, Jer. xxxi. 31, 32., and the same expressed by διαθηκη, Heb. viii. 8-10. But the apostle intimated that a testamentary disposition is intended by it, Gal. iii. 15, 17.; as if Jesus Christ, by fulfilling the condition of the covenant of grace, had turned it into a testament, the blessings of it being now legacies absolutely promised to us in the new.

It will be necessary here to inquire, what is the worse covenant, and what is this better testament which is compared with it?

Answer 1. The worse covenant is that conditional divine grant of blessings, upon the obedience required in the law of Moses; or that old covenant which was made at mount Sinai. This is undoubtedly it which is compared with the other; for it is that which the Levitical priesthood did belong to which the priesthood of Christ is compared with, as is manifest, Heb. vii., viii. and ix. chapters. *It is that covenant which the Lord made with the Fathers, in the day when he took them by the hand to lead them out of the land of Egypt,* Heb. viii. 9. And therefore undeniably it was the Sinai covenant, for then that was made with them, Exod. xix. 1-5, &c. *In the third month, when the children of Israel were gone out of the land of Egypt, the same day they came to the wilderness of Sinai;* and both the matter of the covenant and manner of its promulgation we see in that and the following chapters.

It is a conditional grant, it promises nothing but upon the condition of obedience. Exod. xix. verse 5. *If ye will obey my voice, and keep my covenant, then ye shall be a peculiar treasure.*—All is upon an *if.* So, Levit. xxvi. 3, 4, &c. *If ye walk in my statutes, and keep my commandments, and do them, then will I give you rain,* &c. The like in many other places; all promises run there upon the condition of keeping his commandments.

The Covenant of Grace

The whole law is generally distributed into three parts, *viz.* moral, judicial, and ceremonial; no precept but may be referred to one of these; and obedience to all of them is required, as the condition of this Sinai covenant, or all are comprised therein.

1. The moral law is such a principal part of it, as it bears the very name of the covenant, and the tables thereof are called the tables of the covenant, Exod. xxxiv. 28. Deut. ix. 9, 11, 15. The terrible appearances of God in thunderings and lightnings, and the noise of the trumpet, was the promulgation of the moral law, before the ceremonial was given forth, Exod. xix. 16.; xx. 1 to 19.

So that the first constitution of the Sinai covenant was only of the moral law. It is very observable, that Moses having rehearsed these very commandments, Deut. v., he closes up thus, verse 22.—*These words the Lord spake unto your assembly, in the mount, out of the midst of the fire, of the cloud, and of the thick darkness; and he added no more:* i.e. in making this covenant, he added no more than these moral precepts, although he reserved to himself a liberty to add the ceremonials afterwards, yet for the present he did not; indeed, virtually, they were contained therein, but not actually before the discovery of them, any more than gospel institutions, which Israel was not obliged to, until revealed, and after that were equally reducible thereunto. The holy God, that he might tame their rebellious spirits, he comes in this terrible way, requiring exact obedience to the moral commandments, and added no more. At the first hand, he revealed no way for their relief and succour, yet then, before any ceremonials were added, it made a covenant, verse 2. Even when the people could see nothing but wrath and a curse before them, they were forbidden coming up into the mount, upon pain of death, and so were not admitted to familiar converses with God, must have dreadful tokens of a divine presence, as a consuming fire; and in that respect the Sinai covenant is opposed to the new, Heb, xii. 18 to 25. *For ye are not come to the mount that might be touched, and that burnt with fire,* &c. That is, ye are not come to mount Sinai, and the terror of the old covenant, but ye are come to mount Sion—*to Jesus, the Mediator of the new covenant.*

2. The judicial laws belong to it; these are called judgments, Exod. xxi. 1., and obedience unto them is urged therein upon as strict terms as to the other—Lev. xviii. 4, 5. *Ye shall, therefore, do all my judgments—Ye shall, therefore, keep my statutes and my judgments, which if a man do, he shall live in them; I am the Lord.* Here, keeping his judicial laws is urged as necessary unto life.

3. The ceremonial law also appertains to the Sinai covenant; for the apostle mentions the Levitical priesthood and sacrifices, &c. as belonging to the old testament, and prefers the ministry of Jesus Christ before it, even in the text, in that he is a Mediator, not of the old but of the new testament, Heb. vii., and viii.; Heb. ix. 1-3, 15.

These ceremonial laws were called by the name of statutes, containing institutions of worship, and are urged also on as strict terms as the moral.—Lev. xviii. 5. *Ye shall, therefore, keep my statutes and my judgments, which if a man do, he shall live in them.* These positive precepts (his statutes) run upon those terms, do and live, and, therefore, belong to the law in the strict sense, Rom. x. 5. Indeed exact obedience to these ceremonials is required, on pain of the curse, Deut. xxvii. 26., compared with Gal. iii. 10. So Levit. xxvi. 2-4, 14, 15., he enjoins reverencing his sanctuary, and keeping his statutes and judgments, threatening death upon the neglect thereof; and verse 46. *These are the statutes and judgments and laws which the Lord made between him and the children of Israel, in mount Sinai, by the hand of Moses:* and also he closes up the book of Leviticus thus, Levit. xxvii. 34. *These are the commandments which the Lord commanded Moses, for the children of Israel in mount Sinai.* By which it is evident, that those laws contained in that book of Leviticus (of which many are ceremonial and judicial, as well as moral) do belong to the Sinai covenant. So also do some contained in the book of Numbers; compare Num. xix. 3, 4., with Heb. ix. 13., and xiii. 11. And also some contained in the book of Deuteronomy; for the apostle mentions that as part of the law, Gal. iii. 10., which is drawn from Deut. xxix. 26. I do not say that all things in these books are to be esteemed as parts of the Sinai covenant; for some matters are not of a federal nature, as the taking the sum of the congregation, Numb. i., the order of the tribes, Numb. ii., the stories of their murmuring, Numb. x. 33. to the end, xi. 1., &c. of Miriam's case, Numb. xii., of the spies searching the land, Numb. xiii. and xiv., of the rebellion of Korah, Numb. xvi., of Balaam and Balak, chap. xxiii. and xxiv., of Israel's journeys, chap. xxxiii., and many other stories, as Deut. i., ii. and iii. These are not included in it; but whatever, scattered up and down in those books, has the nature of such a covenant in it, whereof obedience is the condition, that is to be deemed as belonging to the Sinai covenant.

The ceremonial law came in by way of addition to the other, after an apparent interval, upon their desiring a Mediator, that might receive the law for, and declare it to them, Exod. xx. 19, 24-26., and chapters xxi., xxii., and xxiii. There was a solemnization and ratification of all, upon the people's promising to fulfil it, Exod. xxiv.

God himself uttered the moral law to the people with great terror, but the ceremonial (although it did after belong to the Sinai covenant) yet was revealed to Moses in the mount, without those thunderings and lightnings which the other was attended with. I have wondered what should be the reason of these additional things.

But I consider, that temporal mercies being promised by that covenant unto Israel upon their perfect obedience, they would have been hopeless of enjoying these, if such a typical expiation and atonement had not been provided, that their sins might not hinder their arriving at them. So that morals, ceremonials, and judicials, did belong to (and with the promises and threats annexed, made up) the Sinai covenant.

Answer 2. The better covenant is an absolute divine grant, by way of promise, of those great blessings which come in by the mediation and ministry of Jesus Christ. As its excellence, it is said to be that whereof he is Mediator, and so it is the new covenant or testament, Heb. ix. 15. and xii. 24; that it runs upon absolute terms, may be seen, Heb. viii. 7. to the end; and it is declared, that it is not according to the old, verse 9. Therefore the chief scope and design of the apostle, in mentioning these promises, rather than any other, is, the discovering wherein especially the new is differenced from, and is said to be better than, the old.

Here are four grand promises of the new covenant instanced in, which are so comprehensive, as all others made to us are some way reducible to them.

1. The inscription of the divine law in the hearts of men—Heb. viii. 10. *I will put my law into their mind, and write them in their hearts.* In the state of innocence, the law was found in lively characters there, but, since the fall, it needs to be transcribed, or written over again. The old covenant had the law written upon tables of stone without; not absolutely promised, and but rarely found within; insomuch as the Lord even weeps over them, Deut. v. 29. *O that there were such a heart in them, that they would fear me, and keep all my commandments.* But in opposition to the old, here the Lord undertakes to write it upon better tables, even of the heart; importing his affording an inward frame, disposition, and inclination, for an universal compliance with the divine will; and then no sooner is any thing offered of a divine stamp, but all the faculties of the soul, understanding, will, and affection, with the greatest readiness, stand bent for a conformity to it; indeed, the

soul is carried forth that way, not so much by legal external enforcements, as by internal powerful obligations. That whereas the old had a large volume of laws, institutions, and ordinances, which they were commanded to yield obedience to; in the new, all is comprised in a little room, and turned into promise, *I will write my law in their hearts;* the spiriting for all, is assured to them. Here the promise leads the way to the obedience; and O how sweet is it, when it begins with, and is the fruit of a divine promise!

2. A mutual relation between God and souls, Heb. viii. 10. *I will be to them a God, and they shall be to me a people.* Here is propriety each in other. By the old covenant, they were externally interested in God: but as by that with Abraham then, so by the new since, it is more absolutely promised unto some, that he will be their God; which must import that they shall have more sweet converses and communion with him, under the new than under the old, and have higher manifestations of their enjoyment of him. And *happy is that people whose God is the Lord,* Psal. cxliv. 15. What then can they want? All creatures are theirs, Christ theirs, grace theirs, glory theirs, all the attributes of God theirs, his wisdom, power, goodness, faithfulness, loving kindness, all theirs, all his promises, his all-sufficiency theirs, and what can they desire more than to have him who is all in all?

Also, *they shall be to me a people;* that is, I will own them in a clearer, more eminent, and glorious way, than under the old. There shall be a greater separation in their spirit, and in their whole course from all corruption, from sin, Satan, the world, and a greater dedication unto God, 1 Cor. vi. 19, 20. and 2 Cor. vi. 17.; Zech. xiv. 19, 20. *In that day every pot in Jerusalem and in Judah shall be holiness to the Lord:* there shall, be an universal tincture of holiness—Isa. xliv. 5. *And one* (*i.e.* one by one) *shall say, I am the Lord's.* There shall be a more voluntary and free self-resignation unto him; indeed, when they find their hearts stand off and hang back from God, it is under promise, (they shall be to me a people), they may plead the promise for enablement to make over themselves in a fuller way unto God than formerly.

3. Special illumination is promised—Heb. viii. 11. *They shall all know me, from the least to the greatest.* There shall be an enlargement of their knowledge and acquaintance with God and divine things. It would seem rather to exclude private teaching than public, (they shall not teach every man his neighbour, and every man his brother), but it is not absolutely exclusive of outward teachings by instruments and means; but comparatively it holds forth how surpassingly excellent those discoveries under the new testament should be, above those under the old; they far transcend and go beyond these, are more eminent and universal; not only some but all shall know me, &c. Yet public and private teachings were to be attended to, as means conducing to this end, Mat. xxviii. 19, 20. Ephes. iv. 11-13. and vi. 4. Col. iii. 16. Those teachings then of the divine spirit do not render the other void or unnecessary. Under the old, they had some dark, typical, shadowy representations of God and Jesus Christ; under the new, they shall have those that are more clear, and out-strip the other. It is under promise, (they shall all know me), and, therefore, they are to make an improvement of that, toward the gaining a more eminent measure of knowledge than those in old testament times arrived at.

4. Remission or pardon of sin is promised—Heb. viii. 12. *For I will be merciful to their unrighteousness, and their sins and their iniquities will I remember no more.* That particle *for*, argues it to be a reason of his affording other federal blessings: he will write his law in their hearts, for he will forgive their sins; he will be their God, and they shall be his people, for he will pardon their iniquity. Forgiving grace is the very spring of other mercies; that makes way for sharing in them, and nothing without that.

There was a typical forgiveness in the old covenant, Heb. ix. 9, 10, 14. and x. 1-3. &c. but there is real remission in the new, Heb. x. 16, 17., and by this the whole of our justification is noted out: whence the apostle, Rom. iv., from the way of the non-imputation of sin, proves our justification to be by faith, and not by the works of the law.

But pardon of sin denotes:—

1. Freedom from an obligation unto the punishment of the law; for pardon is opposed to guilt, which properly is obligation to punishment—Exod. xxxiv., *Pardon our iniquity and our sin;* that is, do not hold us as guilty. It is noted, by not imputing sin, Psal. xxxii. 2. that is, do not charge it upon us. It is called a covering of it, a blotting of it out, as when a man crosses a debt book; and Heb. viii. 12. *a remembering it no more;* that is, he will not so remember it, as to keep it upon record, and hold the person obliged to its penalty.

2. Pardon notes impunity, or a discharge from the punishment of sin. When pardoning mercy is extended to a soul, the Lord does give a freedom from the punishment itself that is due to sin, as well as from the obligation to it—Numb. xiv. 9. *Pardon, I beseech thee, the iniquity if this people,* &c. *i.e.* do not inflict deserved punishment. The Lord had threatened to cast them off, to disinherit them, and kill them, as one man, verses 12, 15. Moses intercedes, and the Lord answers, verse 20. *I have pardoned, according to thy word;* that is, I will not punish, and execute the fierceness of my wrath upon them; yet he swears, that they should not enter into the promised rest, verses 21-23. The Lord then may pardon, so as not to deal in utmost severity with a people, and yet may reserve to himself a liberty to chastise them, by withholding some desired enjoyments from them. Indeed, in this sense, so far as he does not chastise them, he may be said to pardon; when her *(i.e.* Sion's) warfare is accomplished, then it is said, as Isa. xl. 2., that *her iniquity is pardoned, i.e.* the Lord will not visit for her iniquity as

he did before—(*she hath received if the Lord's hand double for all her sins*); not that her suffering had given the least satisfaction to divine justice for her sin, that belonged to Christ alone, but she had experienced a large measure of fatherly chastisement, and now, being released from this, she is said to be pardoned—Isa. xxxiii. 24. *The inhabitant shall not say I am sick, the people that dwell therein shall be forgiven their iniquity.* As there is a freedom from sickness, and tokens of fatherly displeasure, so, in this sense, sin is said to be forgiven.

Now, in the new covenant, the Lord's remembering iniquity no more, implies this also, his not executing eternal wrath upon the sinner; nothing vindictive, or satisfactory to divine justice, will ever be laid upon him: in fact, fatherly chastisements will be taken off; so far as may be good for him.

And now, what a rich treasury is this new and better covenant? It has enough in it to supply all the wants, to answer all the grounded desires of poor souls. If they want an obediential frame of heart, here it is promised—*I will write my laws in their hearts.* If they desire interest in God, as that only which will satisfy their immortal souls, behold it is promised—*I will be to them a God.* Do they find a backwardness to giving up themselves to God? here it is promised—*they shall be to me a people.* Do they find cause to complain of spiritual blindness, darkness, and ignorance? it is promised—*all shall know me.* Does sin sadly threaten? it is promised—*their sins and iniquities will I remember no more.* And O how miserable are all unbelievers, who want an interest in this new covenant; they have not this law of grace written within; are without God, and a due knowledge of him, strangers to forgiving grace: in these is the sum of all unhappiness.

Quest. Whether this better covenant (wherein the ministration of Jesus Christ does lie) be distinct from that at mount Sinai? Are they two covenants, or but one?

Answer. That new or better covenant is distinct from that at mount Sinai. It is usually said, that they are two administrations or dispensations of the same covenant: I think, they are not merely one and the same covenant, diversely administered, but they are two covenants.

Yet, to prevent mistakes, I would explain my meaning herein. I grant that the Sinai covenant had a special relation to the covenant of grace, and was of great use thereabout: also, I am far from thinking that there are two covenants of grace, if thereby be meant two ways to life and salvation, specifically and essentially different each from other. I conclude, that the elect were saved in one and the same way, for substance and essence, in all ages, *viz.* by grace through a Mediator, by faith in him. The grand covenant of grace was made with Jesus Christ, and us in him, and is essentially one in all times; so as no one of those federal expressures to Adam fallen, or to Abraham, or to David, can rightly be deemed the covenant of grace itself; (unless summarily, or as an epitome thereof), but only discoveries of some small parcels and branches thereof; and differ from it, as a part from the whole, or as a particular article from a whole federal transaction, which consists of many more; that comprises all the promises of furnishing Jesus Christ for the work, and rendering him prosperous and successful in it, Isa. liii. 10-12., as well as promises of what he will do for us; and one article may be distinct enough from another. As among men, a father, by an indenture, containing many articles, may settle an inheritance upon his son and his posterity, and all make up but one covenant in the main; yet one article may be distinct enough from another, and any one may be called a distinct covenant, when it is compared with another; one covenant may be concerning some condition to be performed by the Son, another covenant for the Father to acknowledge a fine, or give a further assurance, another to free from encumbrances;

so the great God settles an everlasting inheritance upon some of the sons of men, by one grand covenant of grace made with Jesus Christ, as their head, which has many articles and matters belonging to it, distinct enough each from other; as, one covenant concerning a condition to be performed by men in their surety, Jesus Christ, this is that at mount Sinai; another covenant concerning the privileges which shall be afforded by him, that condition being performed, this is the new covenant—Jer. xxxi. 31. *Behold the days come, saith the Lord, that I will make a new covenant.* Here is a covenant to give further assurance, and of what; and thus although the grand covenant be but one, yet these several articles thereof, compared each with other, are clearly enough distinct, and so that at Sinai and the new are two covenants; as may appear these ways.

1. The Sinai covenant is denied to be made before Israel's coming out of Egypt, and, therefore, must be distinct, or another covenant from that which promised special blessings in Christ; for that was made with the patriarchs, as Abraham, Isaac, and Jacob, &c. long before Israel's deliverance out of Egyptian bondage, Gen. xii. 1-3, &c.; Gen. xvii. 2, 7. The apostle asserts the stability of the covenant with Abraham and his seed, and proves it in this, way, Gal. iii. 15-17. *This I say, that the covenant that was confirmed before of God in Christ, the law, which was four hundred and thirty years after, cannot disannul.* Where he argues thus—that which was made at mount Sinai, coming after, could not disannul that with Abraham, which was of a more ancient date, or long before it. He speaks not of the moral law barely as a rule of life, for so, even before Abraham, it was; immoralities were ever sinful, and exposed those that were guilty of them unto dreadful judgments, as Sodom and Gomorrah to fire and brimstone, and the old world to a deluge of water; therefore he must speak of the law, considered as a covenant given at mount Sinai,

THE COVENANT OF GRACE 105

and thus it was not till four hundred and thirty years after that with Abraham, and so these must be two distinct covenants, of vastly different dates, else the apostle's argument, which is built upon their difference in respect of time, is not cogent; it is of no force, if they be of the same date, one as early as the other; for the false apostles among the Galatians might have said, the law as a covenant was as early as Abraham, for substance, though not for form and administration; this had been enough to elude his plea, which was grounded upon the time of it; especially seeing the law was urged amongst the Galatians, not merely as to any circumstances in that new ministration, but as to the substance of it; the question then being, Whether justification and the eternal inheritance were by the works of the law, or by grace, and in a way of faith? The apostle argues, that this federal transaction at Sinai not having a being till Moses, so long after that with Abraham; hence it could not establish another way of life opposite to that, *viz.* by works of the law.

Also, Deut. v. 2, 3. *The Lord our God made a covenant with us in Horeb; the Lord made not this covenant with our Fathers, but with us.* The Sinai covenant is clearly intended here, by that at Horeb, (compare Deut. iv. 10-13. with Exod. xix. 1, 8, 9.); and this is expressly denied to be made with their fathers; the Sinai covenant then was not made with the patriarchs, not made with Abraham, Isaac, and Jacob, or with any that lived before the time of Moses; they that were alive at that day are intimated to be the first with whom it was made; it was not with our Fathers, but with us, *even with us who are all of us here alive this day.* Those then, who, before the time of Moses, were dead, had not this covenant made with them, and, therefore, it is distinct from that which was made with the fathers Abraham, Isaac, and Jacob, &c. He does not say, the Lord made not this administration of it with our Fathers, or he made it not in this form, but the Lord struck not this covenant, he denies the covenant itself to be cut, with them. It is an adding to the word, to put in (as some do) *tantum,* as if the meaning were this—not only with our fathers, but also with us. This is to say, it was made with the fathers, when the Holy Spirit expressly denies it. Such additions admitted elsewhere in scripture would be found to be desperately dangerous; and here can by no means be allowed, seeing the apostle gives it an after date, Gal. iii. 17.

2. The better covenant and that at Sinai are contradistinguished, and so must be two distinct covenants; else the opposition were groundless—Jer. xxxi. 31, 32. *I will make a new covenant, not according to the covenant I made with their fathers;* i.e. not according to the Sinai covenant; for that was it which was made when they were brought out of the land of Egypt. He does not say, I will set up a new administration of my covenant, (though that had been true), but a new covenant; there is a plain opposition between covenant and covenant, and therefore the new and that at Sinai must be two distinct, and not one and the same, in different forms; and the rather, because this new covenant is not opposed to the covenant with Abraham, and to that with David, but only to that with Moses and Israel at mount Sinai. Let any instance be given of any thing that is found contradistinguished in such a manner as these are, when only some modification and different respects of the same subject is intended to be signified thereby.

3. The betterness of the covenant were not a sufficient evidence that the ministration of Jesus Christ is of greater excellence than the other, if they were not two distinct covenants. The apostle proves, that Jesus Christ has obtained a more excellent ministry, by this medium—Heb. viii. 6: *By how much also he is a Mediator of a better covenant.* He does not say, only a better administration, but a better covenant; and much of the force of his argument were lost, if the ministry of those Levitical priests,

and also Christ's, were conversant about the same covenant; but if they be two, then it is very forcible: they ministered about one covenant, and Christ about another and a better, and, therefore, his is the more excellent ministry. Besides, it is taken from his being a Mediator of that better covenant, which implies that he was not then a Mediator of that worse Sinai covenant, (though of old typified therein), which their ministry related to. Indeed, it had been a slender proof of the excellence of his ministry, if the better covenant were the same for substance with the worse, seeing then that at Sinai must be still continuing, and so Jesus Christ, not only in his type, but in his own person, must be Mediator thereof, ministering therein, which that text does not give the least countenance to, but there, and also elsewhere, Christ is called *the Mediator of the new covenant,* in opposition to the old, Heb. xii. 18-20, 24., ix. 15., even in the satisfying the old by his death; and, therefore, they must be two distinct covenants.

4. The many notes of distinction that are given of them argue that they are two covenants. They are not only called the old and the new, (this possibly might be said of the same subject, as we say the old and the new moon, and yet one and the same moon), but the first and the second—Heb. viii. 7. *If that first covenant had been faultless, then should no place have been sought for the second.* As Dr. C. says, that it should he affirmed of one and the same covenant, that this is the first covenant, and that is the second, and yet those two should be but both one—that is strange.

5. They are successive; the second comes in the place of the first, and so they must be two distinct covenants— Heb. x. 9. *He taketh away the first, that he may establish the second.* Nothing comes in the room and stead of itself, but of something else; now the second better covenant comes in the place and stead of the first; so as the one must be removed, and taken away, that the other may be established, and so they must be two distinct covenants:

the first is old, and Heb. viii. 13. *That which decayeth and waxeth old is ready to vanish away—Heb.* vii. 18. *There is verily a disannulling of the commandment going before,* i.e. of the first covenant. The old then is, such as it, is, disannulled, and vanishes away; whereas the new covenant cannot be disannulled, never vanishes away. Neither is it said that one administration vanishes, is disannulled, and taken away, that another might succeed, (though, this is true), but one, *viz.* a first covenant itself, is taken away, that a second may come in the room of it.

6. They are expressly called two covenants or testaments. The apostle mentions Abraham's two sons, the one by a bond-woman, who was born after the flesh, the other by a free-woman, who was by promise, and makes this application of it, Gal. iv. 24. *Which things are an allegory, for these are the two covenants or testaments, the one from the mount Sinai, which gendereth to bondage, which is Agar.* What can be more plain? Here it is expressly affirmed, that there are two covenants or testaments, and neither of these two was formally (though materially one might be) the covenant of works or of friendship made with the first Adam in his state of innocence; for then, man himself must have been the worker for life, and therefore, of necessity, there must he two covenants besides; and so it is no way incongruous to speak of three covenants, seeing that with Adam is generally acknowledged to be one, and here the scripture expressly speaks of two covenants, and that with Adam is none of them. It is not that signified by the free-woman and her son Isaac, for that, in opposition to the other, is said to be free, and to be by promise, verses 23, 26, 31. Neither is it signified by the bond-woman and her son, for after he said, *these are the two covenants,* it immediately follows, verse 24. *The one from the mount Sinai, which gendereth to bondage, which is Agar.* So then, not the covenant of works, as made with Adam, but the Sinai covenant, is

the other here intended. And plainly he speaks of both, according to divine ordination or institution, and concludes them so to be two covenants. In this allegory, he does not mention them considered abusively, according to the intention of the Judaizing prophets, but in themselves—verses 21, 22. *Ye that desire to be under the law, do ye not hear the law, for it is written, Abraham had two sons,* &c.; therefore, as they warrantably heard the Sinai law, so it and the free promise made two testaments.

In the times of the old testament these were kept very distinct: hence it is observable, that when the children of Israel had sinned egregiously in making the calf, and the Lord severely threatened even to consume them, Exod. xxxii. 10, 11. Moses, in interceding for them, does not plead the covenant newly made at mount Sinai, but that with Abraham—verse 13. *Remember Abraham, Isaac, and Israel, thy servants, to whom thou swearest,* &c. He saw he could not ground his plea upon the Sinai covenant, already violated by them, and, therefore, he flees to another, founded upon free grace. So, Deut. ix. 27. 2 Kings xiii. 23. *The Lord was gracious to them, and had compassion on them, and had respect to them.* He does not say, because of his covenant with Moses at mount Sinai, but because of his covenant with Abraham, Isaac, and Jacob, &c.; so that whilst the Sinai covenant was in force, yet that with Abraham (which went before) was not swallowed up or mixed in it, but remained entire and distinct still, dispensing out blessings to the subjects of it; they were not one and the same covenant in that day.

O then let Christians beware of mixing and confounding the old and new covenants, which are so distinct. It is the great design of the Epistle to the Romans and Galatians to beat off from this mixture: both have their great use, but they must have their due place—Gal. iv. 24. *Ye that desire to be under the law,* &c.; there is a great aptness to legalize, or desire to be under the law.

The false prophets were ready to be branding Paul for an Antinomian; as if he rendered the law unprofitable by his preaching the doctrine of free grace. For the taking off this aspersion, he puts the question; Gal. iii. 19. *Wherefore then serveth the law?* that is, if the law does not justify, why then was it given? or what use was it of? He answers, *It was added because of transgression, till the seed should come, to whom the promise was made.*

Where observe, how carefully the apostle does distinguish these: he does not make the Sinai law or covenant one and the same with the promise, but something added or put to it, a distinct thing; it was additional, and so not the promise itself, but yet was of admirable use; it was added *because of transgression,* say some, to reveal and discover sin, and lay restraint upon men that they run not into it. But the law in the hand of Christ is of such use to believers still; whereas he speaks of such a use of it as lasts only till the coming of the promised seed; and, therefore, I understand it thus— (because or for the sake, of transgression), *viz.* that Jesus Christ, by coming under it, might make full satisfaction for that transgression which man was in: it was added, not for justification, but for transgression's sake, that its curse might be endured and removed; and this additional use of the law was but till the promised seed came, then it ceased, having its accomplishment in him: the Lord was added, that he might *finish transgression, and make an end of sin,* as Dan. ix. 24. And this way was made for the divine promise to pass upon us.

Now there is a sinful mixing these two covenants, the old and the new, which are distinct.

1. When there is a joining any thing of ours with Jesus Christ, in the matter of acceptation unto eternal life. This was the case of those Judaizing prophets—Acts xv. 1. they taught, *except ye be circirmcised after the manner of Moses, ye cannot be saved.* The like we have, Gal. v. 2. *If ye be*

THE COVENANT OF GRACE 111

circumcised, Christ shall profit you nothing. They expected advantage by Jesus Christ, else this argument would have been of no force to them, verse 4. *Christ is of no effect to you.* &c. They were, therefore, jumbling works of their own and Jesus Christ together, mixing these in the matter of their acceptation unto life; and this is intimated to be desperately dangerous.

Christians ought to perform all duty, in conformity to Jesus Christ, in the way to salvation, but not in the least as that which justifies or saves. See what earnestness and vehemence the apostle uses here, verse 3. *I will testify again to every man that is circumcised, that he is a debtor to the whole law.* Where is intimated, that an acting in any work upon a legal account, or on a legal ground, is putting ourselves under the obligation of, and is all one as if we sought life altogether by the law: for, if they were circumcised upon a principle or opinion of its conducing to their justification, they became debtors thereby to the whole law; though they did not think other services required, or themselves obliged to them; yet by one they put themselves under the bond of the whole. Thus then, if any should act in any gospel institutions, as baptism or the supper of the Lord, upon a like account as they did take up circumcision, *viz.* with an opinion of their conducing to justification and acceptation with God unto eternal life, they would thereby make themselves debtors to the whole law: so if they should give repentance, mourning for sin, self-emptiness, indeed faith itself, the same place, and act therein upon such a ground as they did in circumcision, Christ would be rendered of no effect unto such souls.

2. When there is a living in the spirit of the old covenant, in dealing with the promises of the new, then indeed there is a mixing of the two covenants, which are so distinct: the old covenant carried with it a spirit of bondage and terror, Rom. viii. 15. Heb. xii. 18.; and if souls, in looking to the

promise, carry it as if they were conversing with God upon the burning mount, eyeing chiefly divine wrath, dwelling more upon a divine curse than upon the grace of God in the free promise, in looking for mercy—here is the spirit of the old covenant: so, when souls are shy of the promise, and ready to stand at a distance from it; when they carry it towards God, as if Jesus Christ had not satisfied the curse of the law, and yet in part look to the promise.

The old covenant did run upon do and live, intending that Jesus Christ should be the doer, in reference to eternal life; but when souls are like those who were hired into the vineyard, Mat. xx. 1, 2. &c., when they are indenting with God for their penny, when they must have such incomes and such enjoyments from God, in case they act in duty, when they seek the reward upon their own doing, they may work hard and sink under their burden, and have little thank for their pains, as that parable shows. When duty is not managed with a gospel spirit, when the divine spirit is not acting the soul, by the promise of the new covenant, it comes to little.

The old covenant did run upon condition, and so when souls dwell upon conditions performed by, or wrought within themselves, and build their hope, peace, and comfort upon them, so as they look little or nothing to the free grace of God in absolute promises, make but little use of these in comparison with the other, then they are too much in the spirit of the old covenant, and mixing with the new.

CHAPTER VII.

Of the Nature of the Mount Sinai Covenant.

IT will now be asked, What manner of covenant was that at mount Sinai, which is called the worse covenant? What kind of covenant was it?

Sol. In general, it was a covenant of works, as to be fulfilled by Jesus Christ, but not so to Israel. Or, it was the covenant of grace as to its legal condition to be performed by Jesus Christ, represented under a conditional administration of it to Israel.

This a knotty puzzling question in divinity; for the clearer opening of it, I must answer both negatively and affirmatively.

SECTION I.

Answer 1. Negatively, in four propositions:—

Prop. I. The Sinai law was not given as a covenant of works to Israel. It was designed to be a covenant of works, as to be accomplished by Jesus Christ, as will appear afterwards; but the end of the Lord was not that it should be so to Israel; for,

1. The nature of a covenant of works, and also the general current of scripture, denies the Sinai law to be such.

A covenant of works requires perfect personal obedience, promising life, or a reward of justice thereupon, and threatening death upon the least violation thereof.

This is evident from the covenant with Adam in innocence, Gen. ii. 17. He obeying, it is implied he should live; he disobeying by eating the forbidden fruit, the sentence of death passed upon him: and apparently this is a true description of a covenant of works, for whatever is opposite to this speaks grace. If justification and eternal life be attained by another righteousness or obedience, (without their personal performance of it), there is grace herein; if the reward be not of justice, it must be of grace; if imperfections and sinful failings be not followed with death, there is grace in that also.

Now the design or intendment of God, in giving the Sinai covenant, was not, that Israel should, by their own obedience, obtain eternal life and salvation. Indeed, the false apostles, in gospel times, did put upon personal obedience, they urged circumcision, and other works of the law, as necessary unto justification and eternal life; but, in opposition to them, the apostle argues, in diverse chapters in the Epistles to the Romans and Galatians, proving that they come by a righteousness performed for us by Jesus Christ—Rom. iii. 20: *Therefore by the deeds of the law* (*i.e.* as performed by themselves) *shall no flesh be justified in his sight;* it is, verse 28. *without the deeds of the law,* Gal. ii. 16., iii. 10. *As many as are of the works of the law* (*i.e.* as performed by themselves) *are under the curse,* and verses 11, 12., Gal. v. 2, 3. Indeed, *our salvation is not of works,* Ephes, ii. 8, 9. 2 Tim. 2. 9, 19. Adam forfeiting life, when he might have had it on the terms of his own doing, hence the Lord would never deal with man in that way any more. And lest any should think that this was only since the Sinai covenant was at an end, the apostle proves that our works are now excluded from the instances of Abraham and David—Rom. iv. 2, 3. *For if Abraham were justified by works, he hath whereof to glory, but not before God;* and adds, *it is to him that worketh not*—verses 5 and 6. *Even as David also describeth the blessedness of the man unto whom God imputeth righteousness, without works.* Where it is plainly intimated, that we are justified in gospel times in the same way, for substance, with them of old, and he expressly says, that this was not by works of their own performance; no, not by such as they came up to, after they were in a state of grace, much less by any works of theirs before they did believe, else the apostle's argument were not cogent; for the false prophets might easily have answered, that now, in gospel times, we are not justified as Abraham and David were, and so they might have waved whatever is urged from these instances, seeing all that he says is built upon this very foundation, that we are justified as they were: only this can hardly be evaded, that David (who lived under the Sinai covenant) yet is denied to be justified by works of his own. Indeed, the apostle excludes them even from the nature of a covenant of works; which is such a ground as denies lapsed man, in any age, to be saved by his own obedience, verse 4. *Now to him that worketh is the reward not reckoned of grace, but of debt.* Therefore, unless it could be said that those under the Sinai law had eternal life, *not of grace, but of debt,* it must be said that they had it not in the way of a covenant of works.

2. Moses and the children of Israel were antecedently under a covenant of grace, or before the making that at mount Sinai; therefore, that could not be a covenant of works. In the very preface, he says, Exod. xx. 2, 5. *I am the Lord, thy God:* the Lord did not first become their God by that, but was so before, as they were the seed of Abraham, and under that with him—Exod. ii. 24. and iii. 6, 7. *I have seen the affliction of my people,* verses 15, 16. And Moses himself entered into the same Sinai covenant with the people, Exod. xxxiv. 27. *I have made a covenant with thee, and with Israel;* not only with Israel, but with him also.

Now it is not imaginable that the Lord would reduce them, and Moses himself, from a covenant of grace, back to that of works. Surely the Lord would advance them higher, rather than bring them lower. He is ever one and the same in his grace and promises unto souls; no such inconstancy and changeableness is found with him.

3. The Sinai testament typically revealed mercy for sinful men, and, therefore, was not a covenant of works; for, that being once violated and broken, holds forth nothing of mercy to the sinner, whatever his repentance be; gives no hope of salvation, but denounces judgment, death, and utter destruction against him; Adam having eaten the forbidden fruit, that says, Gen. ii. 17. *Dying thou shalt die.*

Whereas the Sinai covenant includes the ceremonial law, as well as the moral, as is plain, Heb. ix. 1, 2, 3. &c. *The first testament had ordinances of divine service, and a worldly sanctuary, a tabernacle, priests and sacrifices, offerings for the errors of the people,* &c. Although these services did not of themselves expiate sin, and purge the conscience, yet they did point out a way wherein they might have an expiation of, and freedom from, sin, which a covenant of works gives not the least intimation of.

The Sinai covenant was ordained by angels, Gal. iii. 19., in the hands of Moses, a typical Mediator; and this argued a variance between God and Israel, else no need of any, and there is grace in a covenant that admits of any way for the making up of such differences; there was abundance of grace wrapt up in many types and ordinances in the Sinai covenant; it was confirmed by blood and sprinkling, called *the blood of the covenant,* Exod. xxiv. 3, 4, 5., which typified the blood of Jesus Christ, and therefore it was no covenant of works, for that speaks nothing thereof.

4. There had been an utter impossibility for Israel, or any other, to have attained unto eternal life and salvation, if they had been under that at Sinai as a covenant of works: for they could never have performed the works which were the condition of it, and so must have been hopeless of the benefit which was promised thereupon—

Gal. iii. 21. *If there had been a law that could have given life, righteousness had been by the law.* This clearly concludes, that righteousness did not come by the law, *i.e.* as performed by us in our own persons; and also, that the law could not give life, no eternal life to be expected by it; and he speaks of the Sinai law, as is clear, verse 17.; and, therefore, that could not be a covenant of works to Israel or us for eternal life—Rom. viii. 3. also proves, the law could not free from condemnation, in that it was weak through the flesh, and so no eternal life was attainable thereby.

5. That way which the Lord had established with Israel for life and salvation before the Sinai covenant, was utterly inconsistent with that of works, and, therefore, that could not be a covenant of works—Gal. iii. 18. *For if the inheritance be of the law, it is no more of promise.* These two ways cannot stand together; if it be by one of them, then it is not by the other; they carry a contradiction each to other. If *Israel had the inheritance by the law, i.e.* by works performed by themselves, then it could not be by the obedience of another, of Jesus Christ for them: if it were by their own righteousness of the law, then it could not be by the righteousness of Jesus Christ entertained in the promise by faith: one of these ways does necessarily subvert, overthrow, and destroy the other, so as the same person, at the same time, cannot have it both ways.

Now such an opposite way of a gospel promise was established with Israel, long before the Sinai covenant— Gal. iii. 16, 17. *They were the seed of Abraham;* and he concludes, that the Sinai covenant, coming so long after, could not disannul the Abrahamic covenant or promise, (wherein they had interest), which was so long before it; and consequently it was no covenant of works to Israel, for then it must necessarily have disannulled the foregoing promise, as that demonstration, verse 18., evidences.

SECTION II.

Prop. II. That the Sinai law was not a mixed covenant for eternal life to Israel. It was not partly a covenant of works to them, and partly of grace: for—

1. It is an undoubted obstacle or hindrance in the way of salvation, to be seeking it in a covenant of works, by personal performances; and, therefore, that at Sinai could not be so much as in part such a one to Israel. The reason why Israel obtained not righteousness (and so life) was, because they sought it not by faith, *i.e.* in another, in Jesus Christ, *but as it were by the works of the law,* Rom. ix. 31, 32. He doesn't say, they sought it altogether by their own works, but after a sort, *(as it were),* and thus obstructed or hindered their arriving at it. Thus their coming short of salvation is resolved into the same cause, Rom. x. 1, 3. *They going about to establish their own righteousness, have not submitted themselves unto the righteousness of God.* A seeking salvation then by our own works (which are our own righteousness) prevents a submission unto that righteousness which is necessary unto eternal life; and, therefore, if it were a mixed covenant, one part of it would hinder another, as if the Lord, in the same dispensation, should pull forward and backward, do and undo, put upon seeking life, and yet on that which is a let in the way to it, which were an impeachment to the wisdom of God for any to assert.

2. Legal works are excluded out of justification and salvation, in conjunction with Jesus Christ, and, therefore, the Sinai law could not be a mixed covenant—Gal. v. 2, 3. *I, Paul, say unto you, that if you be circumcised Christ shall profit you nothing.* Verse 4. *Christ is become of no effect to you, whosoever of you are justified* (*i.e.* seek to be justified) *by the law, ye are fallen from grace*—(Acts xv. 1, 11; Ephes. ii. 8, 9.). This implies, that, they urged circumcision, or works of the law, and Christ too, for justification and life; the argument had been insignificant

to them, if they had not expected profit and advantage by Jesus Christ, and by the works of the law too; and the apostle concludes one of these to be exclusive of the other, *a mixture of our own works is a falling from the way of grace,* a taking any of our senses, in conjunction with Jesus Christ, in that matter, is enough to shut out from all benefit and advantage by Christ; he shall profit nothing, if he alone be not owned herein.

3. After a violation of a covenant of works, nothing less than utter ruin and destruction are threatened therein—Gen. ii. 17. *In the day thou eatest, thou shalt die.* There is nothing promised by it ever after, whatever services be performed, nothing but death thenceforth to be expected from it, and, therefore, the Sinai law could not be a mixed covenant; in regard Israel is often accused by the Lord for breaking of it—Jer. xxxi. 32. *Which covenant they brake,* &c., no good could be reaped from that part which was supposed of grace, the death threatened in the other part hinders all good; so that, unless Israel could have kept it without violation, (which they could not), it must have been altogether unprofitable to them; for, as Dr. Bolton says, man was not able to stand to the lowest terms, to perform the meanest condition.

4. There is such an opposition between our works and divine grace, in relation to eternal life, that they are inconsistent each with other; therefore, the Sinai law could not be a mixed covenant. There is no *medium participationis,* or so as to partake of both; there was an impossibility of having life both ways, this I cleared before, from Gal. iii. 18. which is equally strong here.

It is further proved, Rom. xi. 4, 5. It is said to be by grace, verse 6. *If by grace, then it is no more of works, otherwise grace is no more grace; but if it be of works, then it is no more of grace, otherwise work is no work.* Which clearly intimates, that the way of grace and works are so mutually destructive one to the other, that if it be by one it cannot be by the other. If Israel had been to do any thing for eternal life, though never so small, it would have denied it to be of grace.* Grace is no way grace, unless it be every way free; and, therefore, seeing Israel was justified and saved as we are, Acts xv. 11., and we are justified freely by his grace, Rom. iii. 24. *and saved by grace,* Eph. ii. 8.; hence the Sinai law could not be a mixed covenant, partly of works, and partly of grace, the one being so diametrically opposite to the other.

SECTION III.

Prop. III. That the Sinai law was not only a covenant for temporal mercies, as the land of Canaan, and such like, but did in some further way belong to the covenant of grace, and had the great concernment thereof, even our eternal salvation, as its principal aim and end.

Temporal blessings were dispensed out, (and possibly those only), by virtue of the Sinai covenant, upon Israel's performance of it; but yet as it was to be performed for them by Jesus Christ, so it respected the great matters of the covenant of grace, even spirituals and eternals, as may appear; for,

1. There are typical representations in it of spiritual and eternal blessings: there was abundance of the gospel wrapt up in those legal types and shadows of old.

There were priests and a high-priest, an eminent type of Jesus Christ, who is therefore called a high-priest also, Heb. viii. 1., and elsewhere.

O what an advantage was it, so long before the incarnation of Jesus Christ, to have such a lively emblem of this his glorious office, which our everlasting salvation had such a necessary dependence upon! That as the Levitical high-priest did stand and appear for the people,

---

* *Gratia nullo modo gratia nisi omni modo gratia*—Aug.

THE COVENANT OF GRACE 121

in many ways, and for many precious ends, that none else could, so they might expect that Jesus Christ would do the like for them. As the priests did offer sacrifice for the errors of the people, so they might look that the Lord Jesus would offer a better sacrifice for them. They might easily guess that the anti-type, Jesus Christ, would far excel, outstrip, and go beyond the types; the substance beyond the shadow, so Jesus Christ would be far more excellent than any of those figures of him. What a privilege was it to have some lively resemblance of all this so long beforehand, Heb. ix. 23, 24. Those things under the Sinai first testament are intimated to be patterns of things in heaven, and figures of the true. There was a holiest of all, which the high-priest alone went into, once every year, not without blood; signifying that the holiest of all was not made manifest, while the first table was standing—verses 3, 7, 8. This intimates, that Jesus Christ, the great high-priest, should enter into that which was truly the holy of holies, to appear in the presence of God for us, verse 24.; and so that their holiest of all was a type of heaven.

A like type thereof was the land of Canaan, and, therefore, it bears the very name that heaven itself is set out to us by; it is called the *rest of the Lord,* Psal. xcv. 11. *If they shall enter into my rest, i.e.* into the land of Canaan, Deut. xii. 9. This was another type of the rest in heaven, Heb. iii. 19., compared with Heb. iv. 8, 9. Many other instances might be given, wherein the Sinai covenant represented matters of the covenant of grace, even spirituals and eternals, to Israel.

2. Some of the same promises of spiritual and eternal blessings which are found in other federal expressures are under a conditional form in the Sinai covenant, and, therefore, that appertains some way to the covenant of grace, and not only temporals are respected therein.

In the preparation to it, the Lord says to Israel, Exod. xix. 5, 6. *If ye will obey my voice, and keep my covenant, ye shall be a peculiar treasure to me above all people, and ye shall be to me a kingdom of priests, and an holy nation.*

Indeed this cluster of promises has an *if* hanging upon it, or is under a condition that obedience be yielded to the Sinai covenant, and then the wine in it may flow out, and all temporal enjoyments which the world affords are nothing to one drop hereof. It is true, *conditio nihil ponit in esse,* therefore we must know, that the Sinai covenant did hold forth the condition upon which not only temporals, but spirituals and eternals, are vouchsafed, which then was unperformed, but since is fulfilled by Jesus Christ. Besides, the apostle applies it to the saints, in gospel times; this is evidence enough that the Sinai covenant (to which it belonged) had a notable relation to the covenant of grace— 1 Pet. ii. 9. *But ye are a chosen generation, a royal priesthood, an holy nation, a peculiar people.* These are reckoned up among gospel privileges, and attainable only by Jesus Christ, Rev. i. 5, 6.; and indeed they are glorious advantages. To be *a peculiar treasure* implies, not only his acceptation into favour above others, his claiming a special relation to, and propriety in them, but his highest estimation of them; they shall have peculiar preservations, peculiar affections, peculiar influences, and peculiar consolations: *a kingdom of priests, i.e.* they shall have an eminent separation to the highest services or employments, and be admitted to nearest approaches unto God; shall partake of spiritual anointings, the holy unction of the divine spirit for that end, and shall enjoy intimate fellowship and communion with the Lord himself: *an holy nation,* when others are left in their sin and pollution, under their profanity, they shall have the image of God in a transparent manner found upon them, appearing in a holy profession; O how far is this beyond temporals! There are other conditional promises in the Sinai covenant of the Lord's dwelling among the children of Israel, and being their God. Exod. xxix. 45, 46. with Levit. xxvi. 3, 11, 12., and so elsewhere, which undoubtedly hold forth privileges of the covenant of grace, but the condition was to be performed by Jesus Christ.

3. The nature of many services in the Sinai covenant was such as argued its special respect to the great matters of the covenant of grace, and its intending higher things than merely temporals: there were sin offerings in it, for the ignorance of the priests, of the congregation, of the rulers, of the people, Levit. iv., and intimations of atonement and forgiveness of sin. Not that these offerings did make atonement of themselves, but they pointed out Jesus Christ, by whom we have atonement. The like may be urged from the scape-goat, &c.

I may add, that some of those arguments under the affirmative part, to prove its containing the legal condition of the covenant of grace, will be equally strong to evidence that this Sinai covenant had not temporals as its only end.

SECTION IV.

Prop. IV. That the Sinai law is not merely a gradually different administration of the covenant of grace to Israel, from that with us in the new and better covenant.

Many suppose that this was only a federal transaction with Israel, so as that obedience which is the condition of the Sinai covenant, (on which all the blessings of it do depend), is nothing else but the same which is to be yielded by us in gospel times; only then it was exacted with dreadful terrors, thunderings; and lightnings—now in a sweeter milder way; but certainly a higher matter, a perfect obedience, is aimed at therein. It is true, Christians are obliged unto all duty, under the better covenant; there is a promise in it of writing the divine law in their hearts, for that end. All the difficulty then in the Sinai dispensation arises not merely from its enjoining doing, (all runs upon doing there, not upon believing), but also from its annexing life thereunto—*this do, and live;* and a curse to the contrary. If it had contained all the laws that are in it, even all the ceremonials, these indeed would have rendered it more burdensome than other dispensations, yet it would as manifestly have belonged to the covenant of grace still as that with Abraham and others, under which were some sacrifices, and other typical ceremonies. If this doing had not been for life, there had been no more difficulty in this Sinai law than in any other federal expressure; its running upon *do, and live,* this has caused many to doubt of the nature of it, and, therefore, the great matter to be cleared is, upon what account it stands in this form? and this will evidence, that, though there was an administration of the covenant of grace in it to Israel, yet there was a higher intendment therein, *viz.* a performance of it by Jesus Christ, for impetration, or the procurement of federal blessings for us; and, therefore, that it was not only a gradually different administration to Israel, from the other new covenant to us. For,

1. The Sinai covenant obliged unto such doing as makes up a righteousness unto life—Rom. x. 5. *For Moses describeth the righteousness which is of the law, that the man which doth these things shall live by them.* He speaks undeniably of the Sinai law, for the text here alleged is Levit. xviii. 5., and the doing enjoined, the apostle says, is a description of a righteousness unto justification and life. Neither is taken here abusively, as urged by the false prophets, but he says, Moses describes the righteousness of the law thus. Therefore, not only according to the opinion of the false prophets, but according to the intention of Moses, the Sinai law did hold forth a doing as a righteousness: this was the tenor of it, *do, and live.* The same may be urged from Gal. iii. 12.; and, therefore, a vastly different obedience (in respect of its end) was required in the Sinai covenant from that which could be yielded by Israel then, or by Christians now, under the new covenant; for, their doing was not to work out a righteousness unto their own justification and life.

2. The Sinai covenant obliged unto such doing, as stood in a contradistinction unto faith. The apostle, Rom. x., having told us of the law doing, by way of antithesis or opposition, he adds, verse 6, *But the righteousness which is of faith speaketh on this wise,* &c. where he plainly makes the doing, which, according to Moses, was the righteousness of the law, and that which is the righteousness of faith, *membra dividentia,* and so they stand upon opposite terms each to other. Thus Gal. iii. 12. *And the law is not of faith, but the man that doth them shall live in them.* Where he speaks of the Sinai law, verse 17., and gives the same proof as before, *viz.* Levit. xviii. 5., and that doing he denies to be of faith. It is evident then, that the Sinai law obliged to such doing, as was not of faith, and, therefore, to an obedience specifically different (in its use or end) from that which was to be performed by Israel then, or by Christians now, which flows from faith. And this, with the former particular, shows the invalidity of what is said by some for the unfolding the meaning of *do this, and live,* as it stands in the Sinai covenant, as will appear especially under the sixth particular—in the affirmative part.

SECTION V.

Answer 2. Affirmatively, the Sinai covenant was a covenant of works, as to be fulfilled by Jesus Christ, represented under an imperfect administration of the covenant of grace to Israel. Or thus—

The Sinai law is, the covenant of grace as to its legal condition (even for eternals) to be performed by Jesus Christ, held forth under a servile, typical, conditional administration of it, for temporals, unto Israel.

It promised its blessings, especially eternal life, upon the condition of the perfect obedience of Jesus Christ; thereby was the procurement of all.

It promised temporal mercies to the children of Israel, upon condition of their due obedience; thereby was the obtainment of them.

There were many articles between the Father and the Son, which are not found in this Sinai dispensation; so that it was not the whole covenant of grace, but referred to it, *viz.* it is a covenant for the performance of its legal condition, both in respect of duty and penalty.

The covenant of works being broken by us in the first Adam, it was of great concernment to us that satisfaction should be given to it, for unless its righteousness were performed for us, the promised life was unattainable; and unless its penalty were undergone for us, the threatened death (Gen. ii. 17.) was unavoidable. All this condition, in Moses' time, was unfulfilled, and so the Lord putted, Israel (who belonged to the principal party guilty, *viz.* mankind), upon entering into a solemn covenant at mount Sinai, therein owning their just debt, and acknowledging their owing perfect obedience to God, and deserving an eternal curse upon the least failure therein, and promising a full payment of the whole debt: *all that the Lord hath spoken, we will do,* Exod. xix. 8., xx. 19., xxiv. 3, 7. Not only some of his words, but all that the Lord has said will we do. Yet the Lord intended, that not Israel, (the principal debtor), but Jesus Christ, the surety, should perform for them the obedience therein required unto life; his pay should be accepted for what Israel had hereby covenanted to yield, and, through inability, was never able to perform; this much is manifested in the very dispensation itself, in those many types and other services contained in it, they all intimate, that the performance should be by Jesus Christ for them.

In one and the same Sinai covenant, the all-wise God exacted a double obedience, for vastly different ends, *viz.* a perfect obedience to be performed by Jesus Christ, as the legal condition of the covenant of grace, as the principal end: and also an obedience to be performed by

Israel belonging to the administration of it, in order to their fruition of temporal enjoyments: under this latter, the former is represented. These are so twisted into one and the same law, as in the same breath the Lord demands both of Israel, the principal debtor, who covenants universal performance; but the Lord had this intention, that Jesus Christ should fulfil the former, on their behalf.

I shall endeavour the clearing of this matter, under two propositions.

SECTION VI.

Prop. 1. That the Sinai covenant did hold forth the covenant of grace, as to its legal condition, to be performed by Jesus Christ, and so was a covenant of works, as to be fulfilled by him. Or,

It conditionally promised its blessings, especially eternal life, upon the perfect obedience of Jesus Christ, then (in Moses' time) not fulfilled.

The Sinai covenant did not intend only an obedience to be performed by Israel, but also a further and higher obedience to be yielded by Jesus Christ. Indeed, Israel did undertake, in a federal way, the yielding thereof, and so was obliged, by that visible dispensation, to perfect obedience; they being of the principal debtors, they came under the obligation to it, by their own act, yet the intendment was that the performance should be by their surety, Jesus Christ, for them; so as *do and live,* in that Sinai covenant, primarily had respect unto the doing which was only by Jesus Christ, for us. This appears in these ways:—

1. The Sinai covenant exacts a perfect obedience, which makes up a righteousness unto life, and, therefore, was the legal condition of the covenant of grace to be performed by Jesus Christ alone; for it is impossible that Israel, or

any of the sons of men, should perform such a perfect obedience for themselves, Gal. iii. 21., and so they must miss of eternal life, if he did not perform it for them.

That such a perfect obedience is indispensably required in the Sinai covenant, as a condition of life, is evident, Levit. xviii. 5., compared with Gal. iii. 10, 12., it is such as stands upon opposite terms to faith, and is impossible for any man to perform, as I have proved, and such as is a righteousness—Deut. vi. 25. *And it shall be our righteousness, if we observe to do all these commandments, before the Lord our God, as he hath commanded us.*

Also in Rom. x. 5. he evidently determines that the Sinai law imposes that doing which amounts to a righteousness unto life, and must be a perfect obedience, which man is utterly unable to yield for himself: and therefore, admirably to our present purpose, it is added, verse 4. *For Christ is the end of the law for righteousness to every one that believeth.*

This intimates, that the law has an end to be attained, and that is righteousness, and that Jesus Christ performs it; he becomes that end of it to believers, not only accidentally and indirectly, as the law discovers duty impossible for any man to perform, and a necessity of looking to another for relief; but, directly, Jesus Christ has wrought out and fulfilled that righteousness which the law exacted, and so is *the end of the law;* for it is here opposed unto that righteousness which is of a man's own working out, verse 3.

We must know, that when Adam was in innocence, the Lord required a perfect fulfilling of the law, in order to his preservation in life, and now man is in a fallen state, the Lord will abate nothing of it; still, without a righteousness specifically the same, no eternal life to be had—Rom. i. 17., iv. 6., v. 18, 21., 2 Cor. iii. 9. &c. That end of the law, *viz.* righteousness, must still be come up to; only under the covenant of works man was personally to perform it for himself, but now Jesus Christ is admitted to work out this perfect righteousness of the law for him—Rom. v. 18, 19. *By the obedience of one* (*i.e.* of Jesus Christ) *many are made righteous.* Hence he is said *to be made of God to us wisdom and righteousness,* 1 Cor. i. 30.; and we are said to be *the righteousness of God in him,* 2 Cor. v. 21.—It is not the righteousness of a mere man, but of one which is also God, that we must stand in.

Now the Sinai covenant is a platform of the legal righteousness which was indispensably necessary unto life; there it is deciphered, delineated, and described, more clearly than in any other federal expressure. The Sinai covenant excels all other, in discovering what that righteousness is, upon which we enjoy eternal life.

The promissory part of the covenant of grace is more fully revealed in other federal expressures, as that with Abraham, David, and the new covenant; but the mandatory and minatory part of it, in order to life, the duty to be performed, and the curse to be endured; is most fully set forth in that at mount Sinai. Adam was obliged to a righteousness, in obedience to a positive command of not eating of the tree of knowledge, Gen. ii. 17., as well as to moral commands: answerably in the Sinai law there is a righteousness required, of the same kind, standing in obedience to many positive and ceremonial commands, and this was fulfilled by Jesus Christ; he did take it as his office to fulfil, not only some, but all righteousness, Mat. iii. 15.

And also the righteousness of the moral law, Mat. v. 17, 18.; he came *not to destroy the law, but to fulfil it;* he yielded obedience to the moral commands; in fact satisfied (Heb. ix. 15.) even for transgressions that were under the first testament.

2. The Sinai covenant denounces a dreadful curse (which can be undergone by none but Jesus Christ) upon the least failing of perfect obedience, and, therefore,

expresses the legal condition of the covenant of grace to be performed by Christ, or is a covenant of works as to be fulfilled by him; for that only threatens a curse upon the least imperfection, in point of obedience.

Now the Sinai law does that—Gal. iii. 10. *For as many as are of the works of the law are under the curse, for it is written, Cursed is everyone that continueth not in all things which are written in the book of the law, to do them.*

The law then runs upon such terms, as if a man should perform never so many acts of obedience, yet if he should not come up to *all* that is written in the book of the law, it curses him. If he should come up to all, yet if he did not continue therein, it curses him: it exacts perfect obedience, upon pain of a curse.

Nothing can more fully express the nature of a covenant of works than this; that with Adam, in innocence, cannot be one, if this be not so; for there is no more in that than *if thou eatest, thou shalt die*—and there is as much here, *if thou dost not all; thou shalt be cursed:* and yet the apostle is not speaking here of the very covenant with Adam in innocence, but of one in the matter of it resembling that, made a long time after, even at mount Sinai; for, he says, *it is written thus:* now it is in Moses' law (long after Adam) that this was written, *viz.* Deut. xxvii. 26. He speaks of it as belonging to the Sinai law, as expressing the tenor of that; and he does not mention it only as the opinion of the false prophets among the Galatians, but as the intention of the divine law itself—*It is written, Cursed is everyone that continueth not in all.* Further, let it be observed, the scope of the apostle is to evidence the impossibility of attaining justification by the works of the law; for, says he, *as many as are of the works of the law, are under the curse*—and why? Because it is impossible that any mere man should continue in all that is written in the law; the best of men will have some sinful infirmities and imperfections, and the least transgression lies under a divine curse, according to that law, which must be undergone, either by men themselves, (and that would sink and ruin them for ever), or else by Jesus Christ, and then the legal condition is performed by him for them.

3. Jesus Christ, by coming under, and fulfilling the Sinai covenant, did work out redemption for us, and, therefore, that did hold forth, not only an obedience to be performed by Israel, but also such as was a legal condition of the covenant of grace, to be performed by Jesus Christ: for surely that whereby we are redeemed was not any work of Israel, (they did not redeem themselves or us), but a work of Jesus Christ, answering the demand of the covenant of grace, which is for redemption.

Now, Gal. iv. 4, 5. *God sent his Son, made of a woman, made under the law, to redeem them that were under the law.* He speaks of that law by which, they were held in bondage, before the incarnation of Jesus Christ, verse 3., which was that at mount Sinai, verse 24.; and a great design or end of his coming is said to be *to redeem them that were under the law;* how this was accomplished or brought about, is declared, *viz.* by his being *made under the law,* and, therefore, thereby he performed the condition of redemption.

Indeed, I think, one great end of God in bringing Israel under this Sinai covenant, was to make way for Christ, his being born or made under the law, in order to the fulfilling of it for us. I do not see how (by any visible dispensation) Jesus Christ could have been born actually under the law, if this Sinai covenant had not been made; for, the covenant of works with the first Adam being violated, it was at an end as to the promising part; it promised nothing; after once it was broken, it remained in force only as to its threatening part, it menaced death to all the sinful seed of Adam, but admitted no other into it who were without sin, either to perform the righteousness of it, or to answer the penalty; it had nothing to do with an innocent person, after broken, for it was never renewed with man again, as before: therefore, an admitting an innocent person (as Jesus Christ was) into it, must be by some kind of repetition or renewing of it, though with other intendments than at first, *viz.* that the guilty persons should not fulfil it for themselves, but that another, a surety, should fulfil it for them.

Some medium or means there must be, whereby this innocent person, Jesus Christ, might be taken into it, and come under the very same law that was broken, to fulfil the righteousness, and satisfy or undergo the penalty, which the Lord still required, without substantial abatement.

Now, in infinite wisdom, the Lord contrived this way of the Sinai covenant, wherein Israel (who were guilty), by voluntary compact and agreement, obliged themselves and their seed to the perfect obedience which the law required, and that under pain of the curse; and Jesus Christ being born of their seed, and under the Sinai dispensation or covenant, was born under the same law, which the guilty persons were included in. I see not how that could have been, though he had been born of the seed of Adam; without this renewing of it at mount Sinai.

If he had not been born under the very law, as a covenant of works, he should not have satisfied it, by answering the penalty or fulfilling the righteousness of it; but had only done and suffered something in lieu and stead thereof; it would not have been the *idem* for us; and this shows how exceedingly necessary the Sinai covenant was.

It is true, that there was an agreement between the Father and the Son from eternity about it, the covenant of grace was then struck, and, had a being; but the Sinai covenant was a necessary medium or means for the execution thereof.

4. Jesus Christ actually underwent the very curse of the Sinai law, so as thereby he has obtained our freedom

from it, and, therefore, that held forth the legal condition of the covenant of grace, to be performed by him on our behalf: how else should his undergoing the Sinai curse give us immunity from it?

Now it is said, Gal. iii. 13. *Christ hath redeemed us from the curse of the law, being made a curse for us,* &c., *that the blessings of Abraham might come on the Gentiles,* &c. Here, is our privilege; we are sharers in the blessings of Abraham, we are redeemed from the curse of the law, of the Sinai law, for of that he speaks, verses 10, 17.; and in order to our fruition of this privilege, Christ was made a curse for us; he actually underwent the very Sinai curse, that we might be delivered from it. And the scope of the apostle here is, to discover how we attain unto justification and eternal life, it is by Jesus Christ, his redeeming of us from the curse of the law; and, therefore, his bearing of it is the condition of our salvation, as to penalty, even as his active obedience is the condition of it as to righteousness.

And let it be observed, these Galatians were Gentiles, and yet, before their conversion, they were under the curse mentioned in the Sinai covenant, and needed to be redeemed from it by Jesus Christ, as well as Jews, though the Sinai covenant was made only with the Jews, the Gentiles were never formally under it; that expired, as a covenant, before the conversion of the Galatians, Gal. iii. 13., iv. 21. and v. 1. Jesus Christ did bear the curse, not to prevent these Gentiles coming under it, but to redeem them from it.

And, therefore, in the Sinai dispensation was contained the condition of the covenant of grace, which Gentiles were concerned in, as well as Jews.

5. Many ceremonial services in the Sinai covenant did typically point out the sufferings of Jesus Christ for us, and, therefore, the design of that covenant was to hold forth the legal condition of the covenant of grace.

It may stumble some, that in the Sinai covenant all seems to be between God and Israel, and the obedience of it to be required at the hands of Israel, not of Jesus Christ.

But let them know, that Israel's obedience enjoined therein, was not only about morals, but also about ceremonial services, Levit. xviii . 5. and xxvi. 46. his statutes or institutions, which clearly typified Jesus Christ, and that in his passive obedience, his shedding of his blood, which was the great requisite to our redemption and salvation; these were as much imposed upon Israel as the other, and yet Jesus Christ must be principally intended therein, so as Israel could not have any share with him in making the least satisfaction for sin by all those sacrifices, offerings, and sheddings of blood; therein Christ was alone, and there was none with him.

Now, if the principal condition of the covenant of grace, for remission of sin, be undeniably wrapt up in those ceremonial services of the Sinai covenant, why should it seem strange to any, that under the obedience to the moral commands imposed upon Israel, should also lie wrapt up the perfect obedience of Jesus Christ for our righteousness, as the principal aim and intendment thereof?

We are not to think that those legal sacrifices did expiate sin *realiter,* but *typice,* they were patterns and shadows of better things, Heb. ix. 9. They offered both gifts and sacrifices that could not make him that did the service perfect, as pertaining to the conscience: those services, though imposed by God himself, did not please him *ex opere operata,* from the work wrought; they did not sanctify the inward man, the conscience of the sinner, but directed to Jesus Christ, in whom alone they might have remission of sin, and sanctification—Heb. vii. 19. *The law made nothing perfect,* Heb. ix. 12, 13, 14.

Israelites were obliged, typically, by their priests, to offer sacrifices for sin, and make atonement, upon pain of the curse, and to do many such acts that did bear relation to the passive obedience of Jesus Christ, but yet Jesus Christ alone was the real atonement. It is certain, the intendment was not that Israel, by their own works, should attain eternal life; and seeing both the ceremonials and morals are, in the same manner, urged upon Israel in the Sinai covenant; and seeing also such an obedience to the moral law was unquestionably performed by Jesus Christ, as our righteousness; hence all the inconveniences that lie against the one for expressing the condition of the covenant of grace, do also lie against the other, where yet it must be acknowledged.

If any will yet urge, that the Sinai covenant was between God and Israel, not between him and Jesus Christ, let them consider, that in old testament times things were expressed very darkly, and seemed at the first blush to have relation only to some lower matters; these were most obvious, when other higher things were principally intended in them.

Thus, many passages, to outward appearance, seem to relate only to David or Solomon, (who indeed had their share in them), but yet they were prophetical or typical of Jesus Christ, and under them he was principally intended, as the interpreting and applying of them to him does frequently evidence, as Psal. xvi. 10., compared with Acts ii. 31. and xiii. 35.; Psal. lxix. xxii. 18. with John xix. 24.; Psal. lxxxix. 36. with Luke i. 32, 33. So, in like manner, in the Sinai covenant, (which was a dispensation full of darkness, noted by the veiling of the face of Moses, 2 Cor. iii.) Israel's obedience is required for its due and proper end; but yet, under that, the perfect obedience of Jesus Christ is principally intended for a higher end, *viz.* eternal life, for it is applied unto Christ, and the fulfilling of the law and delivering us from it, is ascribed unto him.

6. The great difficulties about this Sinai covenant vanish; if we understand it primarily of the legal condition of the covenant of grace to be performed by Jesus Christ, and any other way they will hardly be removed.

The tenor of it plainly is, *do and live,* and *cursed is he that doth not;* here lies the difficulty of it.

Hence, on the one hand, some account that at Sinai a covenant of works to Israel, and deny it to be a covenant of grace, or to belong to that, it requiring perfect obedience, and not dispensing with one offence, Gal. iii. 10. *There being a curse annexed to the breaking of it, as a blessing to the keeping of it, even to doing,* verse 10. *The seed of it being out-casts,* Gal. iv. the latter end.

Now all such objections melt away, if we understand it of the covenant of grace, as to its legal condition, to be fulfilled by our Surety: immediately it was thus covenanted by Israel, but terminatively it looked at a performance by Jesus Christ, that he should be the only doer for life; and thus a perfect doing was aimed at in the Sinai covenant, and thus it was perfectly fulfilled by Jesus Christ, no offence dispensed with, the curse fully undergone by him; and they that crowd into the place of Jesus Christ in it, and would fulfil it for that end he did, even for eternal life, they are the seed which are the out-casts.

On the other hand, some assert the Sinai dispensation to be an administration of the covenant of grace only gradually or accidentally, and, in some circumstances, differing from other federal expressures, even from the new covenant.

Whereas, all the blessings of the new are promised, as precious fruits and effects of a presupposed accomplishment of the old by Jesus Christ.

It is easy to discover the invalidity of other interpretations of *do and live,* in the Sinai covenant, which confine the doing to Israel, and do not extend it primarily to Jesus Christ. As,

Say some, it is not spoken of the law, abstractly and separately considered, but of the law and the promise jointly, or as including the promise.

But this does not satisfy, for the apostle says, *the law*

is not of faith, Gal. iii. 12., and adds, *but the man that doth them shall live in them.*

Therefore, the law speaks of such a doing for life, as does not include the promise, for then it should be of faith. Nay, plainly, it is a doing directly opposite to believing, in the matter of justification and life, Levit. xviii. 5. with Rom. x. 5, 6. Gal. iii. 12. *viz.* if any men undertake to be the doers.

Say others, it is not *do and live,* by doing, but in doing; Christians live in obedience, though not by obedience.

But this does not satisfy; for it is such a doing as makes up a righteousness unto life, and is contradistinguished from the righteousness of faith, Rom. x. 5, 6.; and hence it cannot be meant only of sincere or evangelical obedience to be performed by Christians at all times, but vastly differs therefrom.

Say others, this *do and live,* has not reference to the moral law only, but to the ceremonial also.

Neither does this satisfy; for there is no ground to exclude the moral law, it was such a law as concluded all under sin, Gal. iii. 22. Besides, the difficulty is the same, whether it be by one or the other. If in *do and live,* a ceremonial doing were intended for Israel, that would speak as much for its being a covenant of works as if it were a moral doing; even that with Adam, in innocence, did run upon a positive precept concerning eating or not eating that fruit, Gen. ii. 17.

Neither does the Lord here make a repetition of the covenant of works, to put them upon their own choice whether they would be saved by working or believing; for they were already within the covenant of grace, and had the Lord for their God, Exod. xx. 1. And doubtless the Lord would not leave them to a liberty to go back from that grace, much less would he enter into such a solemn covenant (as that at Sinai was) with them, for that end to open a door for their crossing his grand design of free grace.

Say others, If we look upon the law separately, so it stands upon opposite terms, but if you look upon it relatively, as it has respect to the promise, so those opposite terms have their subservient ends to the promise of grace, convincing of our sin and impotency, &c. The law, considered absolutely in itself, as Gal. iv. 21. to the end, so it is nothing else but a covenant of works; but considered respectively and relatively, as Gal. iii. 17. to iv. 21.; and so it is not a covenant of works.

Now, it is true, that the Sinai covenant was designed for the ends of the covenant of grace, or of the gospel; for the apostle putting the question, *Is the law against the promise?* Gal. iii. 21. He answers, God forbid. We must then so understand the Sinai law, as in respect of its design and end it may not be against the promise—verse 24. *The law was our school-master until Christ,* yet it was for a gospel end, not that we might be justified by the law, but *that we might be justified by faith.*

But still the difficulty remains, in that, separately and absolutely considered, it is the Sinai covenant, and runs upon *do and live.* Indeed, *it gendereth to bondage,* Gal. iv. 24., even as it is the Sinai covenant. It would not conduce to those ends, the convincing of sin, humbling for it, exciting to believe, &c. But by its own inability for the getting of life, and the avoiding of the curse, as arguments that way; it is, therefore, presupposed as such a covenant, before its usefulness to these ends. Neither can we imagine that the great God would trifle with men in entering into such a solemn covenant with them on those terms, *do and live;* if there must not be this very doing here intended, by some or other, or else no life to be attained: and it is perfect doing that is called for, as I have proved, which could not be fulfilled by Israel; they were utterly unable for it, Gal. iii. 21., and, therefore, it is a doing by Jesus Christ, for them, that is there intended.

Say others, the law is taken largely, for the whole doctrine and administration of the Sinai covenant, and so it holds forth life, upon believing in Christ, Rom. x. 4.; Gal. iii. 23, 24., and is a covenant of faith: or it is taken strictly, as it is an abstracted rule of righteousness, consisting in precepts, threatenings, and promises, holding forth life, upon an impossible condition to lapsed man, perfect doing; in this sense Moses gave it not, nor is it a covenant of faith, but of works.

But this does not satisfy; for, I see no ground for that large acceptation of the law. Rom. x. 4. speaks of *the law for righteousness,* and so is taken as strictly as verse 5.; only it is said to be performed by Jesus Christ, and then, by believing, souls are interested in his performance, and Gal. iii. 12, 23, 24., he speaks of the law as a schoolmaster to Christ, which we are not under. Besides, the law in that strict sense (wherein this objection grants it to be a covenant of works) is that in which it was given at Sinai. Rom. x. 5. *Moses describeth the righteousness of the law— he that doth them shall live in them.* Therefore the law was given in that restrained sense by Moses.

Further, in that large acceptation, it cannot be proved to be clothed with the nature of a covenant; whatever in that is of a federal nature, or can belong to it as a covenant, runs upon the terms of that perfect obedience, and in that strict sense, *do and live;* and so apparently it puts on the nature, even of a covenant of works, though not intended to be performed by Israel for life, but by Jesus Christ for them.

SECTION VII.

Prop. II. That the Sinai covenant, under a typical servile administration of the covenant of grace, promised temporal mercies to Israel, upon the condition of their obedience.

Its servile and typical nature is clearly held forth, Gal. iv. 3, 24.; Heb. viii. 9., and will be more fully manifested elsewhere.

Its conditional form is obvious; it promises nothing but upon the condition of obedience, and that not only to be performed by Jesus Christ, but also by Israel—Exod. xix. 5, 6. *If ye, Israel, will obey my voice, and keep my covenant,* &c. Deut. iv. 13. *He declared unto you his covenant, which he commanded you to perform, even ten commandments:* you, *i.e.* Israel, (as. v. 1.) are required to yield obedience, or commanded to perform it; and he speaks of the same covenant made in Horeb or at Sinai, when the Lord spoke to them out of the midst of the fire, verses 10-12. Yea, Israel is blamed for violating that covenant—Jer. xxxi. 32. *Which covenant they brake,* &c.; therefore, it was their duty to keep it.

That it promised temporal mercies to Israel, upon the condition of their obedience, is manifest—Levit. xxvi. 3, 4. &c. *If ye walk in my statutes, and keep my commandments, and do them*—what then? *then will I give you rain in due season, and the land shall yield her increase,* &c.; these are outward mercies. Verse 6. *I will give you peace in the land,* &c.; there is another temporal mercy.

And not only obedience to the judicial commands, (which respects them as a commonwealth), but to all moral and ceremonial precepts, is required to these ends. The ten commandments are rehearsed, Deut. v., and then statutes and judgments mentioned, and observing all is urged to this end, *that they may live, and enjoy the land of Canaan, and length of days therein*—verses 31-33. Deut. vi. 1-3, 17, 18, 24. and xi. 8. *Therefore shall you keep all the commandments which I command you this day.* Here a universal obedience is enjoined; they were to keep not only some, but all the commands: and what will follow? Verse 9. *I will give you the rain of your land in his due season,* &c.; by all which it appears, that Israel's obedience

THE COVENANT OF GRACE 141

to the whole Sinai covenant was required, in order to their fruition of temporal blessings.

It was not only external, *viz.* that of the outward man, but cordial obedience is required to this end—Deut. xi. 13. *If ye will hearken diligently to my commandments which I command you this day, to love the Lord your God, and to serve him with all your heart, and with all your soul,* then, verse 14. *I will give you the rain of your land,* &c. *send, grass,* &c.; outward mercies. So Deut. vi. 5. Conscience then was concerned even about these things, and disobedience to moral precepts (which did bind their conscience) was given as a reason of their being excluded from their temporal mercies,—Jer. xi. 8, 10. &c.; xliv. 21-23.

It rests then to be proved, that the Sinai covenant (as to be performed, by Israel) did belong to the administration of the covenant of grace, or had grace in it to them.

It is true, it required of them not only sincere but perfect obedience, even in order to temporal mercies, it must be to all commands, with all the heart, as I have proved; their coming short of it was sinful, for in that very covenant some sacrifices were appointed, where sincere obedience was performed, for sins of infirmity as of ignorance, &c., as well as for others.—Lev. iv. 26, 29, 31, 35. and v. 10, 13, 16, 18. and, elsewhere.

This providing a relief, a remedy, implies, that Israel would fail, would, sin, and stand in need of that forgiveness, which, in many cases, was here promised; yet, in pursuance of these directions, (which are punctually given by the Lord), in offering sacrifices exactly according to appointment, they should be forgiven; that is, so far as temporal judgments threatened should be averted, and temporal mercies promised should be afforded: these sins should not be any hindrance in the way of them. Thus far it was a real forgiveness, for if there had been no real expiation by those sacrifices, and something forgiven, how could they have been typical of that forgiveness which believers have of their sins; by the true sacrifice, Jesus Christ? It was not real spiritual forgiveness, as to the conscience, that was promised there, so the law could not make him that did the service perfect, as pertaining to the conscience, Heb. ix. 9.

And let it be observed, when the apostle speaks not in relation to temporals, but to eternals, that he mentions the tenor of the same Sinai law to be *do and live, and cursed is he that continueth not in all things,* Gal. iii. 10.; Rom. x. 5. We are not to think that the righteousness whereby we are justified is to be performed by ourselves, as if the sacrifice of Jesus Christ were intended only to expiate and obtain the pardon of our sins in coming short thereof: no, such a righteousness is exacted unto justification and eternal life, as is absolutely perfect, has no flaws or sinful imperfections in it; no forgiveness is needed there, it is such as could not be performed by any but Jesus Christ alone, verse 4.; Rom. v. latter end. Hence if the Romans and Galatians would so much as attempt the seeking it by any works of their own performance, the apostle tells them, the least sin would lay them under the curse; they thereby would frustrate and make void to themselves the whole undertaking of Jesus Christ, so as they should have no profit or advantage by him. Gal. v. 2, 4. *The Lord exacted perfect obedience, without any abatement in order to eternals; it was a strict covenant of works there.*

But as to temporals, it was otherwise. Although these were promised in the Sinai covenant, upon condition of Israel's perfect obedience, yet when there was a coming short of it, and so a forfeiting them, yet there was provision made for the forgiveness of many sins, so as the Lord would not take the forfeiture, or deal with them upon such strict terms as in the covenant of works; for in case they duly offered sacrifices, they should not lose their temporal mercies: and thus it was an administration with some grace in it unto Israel. This appears these ways:—

1. The laws and ordinances for the public worship of God among the children of Israel, were contained in the Sinai covenant, as part of its condition, and, therefore, it did belong to the administration of the covenant of grace. There is a description of the tabernacle, which was for the worship of God, Ex. xxvi. and in Leviticus; many sacrifices and services are required of the children of Israel, burnt-offerings, trespass-offerings, peace-offerings, &c.; and the rules and directions left by the Lord must be exactly pursued by them, in their several places, at their utmost peril, that they die not, or be not cut off.—Exod. xxviii. 35. and xxx. 20, 21, 33.; Levit. vii. 21, 25, 27.; xv. 31.; xvi. 2, 13.; xvii. 4, 9. and many others.

The Lord would never so punctually have laid out the way of his worship, if he had not intended that Israel should find acceptation, in keeping close to him in those his appointments. The free-will offering must be brought to *the door of the tabernacle,* Levit. i. 3, 4. *and it shall be accepted for him, i.e.* for him that brings it—he shall have acceptance with the Lord to some end; and many of those ceremonial services are said to be *for a sweet savour unto the Lord,* Lev. iv. 31., vi. 15. and xxiii. 18; which implies their acceptation with God in those acts of worship, at least to the affording promised temporals, and to speak their appertaining to the administration of the covenant of grace, for sinners cannot be accepted but in that way of grace, in any service; the Lord owned them with eminent tokens of his presence, when they duly acted therein—Lev. ix. 23. *The glory of the Lord appeared unto all the people.*

2. Israel's obedience was not to be that righteousness which was the procuring cause of those temporal blessings promised in the Sinai covenant, and, therefore, that was an administration of grace: the procurement even of those was by the righteousness of another, by the perfect obedience of Jesus Christ, and, therefore, of grace.

In the covenant of works, man might have expected blessings for his own obedience, but it is otherwise in the Sinai dispensation.—Deut. ix. 4-6. *Speak not thou in thy heart, saying, for my righteousness the Lord hath brought me in to possess this land; but for the wickedness of these nations, the Lord doth drive them out from before thee:* and again, verse 5. *Not for thy righteousness, or the uprightness of thy heart,* &c.; and a third time, verse 6. The fruition of Canaan was a great mercy promised in the Sinai covenant, and with what vehemence the Lord denies that it was afforded for the righteousness of Israel—three times over he inculcates this; and, therefore, they must needs have it in a way of grace and favour.

3. There is intimation in the Sinai covenant of a provision made against the sins and transgressions of persons under it, and, therefore, it was an administration of grace: for a covenant of works reveals no relief or succour, in case of sinning; nothing but death, and a divine curse, is there to be expected, Gen. ii. 17.

But it was otherwise in the Sinai covenant: the children of Israel came exceedingly short of the obedience required therein, yet behold divine indulgence even in the bowels of that very covenant, there is pardoning mercy represented in the ceremonial law: thus, in case the priest, the rulers, and the whole congregation, or any of the common people, became guilty of sins, through ignorance, against any of the commandments of the Lord, there was a sin-offering provided, Levit. iv. throughout; and, pursuing the directions therein, it is said, *they shall be forgiven,* verses 20, 26, 31, 35.; so, in case of sinning wittingly, there were trespass-offerings, Levit. vi. Also, there were *days of atonement, and many washings;* all which intimated, that the Lord would not deal with them in a way of strict justice, according to the rigour of a covenant of works; and, therefore, that was to Israel a ministration of grace.

THE COVENANT OF GRACE 145

Indeed, Israel had stood under an impossibility of reaping any temporal blessings by the Sinai covenant, if they had been held strictly by the Lord to the condition of perfect obedience, without any way to be freed from their sin; for Israel could never have answered the condition of it, and so would have missed and come short of all the good of it, and consequently this covenant for temporal blessings would have been vain and useless, which were an impeachment to the wisdom of God, the maker of it, to assert; there must, therefore, be grace in it.

4. Considerations of mercy are made great inducements to the obedience of Israel, in the Sinai covenant, and, therefore, it was an administration of grace to them.

A covenant of works runs upon perfect obedience as the condition of it, urges duty in a way of justice, as in that with Adam in innocence; the enforcement to obedience was primarily the danger of failing thereof, *viz. dying thou shalt die,* Gen. ii. 17.

Or, on the other hand, the hope of a reward of debt; Adam perfectly obeying, the Lord, in justice, would be obliged to afford what he had promised.

Whereas, in the Sinai covenant, a grand motive and provocation to Israel's obedience, was mercy. In the very preface to the decalogue, Exod. xx. 2. *I am the Lord, thy God;* that denotes covenant interest in him, a choice mercy to a sinful people; *which brought thee out of the land of Egypt, out of the house of bondage;* there was mercy in their redemption, and this is mentioned to urge their observation of the following commandments, verses 3, 4. &c.; so that covenant mercy and redeeming mercy are grand arguments unto Israel's obedience in this Sinai covenant; and, therefore, there was grace in that ministration. Likewise, Deut. xxvii. 9, 10. *Thou art become the people of the Lord thy God;* here is their mercy—what improvement to be made of it? Verse 10. *Thou shalt, therefore, obey the voice of the Lord thy God, and do his commandments and his statutes, which I command thee this day.* Likewise Levit. xix, many verses; Levit., xx. 7, 8.

5. No violation or breaking of the covenant on Israel's part deprived them of those temporal mercies promised, unless it were against the substantials of the Sinai covenant; and, therefore, it was an administration of grace to Israel: for else, every, even the least sin, would have cut them short of all the benefit thereof.

Now, where the Lord speaks of breaking the covenant, it is in some principal matters thereof, as Levit. xxvi. 1, 2. &c. *You shall make you no idols, nor graven images,* &c. despising his statutes and breaking his covenant are in connexion, verse 15. Also Josh. xxiii. 16. *When you have transgressed the covenant of the Lord your God,* which he commanded you, *and have gone and served other Gods, and bowed yourselves to them.* Every sin was some breaking of that covenant, but, upon the account of the covenant with Abraham, they were only such transgressions as serving other Gods and worshipping them, that provoked the Lord to anger against them, so as to destroy them.—See Jer. xi. 10. Deut. viii. 19, 20.

If we view the instances or examples of the Lord's plucking away those temporal mercies from them, the Lord did not take advantage to do it upon every sin of infirmity, but upon grosser failures against the substance of the covenant—Deut. iv. 3. *The Lord destroyed them that followed Baal-Peor:* there is judgment upon transgressors; and, in opposition to them, verse 4. *But ye that did cleave unto the Lord your God, are alive everyone of you this day,* verses 5, 6. Those that were in the firmest adherence unto God, yet were not sinless; but the Lord intimates, that he would not take advantage upon lesser sins of infirmity, to deal in such a way of severity with them, but upon greater miscarriages; they that walked in a believing, careful, conscientious obedience, were spared by the Lord, as here he tells us: so their going into the Babylonish captivity, and other scatterings out of the land of Canaan, and deprivation of their temporal mercies, were upon their crossing some main ends of that covenant, and not otherwise, which argues, that there was grace attending it unto Israel.

6. After a violation of the Sinai covenant by Israel, yet it admitted of repentance, and promised a return of mercy, and, therefore, was an administration of grace to them. Had it been a covenant of works to them, then no benefit could have been expected by it after a violation, whatever repentance had succeeded.

But it was otherwise here, Deut. xxx. 1, 2. when under *scatterings among the nations,* then if, verse 2. *thou shalt return to the Lord thy God, and obey his voice with all thy heart,* &c.; verse 3. *Then the Lord thy God will turn thy captivity, and have compassion upon thee;* verse 5. *And will bring thee into the land which thy fathers possessed, and thou shalt possess it, and he will do thee good; and multiply thee above thy fathers.*

When by their sin they had forfeited their temporal mercies, yet, on the condition of their repentance, they might repossess and enjoy them; and, therefore, to Israel it was an administration of the covenant of grace.

Objection. But did not the Lord dispense out spiritual and eternal mercies of the covenant of grace, by the Sinai covenant, as well as temporals? If so, why is it mentioned as if it were only an administration of it to Israel for temporals?

Answer 1. Many persons under the Sinai covenant did obtain spiritual and eternal mercies, I freely grant; but whether these were dispensed out by that, is questioned. Moses and other Israelites were enriched with faith, Heb. xi., and were saved through the grace of our Lord Jesus Christ, even as we, Acts xv. 11. But they might enjoy those blessings by virtue of the covenant with Abraham, and not by that at mount Sinai.

2. Under those temporal things in the Sinai covenant, many spiritual privileges were typically represented. The dealings of the Lord with Israel in that dispensation are said to be as with an heir, whilst in infancy, Gal. iv. 1, 3. Now, children in their minority are led into apprehensions of, and affections to, things, by the pictures of them, and are not so capable of right conceptions thereof other ways; and, therefore, a great design of the Lord in this Sinai covenant was, to picture and point out many spiritual blessings unto Israel, under these shadows, (Heb. viii. 5.) for the drawing out that faith which they had, by the covenant with Abraham, to be exercised about them; so as their faith might be raised or helped by that at Sinai, though the blessings themselves were not dispensed out thereby, but by that with Abraham.

3. The Sinai covenant must be considered, either as holding forth the condition of the covenant of grace, and so it promised nothing but upon a perfect obedience, and this not to be performed by Israel, but by Jesus Christ; and thus, as it could not give life by any obedience of Israel, Gal. iii. 21.; Rom. viii. 2, 3., so neither did Jesus Christ dispense it out thereby; for he was the Mediator of the new and better covenant, and his ministration did lie there.

Or, we must consider it as it was an administration of the covenant of grace, (though but a servile one), and the obedience thereof to be performed by Israel; and thus *it was added,* Gal. iii. 19.; it was additional, or an appendix to that with Abraham, containing many precepts, rules, and ordinances, of divine appointment, as sacrifices, and other ceremonial services relating to the tabernacle, priests, and external worship of God, not before given forth, and so the persons who were found in a due performance of these, with an eye upon, and relation to, the ancient promise, had many spiritual blessings dispensed out to them; but they might be only externally represented by the Sinai covenant, and dispensed out by their looking from thence to that with Abraham, which it was annexed to, and to be taken in conjunction with.

I cannot think that the Lord would require their exercising themselves about so many acts of worship, without intending that they should enjoy his spiritual presence, and have acceptance in a due observance thereof.

The temporal mercies themselves, promised and afforded to them, under the Sinai dispensation, were fruits of the covenant of grace; no outward mercies can be enjoined by sinful men, in a federal way, but there must needs be grace therein: and thus the matter comes to the same reckoning, in many respects, whether those spiritual privileges were derived to them through the one covenant or the other. I am far from thinking that the Israelites enjoyed only temporal mercies; doubtless they had spiritual also, though possibly by another covenant. But for the clearing of that Sinai dispensation, and preventing some ill effects (even in practice) of misunderstanding the nature thereof, I shall add—

4. It is probable that spiritual and eternal blessings were not dispensed out to Israel, by the old Sinai covenant, but only were typically represented therein. I take the main purport and design of it to be, under that servile administration of the covenant of grace, to point out the higher and more spiritual matters thereof; and to show, that as upon literal Israel's performing the obedience which was required of them, as a condition thereof, they did enjoy temporal blessings, therein promised to them; so, upon the performance of the main condition thereof by Jesus Christ, even perfect obedience, the true spiritual Israel should enjoy the spiritual blessings promised unto them. So that, temporal blessings were afforded by the Sinai covenant, but spiritual blessings were not dispensed out thereby. This (with submission to better judgments) seems to me to be so upon these (among other) grounds.

1. No life was attainable by Israel's performing of the Sinai covenant, and, therefore, other spiritual blessings were not dispensed out to them thereby—Gal. iii. 21. *For if there had been a law given which could have given life, verily righteousness should have been by the law.* The great blessings then of the covenant of grace, *viz.* life, could not be had by their obedience to the Sinai law, of which he there speaks, verse 17.; and, therefore, neither could other blessings be had thereby, which had their dependence upon, and issued from that. As Christians are not now, so Israelites were not then to do, for life. That Moses and Aaron must not enter into the promised Canaan, but go up to the mount, and die, may be to signify, that the Sinai covenant would not give an entrance into the heavenly Canaan; Moses obtained that, not through the works of the law, but in a way of faith.

2. Spiritual blessings were not dispensed out upon the condition of Israel's obedience to the Sinai covenant, for they often violated that covenant—Jer. xxxi. 32. *Which covenant they brake;* and, therefore, their spiritual mercies had been forfeited and lost, if they had been dispensed out then upon the condition of their keeping that covenant, seeing they came so much short of it; whereas there was no falling from special grace in that day, any more than now. When they had made a forfeiture of their temporal mercies, therein promised, by breaking of it, they were forced to make another plea, Exod. xxxii. 13. *Remember Abraham, Isaac, and Israel, thy servants, to whom thou swarest, by thine own self,* &c. When the angel of the Lord waxed hot against Israel, verse 11., for committing idolatry, by making the calf; Moses does not plead that made at Sinai, but flees from that to the covenant with Abraham, for their relief.

Indeed there was an external representation of spirituals in the Sinai covenant; as they making atonement, and offering sacrifices for diverse sins, it is said they should be forgiven them, Levit. iv. 26-29, 31.,

THE COVENANT OF GRACE   151

v. 10, 13, 16, 18.; Num. xv. 28. But no real atonement was made thereby, for the law made nothing perfect, (Heb. vii. 19., ix. 9.). No real forgiveness was afforded by these acts of obedience, unless so far as that those sins should not hinder their attaining the temporal mercies promised in that covenant, or that the temporal curses of it should not be inflicted; these did but typically represent the spiritual forgiveness, which they, by another covenant, even that with Abraham, should attain unto.

Thus their entering into covenant with the Lord is said to be, that he might establish them that day for a people to himself; and that he might be unto them a God, Deut. xxix. 12, 13. They were thereby owned or confirmed in a federal relation unto God, but so as upon their miscarriages he could say to them *Loammi;* Hos. i. 9. *Ye are not my people, and I will not be your God:* and, therefore, it was externally only that they were his, and he theirs, by that covenant.

3. The ceremonials, which seemed most to intimate the dispensing out of spiritual blessings, were only typical representations thereof; these were but *shadows of heavenly things,* Heb. viii. 5. The forgiveness of sin in the Sinai covenant was such as not to have temporal punishments inflicted, and thus it was but a shadow of the real and true forgiveness, which, in opposition thereunto, is restrained unto Jesus Christ, Heb. ix. and x. Their acceptance was unto some end, *viz.* so as to be privileged with their temporal mercies, and it was but a shadow of spiritual acceptation.—Their long life in Canaan a shadow of eternal life in heaven; spiritual blessings seem not to be dispensed out, but only to be signified by these.

4. Those that look for spiritual blessings only by the Sinai covenant, and their personal performance of it, are excluded from being sharers in them—Gal. iv. 30. *Cast out the bondwoman, and her son, for the son of the bond-woman shall not be heir with the son of the free-woman.* The bond-woman

is expressly said to be the mount Sinai covenant or testament; this is Hagar, verse 24., and that as a covenant must be cast out, and also those that are the seed of it, begotten to a profession only in a legal way, by legal duties or terrors; those that stand upon an old covenant bottom, and put themselves under that, shall not inherit, shall not be heirs of the everlasting inheritance; it is another, an opposite seed, begotten by a gospel promise, which shall enjoy that; and, therefore, that Sinai covenant was not intended that souls should have spiritual and everlasting blessings dispensed out by yielding obedience unto that, for then its seed should inherit, as well as the other; but that by the sight of the impossibility of their keeping it, they might be provoked to become the children of the free-woman which are born by promise, by a distinct covenant. Neither does he speak in these things of the law only, taken abusively, in the sense urged and intended by the false prophets, but really in itself, as it was established by God at mount Sinai; for, as an argument to draw them off from the errors of the false prophets, he says, verses 21, 22. *Tell me, ye that desire to be under the law, do ye not hear the law; for it is written, that Abraham had two sons, one by the bond-woman, the other by a free-woman,* &c. And further, that these were an ancient allegory, foreshowing two covenants or testaments, the one gendering to bondage, whose seed must be cast out, as giving no inheritance; and, therefore, he concludes, that the Lord himself, in giving that covenant at mount Sinai, never intended that it should be for communicating of the eternal inheritance unto the sons of men: he tells them, that they did hear the law, and this was the language thereof; that those who are born by it, or are the seed of it, are not of the free promise, and must be cast out; they are excluded, even by the law itself, from the eternal inheritance: therefore, it was always an abuse of it to expect the dispensing out of spiritual blessings thereby; the Lord ordained another way, *viz*. the free promise, for that end.

CHAPTER VIII.

Of the Sinai Covenant, whether ceased or continuing?

IT is questioned by some, whether the mount Sinai covenant be still continuing, so as Christians are laid under the obligation of it in gospel times? I may premise, that it is called *the law,* Mal. iv. 1.; Rom. vii.; and *a covenant, or testament,* Exod. xxxiv. 23. Deut. iv. 13. Jer. xxxi. 31, 32. Gal. iv. 24.

Answer. The moral law, which was contained in the Sinai dispensation, is still obligatory; but consider it as a covenant or testament, and so it is not continuing.*

1. The moral law, as an external rule of obedience, is universally and perpetually obligatory to the sons of men. Some circumstances, as the coming out of Egypt, and prolonging the days in the land, *i.e.* in Canaan, Exod. xx. 2, 12., were peculiar to the children of Israel; and it is union with Jesus, and an internal vital principle, that all acceptable obedience flows from, John xv. 5.; but the substance of the ten commandments is still obligatory. For,

1. The moral law is a perfect rule of righteousness and conformity to the will of God, and, therefore, is perpetual. All good is commanded, and all evil forbidden there—1 John iii. 4. *Sin is the transgression of the law.* The very description of sin is fetched thence; that if we be bound not to sin, then we are to keep the law—Mal. iv. 4. *Remember the law of Moses;* and this refers to the times of the gospel, when the *sun of righteousness ariseth, with healing in his wings.*

---

* *Cessavit lex, ut norma est operum naturæ ex formula federis operum; manet vero iis qui in Christo sunt, ut est regula operum gratiæ,* saith Rolloc. de Vocat. c. 2.

Indeed, it is a repetition of the law of nature, which is engraven upon the hearts of those which are most barbarous—Rom. ii. 14, 15. *The work of the law is upon their hearts;* and, therefore, so long as the nature continues, the obligation to the law of it must also be continuing—Rom. vii. 13. *The law is holy, and the commandment holy, just, and good;* whatsoever, therefore, is opposite to it, must be unholy, unjust, and evil. The same moral law that was delivered at mount Sinai, was, (before and since), as it referred to the free promise, a rule of inward holiness, sanctification, and obedience, and had spiritual enjoyments attending of it: as it had relation to the Sinai covenant, and its end, so it ushered in temporal mercies unto Israel.

2. The Lord has declared his approbation of conformity to the moral law, and with great severity witnessed against disconformity to it in all ages. Long before the Sinai ministration, Abel is commended for his faith, owning and worshipping the true God, and Cain, for the contrary, disapproved, Gen. iv. 1.; Heb. xi. There was a reverend use of the name of God, Gen. xiv. 19, 20., the sabbath instituted, Gen. ii. 3., superiors honoured, Gen. ix. 23. and xxii. 7.; murder witnessed against, in Cain; adultery and unchastity punished, in raining fire and brimstone on Sodom and Gomorrah; Abraham reproved for bearing false witness, saying of Sarah, *she is my sister;* Laban accused for defrauding and coveting, Gen. xxxi. 7-9., so that, though the wording of it in the formality of ten commandments was at mount Sinai, yet immoralities were ever sinful. In the times of the new testament, Jesus Christ declares his observing the ways, actings, and inclinations of men; and some are blamed, others commended, even in his churches, Rev. ii. and iii.; the least swerving from the rule is sinful.

3. The natural tendency of the moral law is to promote love; Jesus Christ himself is giving the epitome and sum of the law, and reduces all the ten to two great commandments, Mat. xxii. 36. to 41., *viz.* love to God and the neighbour.

THE COVENANT OF GRACE 155

Doubtless men are obliged, at all times, to let the streams of their love run out towards God; to love him with *all their heart, with all their soul, with all their mind, and to love their neighbours as themselves;* and upon these two hang *all the law and prophets,* verse 40. The fulfilling of these is the keeping of the law.

4. The moral law is explained, and obedience to it earnestly pressed, in the times of the gospel. To free it from the false glosses of the Jewish Rabbis, Jesus Christ himself gives an explication of it, Matt. v., declaring that not only grosser acts are to be avoided, but whatsoever has a tendency that way, *unchaste looks, unclean thoughts, are sinful,* verse 28. Christians are under an obligation, not only to sincere, but to *perfect obedience, under the royal law of liberty,* Jam. i. 15.; so as the least failing of it is sinful, though it does not bring believers under condemnation. Yielding worship to God is duty still, Mat. iv. 10., as the way to withstand Satan in his temptations, and the duties of the second table, are plainly urged, Eph. vi. 3. Rom. xiii. 8. Love is undeniably a duty in gospel times, and the fulfilling of the law is wrapt up in it—verse 9. *Thou shalt not commit adultery, thou shalt not steal, thou shalt not bear false witness, thou shalt not covet.* These commandments then are in force still, and the Romans (who were Christians of the Gentiles) were under the obligation of them, and, therefore, they are perpetual. Indeed, Jesus Christ owns them as his—John xv. 10. *If ye keep my commandments, ye shall abide in my love,* &c.; keeping these, by believing, and loving one another, is the way to the manifestations of his love: this of love he calls *a new commandment,* John xiii. 34. Indeed, this puts sweetness into it; Christians are under the law, but it is *to Christ,* 1 Cor. ix. 21., to their Mediator, who satisfied for their breaking of it. They take it not from the hand of Moses, in its terror and rigour, but from the hand of Jesus Christ, who has redeemed from the curse of it.

The first tables, which were the work of God, were quickly broken, Exod. xxxii. 16, 19.; but the second tables that were to be hewed by Moses, (a typical Mediator), they were more durable, of longer continuance, and then the Lord proclaims his pardoning mercy, Exod. xxxiv. 1, 4, 6. The moral law, in the hand of Jesus Christ, the true Mediator, is abiding, and pardoning grace and mercy experienced under it. Of old, the ark of the covenant had only the moral law put into it, not the ceremonial, (Deut. x. 2.) to note, this was to be abolished, but the moral to abide with the covenant still; on which account, it is promised of the new covenant, Heb. viii. 10. *I will write my law in their hearts;* all which argue the perpetuity thereof.

2. The mount Sinai dispensation, as a covenant, is not continuing. It is generally granted, that it is abrogated, in respect of some circumstances, fruits, and effects of it— as servile embondaging fear, and such like; but I apprehend, that none are under the obligation of it, as a covenant or testament, in gospel times.

This may appear these ways:—

1. The succession of the new covenant in the room and stead of the old, argue that it is not continuing; for one must be removed when another takes its place, Deut. ii. 12, 21, 22., xxv. 6 and xix. 1. Now, the new covenant succeeds the old. The Hebrews were apt to be doting upon that made at mount Sinai; to take them off from it, he tells them of a better come in the place and stead of it, Heb. viii. 8, 9.; and observe the contra-distinction is between covenant and covenant, not barely between circumstances and accidents of the same covenant—and verse 13., in that he says, *a new covenant, he hath made the first old, now that which decayeth and waxeth old is ready to vanish away.* It is the covenant that is old, and the same is said to vanish away; and, therefore, it must needs be, that the Sinai covenant should cease and come to an end, as Calvin says, "because the second is of

THE COVENANT OF GRACE   157

another quality." It is true, that the new covenant, in the substance of it, or as a covenant, is found in that with Abraham, though not under the notion of new, for that is given it in opposition to the old; but it could not be said to succeed, until the old expired.

2. The ceremonial and judicial laws are generally granted to be abrogated, and so the old covenant, as to them, (which make a considerable part of it), is not continuing: indeed, the judicials, as to their moral equity, are deemed binding, but not as they are a part of that covenant, for then they must oblige exactly as they stand in it: these had a peculiar reference to the Jews.

They are called judgments, Exod. xxi. 1., determining of rights between man and man, and of punishments upon transgressions with reference to the interest of that people in the land of Canaan, says Dr. Owen on Hebrews;* and hence they cannot formally oblige others, who have nothing in that land.

As to ceremonials, the apostle, to evidence that they are abolished, speaks thus, Heb. vii. 11, 12. *If, therefore, perfection were by the Levitical priesthood,* &c. where he asserts perfection, (*viz.* as to remission of sin, justification, &c. Heb. x. 16, 17, 18.) was not obtained by the Levitical priesthood, or legal sacrifices and performances, but only by Jesus Christ, who was typified therein; this he proves thus, *for under it the people received the law,* which imports, that when they arrive at evangelical perfection, they are free from the law, do not receive that, *viz. as a testament,* as verse 22., and he speaks of the moral law as distinguished from the ceremonial: and if perfection were by that, says he, verse 11. *What further need was there that another priest should arise after the order of Melchisedec, and not be called after the order of Aaron?* The necessity of a new order of priesthood argues the

---

* Page 275.

imperfection of the old, and thence he infers the abrogation of the ceremonial law. Verse 12. *For the priesthood being changed, there is made of necessity a change of the law:* there is such a connexion between the priesthood and the law, as they stand and fall together; if one be abolished, (as the Aaronic Levitical priesthood is), of necessity the ceremonial law (by which it stood) must be abrogated also, and he calls it a carnal commandment, verses 16. and 18. *for there is verily* (not only an altering and changing), but *a disannulling of the commandment going before, for the weakness and unprofitableness thereof.*

The same might also be cleared from Heb. ix. where he speaks of ceremonial usages, and they were till the time of reformation, they were the patterns and figures of heavenly things: the substance being come, the shadow must vanish; the antitype, Jesus Christ, being come, the type must cease: And O what a glorious privilege is it, that we have freedom from that load of burdensome ceremonies required in the law. There remains only the moral law, that any can suppose these promises and threats now to be annexed to, and as to that,

3. Jesus Christ has perfectly satisfied and fulfilled the mount Sinai moral law: as it was a covenant for eternal life, and therefore, as such, it is not still continuing. It was impossible for us perfectly to obey the law, by reason of the infirmity of our flesh, Rom. viii. 3, 4.; but whatever is demanded there, in any of its precepts, as the condition of life, Jesus Christ has performed it for us, Mat. iii. 15. and 17., and so has brought in a perfect righteousness to be imputed to us, Rom. x. 4.; 2 Cor. v. 21.; yet we are not exempted from all obedience to the moral law, by his obeying perfectly in our stead, for his righteousness was for one end, *viz. to merit eternal life for us,* Rom. v. 21., our obedience is for other ends, as to testify our conformity and subjection unto God, and so to glorify him, &c.; as his sufferings were for one end, *viz.* to make satisfaction

for our sin, our afflictions and sufferings are for other ends, and not for that.

Also he satisfied all the threats of the Sinai covenant; these all did meet upon him, Gal. iii. 13: *He was made a curse for us;* so that these federal precepts and curses expire by satisfaction, as the judicial and ceremonial laws did by abrogation.

There remain, then, only the promises of it; and upon his satisfying the other, he alters these, and turns them from conditional into absolute, as we see in the new covenant. Hence, whereas in the Sinai covenant, that cluster of promises, concerning there being *a peculiar treasure, a kingdom of priests, a holy nation,* &c. Exod. xix. 5, 6., did run upon the condition of obedience, *if ye will obey,* Jesus Christ having done and suffered all which that covenant could exact, now he has given all forth in an absolute form to believers, and expresses all as already accomplished unto them, 1 Pet. ii. 9. *But ye are a chosen generation, a royal priesthood, an holy nation,* &c., *a peculiar people,* &c. It is not now upon an *If,* as in the Sinai covenant; but the promise is fulfilled to them, and in Christ they are such as it was conditionally promised of old they should be. Thus, Rev. i. 5, 6. *hath made us kings and priests unto God and his Father;* but how? He has loved us, and washed us from our sins in his own blood. It is upon his satisfying the Sinai covenant by his sufferings unto death, as it was the condition of life. Its not continuing as an administration of the covenant of grace, will be cleared in the following particulars.

4. The Lord is not rigorously exacting duty from believers now, upon the legal terms of the Sinai covenant *(cursed is he that continueth not in all),* therefore the Sinai covenant is not continuing: for such a co-action would inevitably follow a being under the obligation of it, in regard that is the very nature and tenor of it, Gal. iii. 10.; Deut. xxvii. 26., and all the promises run upon these terms. If

these curses be not in force against them, then it is ceased as a covenant; if they be in force, then they are under the same rigorous exaction of duty still as Israel was of old, for then the enforcement to it is the same. For, we must know, that the Sinai covenant was not made with pagans, infidels, or professedly unbelievers; the great God would not engage himself by covenant unto such; but it was made with the children of Israel, with those who were the people of God already, by the covenant with Abraham, before they came at mount Sinai: hence the preface runs thus, Exod. xx. 2. *I am the Lord thy God,* &c., not he became their God there, but was their God before. Therefore, if it be continuing to any as a covenant, it must be to the people of God (for it was made with none else), and they must (if any) be under the terror of it.

Whereas it is evident, that Christians are to yield obedience upon more evangelical accounts; the gospel urges upon them duties of holiness, the avoiding apostacy and profaneness, by sweetness and love; not by legal terror, but by their freedom from it, Heb. xii. 14. *to the end.* As if he had said, ye are not come to a legal mount Sinai dispensation, enforcing duty by terror, thunderings, and lightnings; but to mount Sion, to a dispensation of gospel grace, verse 25. *See that ye refuse not him that speaketh,* &c., now the terror is upon abusing grace.

So Rom. vii. 6. Their being delivered from the law in its compelling and condemning power, is made the means to raise up unto new and spiritual obedience. Not so much from *the wrath as the mercy of God,* Rom. xii. 1. from *the constraints of love,* 2 Cor. v. 14. from an eyeing *the promises of God,* 2 Cor. vii. 1. *Having these promises, let us cleanse ourselves from all pollution of flesh and spirit.* And here I may hint one considerable difference between the covenant of works, and that covenant at mount Sinai; the former extended to all mankind, and was made with all in Adam, their common head; but the

THE COVENANT OF GRACE 161

latter was made only with some, with Israel and Judah the people of God.

5. If the Sinai covenant were still continuing, then the people of God within it might still be laying claim to the blessings of it, by virtue of the same promises in the very form as they are found therein; for, if the form be altered, then the claim is by another covenant whereby such an alteration is made. Whereas temporal mercies are promised in a new dialect, more absolutely, Jer. xxxii. 36. to the end, and xxxi. 27, 28, 31, 32.; they are not afforded unto Christians now upon the same conditional terms, that they were to Israel under the Sinai covenant. By way of analogy, those ancient promises may intimate to Christians now, that walking circumspectly is the way to be supplied with earthly blessings that are good for them: but there is no such special contract or distinct covenant (as that made at mount Sinai) whereby they may claim so large a portion of temporal enjoyments, as Israel could by that; rather we find, that those which were most obedient in the first times of the gospel, were put upon an expectation of little in temporals (in comparison), and were to look for a plenty of troubles, losses, persecutions, &c., Mat. vi. 31, 32, 33.; Mat. x. 22.; Acts xx. 23.; 2 Tim. iii. 12.; Acts xiv. 22.; Luke ix. 23.

See Mr. Bisco, in his book entitled *The Glorious Mystery of God's Mercy,* who endeavours to prove, that temporal blessings were made over and dispensed to the Jews under the law, in a peculiar manner, and as never to any people or nation but they.

6. Various expressions holding forth our freedom from the law do conclude that it is not continuing as a covenant; as, Rom. vi. 14. *For sin shall not have dominion over you, for ye are not under the law, but under grace.* Those then that are under the law in the sense here intended, cannot be under grace, and are under the dominion of sin; and therefore the direction of the law for duties of holiness is

not denied here; but they are not under the law as a Sinai covenant, exacting full and perfect obedience upon pain of an eternal curse; nor under it as a condition of life unperformed, for that were inconsistent with grace, and would infer that sin is still exercising lordship over them. Rom. vii. 4. *Ye are become dead to the law by the body of Christ, that ye might be married to another, even to him who is raised from the dead,* &c. He speaks, ver. 1, 2, 3. of the law as an imperious husband (which is by covenant), and thus they are *dead to the law,* not under the power of it; *by the body of Christ,* that is, by his bearing the curse of the law on his body; and therefore they are dead to it as a covenant, for so he had it on his body. Gal. iv. 21, 24, 30. The bond-woman, Hagar, is expressly said to be the covenant or Testament from mount Sinai; and she and her son, all that are of a legal birth, must be cast out, ver. 30.: that covenant, therefore, from mount Sinai, was but temporary, is cast out in gospel times, is not continuing. In some respects that at mount Sinai may be called (as it is by the learned Cameron) a subservient covenant, *viz.* in respect of Israel, as it discovered sin, and provoked to seek after a mediator (Exod. xx. 19.) in promising temporal mercies upon obedience, representing spirituals and eternals; but subservience does not fitly express its federal nature, as it promised life upon doing or perfect obedience, threatening death and a dreadful curse upon falling short of it. I do not call it the covenant of grace, nor the covenant of works; but to express the formality and essential nature of it, I call it the covenant of grace as to its legal condition, or a covenant concerning the legal condition of the covenant of grace, which is held forth under an administration of it for temporals unto Israel.

O let Christians yield utmost obedience to the royal law of liberty, but let all be done in the strength of Christ, and in the way of the new covenant, make use of a promise of grace, in setting about all duty. And beware of seeking

THE COVENANT OF GRACE   163

to keep up the old covenant, which really is not continuing: we seek to keep it up, when we live in the spirit of the old covenant, acting by its enforcements, terror, wrath, curse, rather than by the allurements of grace in the free promise. Also, when there is a grounding acceptation with God upon our own duties and performances: the old covenant did run upon *do and live,* intending a doing for eternal life, which was peculiar to Jesus Christ; but our nature is prone to run our own doing into the place of his, as if we could gain acceptation unto life by our own services, or do something that way. We are apt to build expectations of mercy upon our own doing, instead of building them upon Jesus Christ. Evangelical obedience may be a secondary evidence; but when we dwell more upon any thing done by us, or upon any inherent grace, any thing within ourselves, than upon the free grace of God in Christ, we then make something of our own a ground of acceptance, and not an evidence only; when something within raises our hope of acceptance, more than the grace of God in the new covenant. The promise and oath of God (which are both without us) are the two immutable things of divine appointment, for the raising strong consolation, Heb. vi. 18. All grace within should be improved, for carrying out our souls to God and Jesus Christ therein.

Also, when there is not an improvement of our freedom from the law, towards making out the more after Jesus, and the free grace of God in him, then we seek to keep up the old covenant still. Rom. vi. 14. Being under the law and under grace, are opposites there; the less grace exercises lordship over the soul, the more sin domineers and gets the upper hand of it, and the more it is under the law. The greater freedom from the law as a covenant, the more grace is used towards freedom from the dominion of sin.

Also, when there is a looking for what is promised only in a conditional way, then there is a keeping up the old covenant, which did run upon conditional promises; when souls have acted in duty, and now are ready to count the Lord engaged to give out or afford mercy upon their performing thereof; when they look for nothing but as a fruit of some condition performed by themselves (Isa. lviii. 3.) and their hopes of mercy rise or fall by that rule of their own performance, rather than by the free grace and faithfulness of God, then there is a holding up the old covenant.

CHAPTER IX.

Of the Good that was in the Sinai Covenant.

I SHALL now show what excellence there was in the mount Sinai or worse covenant.

The more good there was in this, the greater excellence will appear in the new, which is a better covenant.

There was excellence in the matter of it. Such precepts were contained in it, as had a stamp of righteousness upon them, Deut. iv. 8., such as did advance Israel above other nations, Neh. ix. 13. Psal. cxlvii. 19, 20. It was excellent, in the manner of its manifestation; there was a dreadfully glorious appearance of the majesty of God in giving it forth, Exod. ix. 16, 17, 18.; he revealed himself in an unwonted way, in thundering, lightning, thick darkness, &c., it was a stupendous dispensation, to humble that rebellious people: the mountain was smoking, the thick cloud covering it, the trumpet sounding, all indications of his divine majesty, that they might discern him from dumb idols, ver. 22. *Ye have seen that I have talked with you from heaven;* as if the Lord himself had spoken in an immediate way. It was not altogether immediate, the ministry of angels was used in it, Acts vii. 38.; but it was by the authority of God himself, with more than ordinary demonstrations and tokens of his Almighty power, such as struck them into a marvellous consternation, and admiration that they were alive. Exod. xx. 19. Deut. v. 26. *Who is there of all flesh that hath heard the voice of the living God speaking out of the midst of the fire, as we have, and yet lived?* O what grace is it, that the Lord is not dealing with us in such a dismaying terrifying dispensation, but in a milder and more familiar way, in the dispensation of the gospel!

It was excellent in the special uses and ends it served to: the two principal I have opened already, which must here be remembered, *viz.* for eternals upon the obedience of Christ, for temporals upon the obedience of Israel. I shall now hint some other uses and ends of the Sinai covenant.

1. To be a provocation unto Israel to look unto a Mediator, the Lord Jesus, to fulfil and accomplish it for them: both the terrible publication and the experienced impossibility of keeping it themselves, were excitations this way, Exod. xx. 19. *They said unto Moses, speak thou with us, and we will hear, but let not God speak with us, lest we die.* Here they asked a typical mediator, and therein a real one, Jesus Christ, for so the Lord expounded their petition, and promises to grant it, Deut. xviii. 15. *The Lord thy God will raise up unto thee a prophet,* &c., *that thou desiredst at Horeb,* &c.; and that prophet is said to be Jesus Christ, Acts iii. 20, 22. They were provoked by the terror of the Sinai law, to ask a mediator, that he would pass into the burning mount, to receive it for them, and give it forth as a law of love; and this request they are highly commended for, Deut. v. 27, 28., so that the use of that fiery dispensation was not, that life should be attained thereby, but to impel to look out unto another covenant for that.

2. To constrain to duty, and restrain from sin, Exod. xix. 9. *Lo, I come to thee in a thick cloud,* but to what end? *That the people may hear when I speak with thee, and believe thee for ever.* It was then to startle them out of their unbelief, and win credit to his word. And in their terror, Moses, for encouragement, says, Exod. xx. 20. *Fear not, for God is come to prove you, that his fear may be before your faces, that ye sin not.* It was then one end of the Sinai covenant to deter them from sin.

3. To be a directory to Israel for the worship of God. The church had been domestic or in families; but the posterity of Abraham swelling into a great number, the Lord would have them become congregational: they must coalesce and become federally united together, the whole to constitute one ecclesiastical body, by this Mosaic dispensation, which had ordinances of worship suitable to that new state of the church now introduced. The Lord gave to Moses a pattern of the tabernacle (which was for public worship), with a strict injunction, Heb. viii. 5. *See that thou make all things according to the pattern that I shewed thee in the mount,* Heb. ix. 1. Exod. xxv. 40. And in that and the following chapters of the book, there are rules about the ark, table, candlestick, and the institution of ministers, used in the service of the tabernacle; as Aaron and his sons in the priests' office: here is direction for the consecration of the ark and tabernacle, the altar of incense, and many ordinances and institutions; which hold forth another use of the Sinai dispensation.

4. To be a platform, model, or rule for government, ecclesiastical and civil. Israel received righteous laws, statutes, and judgments from God himself: Therein they were differenced from, and excelled the nations; that they were more immediately under the government of God as their only law-giver. And not only an eternal curse, but many ecclesiastical and civil penalties, and censures, are threatened upon breaking of those divine laws, Exod. xxii. 1, 4, 20.; Levit. xx.; Numb. v. and xix.; Deut. xiii. and xxv. with many others. This, then, was one use of it, to be an instrument for the government of the children of Israel.

5. Another end of it was, to give a typical representation of many glorious mysteries appertaining to the covenant of grace. These matters were not empty insignificant rites; but, by divine appointment, served as shadows, types, and patterns of heavenly things, Heb. viii. 5, 6. and ix. 23. Even their temporal mercies were typical representations of

spiritual and heavenly blessings. The land of Canaan figured out the heavenly rest. The Levitical or Aaronic priests were eminent types of our great High-priest the Lord Jesus, Heb. 7. The tabernacle a type of his human nature; whence he is said to be *a greater and more perfect tabernacle, not made with hands,* Heb. ix. 11. and viii. 2. It might also figure out *the true church,* Rev. xxi. 3. The *ark,* the furniture for the most holy place, which none but the high-priest might enter into, (Heb. ix. 3, 4, 7.) properly refers to Jesus Christ, who is the great repository in whom the divine law is treasured up for believers; he is their glory and direction unto eternal rest. Many other types there were of him. I might also note that Moses was below with the people, for their encouragement against fear at the promulgation of the law, and making and confirming the covenant; but was called up higher towards the top of the mount, for receiving the tables of the covenant, and the pattern of the tabernacle, Exod. xix. 24, 25. and xx. 1, 20. and xxiv. 12, 18.; all which may typify that Jesus Christ stands with us for our encouragement in receiving the fiery law; and, upon more immediate converses with God, gives forth the frame of his solemn worship. These were the ends of the Sinai covenant.

CHAPTER X.

Of the Differences between the Old and the New Covenant; and the Excellency of the latter above the former.

IT may be enquired, How is the new covenant (in which the ministry of Jesus Christ lies) a better covenant than the old, which was made at mount Sinai?

I would premise, that in Heb. viii. and also Jer. xxxi. 31, 32., the opposition is not between the covenant of works, as with the first Adam and the new, but between the old (made when Israel came out of Egypt at Sinai) and the new covenant. These are they which are compared; and therefore the differences between these, either in their matter or form, must hold forth the excellence and betterness of the new covenant above the old.

1. The new covenant presupposes obedience unto life to be performed already by Jesus Christ, and so is better than the old, which requires an after performance of it. The very tenor of the Sinai covenant was, *Do this, and live,* Levit. xviii. 5. Deut. xxvii. 26. Rom. x. 5. Here Israel was engaged in a federal way to perform the righteousness required in the unspotted law: the very doing is enjoined which our eternal life is dependant upon, even *perfect doing,* Gal. iii. 12. Indeed Israel engaged, yet they were to perform this by their surety, Jesus Christ. But all was then undone, unfulfilled, unperformed, Jesus Christ not being then manifested; and hence the law had then a commanding force, might exact that obedience at the hand of Israel, who covenanted there that it should be yielded in time to come.

But the new covenant takes it for granted, that all this doing for life is over, already past, and not to come, Jesus

Christ being actually exhibited; that as the old covenant seemed to be made of precepts or commandments, so the new is made up of promises; consists of nothing else, Heb. viii. 8 to the end: giving a declaration that all is fulfilled, there remains nothing to be done, either by principal or surety, for that end, *viz.* life. The Lord is so fully satisfied, as in the new he gives a general acquittal, and acknowledges that he hath no more to demand, all is turned into promise, *I will, and ye shall.* Jesus Christ is said to be *the Mediator of the new testament,* verse 6, that is, actually so. To intimate, that in this short term, mediator, we have now in accomplishment the sum of all the doing required in the old covenant; and way is made for our receiving the promise, Heb. ix. 15. Within seventy weeks the Messiah came, Dan. ix. 24. *To make reconciliation, and bring in everlasting righteousness;* before righteousness was commanded, *viz.* in the Sinai covenant, but then it was introduced. *By one offering, he hath perfected for ever them that are sanctified,* Heb. x. 14. Nothing remains to be done for the procurement of these eternal blessings.

Hence in opposition to that Sinai law, which ran upon those terms, *do and live,* under the dispensation of the new, we hear so often of *Believe, and be saved, and he which believeth hath everlasting life,* Mark xvi. 16. John iii. 16, 36. Not that believing now, takes the place of doing in the old covenant; for, then it must be our righteousness unto justification, Gal. iii. 12. Rom. x. 5., whereas that which justifies is called *the righteousness of faith,* ver. 6, and Phil. iii. 9.; and therefore faith is distinct from that righteousness itself, is not the least atom of it. Therefore, not our believing, but the obedience of Jesus Christ, is that which comes in the room and stead of that doing for life intended in the law, Rom. v. 19. *He is the Lord our righteousness,* Jer. xxiii. 6. 1 Cor. i. 30. But to note, that it lies wholly out of ourselves, that it is not by any of our performances, but in another, even Jesus Christ, it is said

THE COVENANT OF GRACE 171

to be by faith, *i.e.* as a means of application. Believe that the work is not now to do, Jesus Christ hath done all; and, says he, John viii. 24. *If ye believe not that I am he, ye shall die in your sins.* Thus the apostle, speaking not merely of the false opinion of the Jews concerning the meritoriousness of their good works, or their external services, being perfect obedience to the law unto life. I say, he, not insisting upon these errors, but having mentioned *the very righteousness of the law,* Rom. x. 5., in opposition to that, he says, ver. 6, 9, 10. *If thou shalt confess with thy mouth the Lord Jesus, and shalt believe in thy heart that God hath raised him from the dead, thou shalt be saved.* It is then a believing in him as already come, and having all righteousness subjected in him, yea, as dead and risen, that is called for. When they were doating upon works of the law as performed by themselves, to take them off from this, he tells them that all this legal doing for life must be found in Christ alone; and, as it follows, *for with the heart man believeth unto righteousness,* that is, as a means unto righteousness. It is not his own working that will be his righteousness, nor his faith itself; only that is a means for the applying that righteousness which is found in Christ alone.

So that the apostle's aim is not to call them off from a legal doing by natural power and ability, and instead thereof to put them upon evangelical believing and doing, as the condition giving right to life; but his design is, to put them upon looking wholly out of themselves and all their own doing, whether by nature or grace, unto Jesus Christ alone for righteousness unto life. If a man should set about any gospel service, upon a legal ground, he would be culpable as the Judaizing professors were. It is such a doing as gives a title unto life (by performing the condition of it), that is rejected, in the epistles to the Romans and Galatians, as dangerous. Evangelical services are required on other accounts, and to be performed to testify conformity to the will of God; and these may evidence life in the way to it: But faith itself, though necessary, yet receives a title from Jesus Christ, does not give one, John i. 12. That axiom, *he that believeth shall be saved,* is not expressive of the tenor of the new covenant. We claim salvation not in right of any act of ours; not upon the rent of faith (as men hold tenements by the payment of a penny, a rose, or such like); no such thing here. All is paid to the utmost farthing by our surety; and we hold, and claim, upon the obedience of Jesus Christ alone, Rom. v. 18, 19, 21.

2. The new covenant represents the Lord as dealing with his people universally in a way of promise; and so is better than the old, which represents him as treating them in a way of threatening.

The new consists all of promises, Heb. viii. 8, &c. as if the heart of God were so full of love, and running over therewith, that he could express nothing else but what he would be to, and do for, his people. The Father having received full satisfaction to all demands in the old covenant, by the mediation of his Son, now he makes it his business to give the fullest assurance by a constellation of promises in the new, that he will fulfil, to a tittle, whatsoever on his part rests for performance. Believers are wholly freed from the curse: *There is no condemnation to those that are in Christ Jesus,* Rom. viii. 1. Heb. xii. 18. *They are under a ministration of righteousness,* 2 Cor. iii. 9.

But the old covenant represented God as a consuming fire, denouncing curses and threats against the children of Israel, who were his own people (for with them was the Sinai covenant made, and not with unbelievers of the Gentiles.) There were indeed some promises sparingly scattered up and down in it; but they run conditionally, and Israel failed to achieve the condition; that if they had not been privileged with the covenant with Abraham, to run unto for relief; what might they think would become of them? By divine appointment, there were some to stand upon mount Ebal to curse, as well as others upon mount Gerazim to bless, Deut. xxvii. 13. &c. There are about twelve curses, which they were enjoined to declare their assent unto, *all the people shall say, amen;* indeed, the last was a general one, ver. 26. *If they continued not in all things, they were liable to it,* Gal. iii. 10.; which shows that, although a temporal curse was not excluded, yet an eternal was also some way intended, on which account it is called, *a ministration of condemnation,* 2 Cor. iii. 7.

It was otherwise with them in reference to that curse, than it is with Christians under the new. Israel, by that voluntary act, the old covenant, passed sentence upon themselves: indeed, the curse of the law was not then actually undergone by Jesus Christ, it was not then satisfied; and so might be presented before them as their obligation or bond, uncancelled, striking fear in them.* But Jesus Christ *hath redeemed us from the curse of the law,* Gal. iii. 13. Now all is discharged for us, and so the new is a better covenant.

3. The new covenant consists of absolute promises, and therefore is better than the old Sinai covenant, which ran upon conditional promises, indeed, had works as its condition. In the times of the old testament, the price of our redemption was not paid by Jesus Christ, and therefore life was then held forth upon the condition of obedience: the Lord said, *Do and live,* Lev. xviii. 5. Rom. x. 5. Gal. iii. 12. As that which under the new seems to be conditionally mentioned in one place, is absolutely promised in another; so, on the contrary, what seems to some to be absolutely propounded in the old, in one part of it, yet is conditionally promised in another, Exod. xxix. 45, 46. *I will dwell among the children of Israel, and be their God.* Indeed this is not properly absolute, but (as

---

* to their great affrightment. *[orig.]*

the foregoing verses show) upon what Aaron (a type of Jesus Christ) should do; however, the very same is clogged with a condition, Lev. xxvi. 3, 11-15. The promise of *circumcising their heart, and the heart of their seed, to love the Lord,* Deut. xxx. 6., runs upon condition: *If thou shalt hearken unto the voice of the Lord thy God, and keep his commandments*, &c. ver. 9.

But the new covenant consists altogether of absolute promises, Heb. viii. 10-13. *I will, and ye shall.*

When the condition of any covenant is performed, it becomes as absolute, as if there had never been any annexed to it. Now, Jesus Christ is mentioned as our *great High-priest and Mediator;* and that, as having finished the work of satisfaction, ver. 1, 2, 6.; and the condition contained in the old being exactly and completely fulfilled by him, it naturally or necessarily must turn into an absolute form, as in the new: because, upon his performance, nothing more is to be demanded of him, but all must certainly be accomplished unto us.

The apostle, in the text, is purposely putting a difference between these; and, seeing the old covenant was unquestionably conditional, and the new here in opposition to it, or distinction from it, is as undoubtedly absolute; must it not needs be concluded, that herein stands much of the excellence of the new above the old?

It was prophesied of Jesus Christ, Dan. ix. 27. *He shall confirm the covenant with many for one week.* A great end of his coming and death was, the confirmation of the new covenant, on the behalf of the many which he stood for; so as now it is turned into a testament, as the word διαθηκη (which generally it is expressed by) doth evidence, Gal. iii. 15, 16, 17. *Though it be but a man's testament, yet if it be confirmed; no man disannulleth or addeth thereto.* The free promise was confirmed by oath before, and by way of testimony since, but especially confirmed by the death of Jesus Christ, by his performing the condition of it; and

THE COVENANT OF GRACE 175

therefore it can admit of no addition or alteration, Heb. ix. 16, 17. *For where a testament is, there must also, of necessity, be the death of the testator; for a testament is of force after men are dead,* &c. It bears the name of a testament, as in relation to his death, so in such a proper sense as it has the laws of a testament attending it; on which account, he mentions a necessity of the testator's death, and its being in force thereupon. Indeed a man may put some conditions into his last will: I do not argue thus, it is a testament, and therefore absolute, but therefore unalterable; and so, being delivered in an absolute form, *I will, and ye shall,* hence it must abide in it, even in its accomplishment. And whereas some argue for conditions from the nature of a covenant, against that it is asserted to be a last will or testament, which may bequeath legacies without any condition.

There is a vast difference between the way of Jesus Christ his acting in the work of his mediation before and since his incarnation, and the latter is much more glorious than the former. Before, he might plead, Father, thou hast promised me, upon my obedience, hereafter to be performed, that those souls which I have undertaken for, should enjoy such blessings: There was a mutual trust between them, and so he might plead it in point of faithfulness. But now, he hath actually performed the condition of the covenant, and may plead it in point of justice. Christ being actually exhibited as a propitiation, upon that, God is said, Rom. iii. 25, 26., to declare at this time his righteousness, &c.: in opposition to the time of the old testament, he says, *at this time;* that is, at the time of the new testament, wherein the blood of Jesus Christ is truly shed: Now God declares his righteousness in the justifying him that believes in Jesus. It is an act of grace to those who attain the remission of sin, but an act of righteousness to Jesus Christ. He may plead, Father, I have made satisfaction to the full for the sin of these souls, now declare your righteousness in pardoning of them: it is that which I have purchased for them, *I have finished the work which thou gavest me to do,* John xvii. 4. I have paid the full price of their redemption, now let them have what I have procured for them. Thus he appears in heaven in our nature, not as a mere intercessor, but as *an advocate,* 1 John ii. 1: to plead that, in law, in right we are to be discharged. And this puts a great excellence upon the new covenant, that it is in itself, and to Jesus Christ, thus absolute.

And note, if some privileges of the covenant were dispensed out properly in a conditional way (as suppose justification were afforded upon faith as a condition, or temporal mercies upon obedience), yet this would be far from proving any thing to be the condition of the promise, or of the covenant itself. Indeed even faith is a particular blessing of it, and therefore cannot be the condition of the whole covenant; for what shall be the condition of faith? And there is no such special covenant now extant, as the old was, for temporal mercies; they are indefinitely promised, and sovereign grace is the determining rule of dispensing out these to the saints when they are wanted, for time and measure, as it is most for the glory of God and their good, Mat. vi. 32, 33. Nothing performed by us, then, is *conditio fæderis,* the condition of the covenant itself; Jesus Christ has performed all required that way.

But whether any thing be *conditio fæderatorum* is now to be considered.

Object. Is the new covenant absolute to us, or conditional? Are there not conditional promises therein to us, as there were in the old unto Israel? Can we expect any mercy, but upon our performing some condition that it is promised to?

Ans. 1. If condition be taken improperly, for that which is only a connex action, or, *medium fruitionis,* a necessary duty, way, or means, in order to the enjoyment of promised mercies. In this sense, I acknowledge, there are some promises belonging to the new covenant which are conditional; and thus are many scriptures to be taken which are urged this way. That this might not be a mere strife of words, I could wish men would state the question thus, Whether some evangelical duties be required of, and graces wrought by Jesus Christ in, all the persons that are actually interested in the new covenant? I should answer yes; for, in the very covenant itself, it is promised that he *will write his laws in their hearts,* Heb. viii. 10., and that implies faith, repentance, and every gracious frame; and those that have the Lord for their God are his people. If the accusation be, that there is a want of interest in Jesus Christ, they need not plead that they have fulfilled the condition of the covenant; but, that the covenant itself, in some promise of it, (which uses to be distinct from its condition,) has its accomplishment upon them therein. And those that are altogether without those precious graces, are strangers to the covenant, Eph. ii. 12.; they cannot lay claim to the blessings of it. It is our duty earnestly to be seeking after what is promised, and one blessing may be sought as a means to another; as, the spirit as a means to faith, and faith as a means to obedience, Gal. v. 6. Believing is a great duty in connexion with, and a means of, salvation; he that believes shall be saved, Mark xvi. 16. John iii. 36. Eph. ii. 8. 1 Pet. i. 5, 9. There is an order in giving forth these blessings to us, and that by divine appointment; so as the neglecting to seek them therein, is highly displeasing unto God. This is our privilege that divine promises are so conjoined and twisted together, for the encouragement of souls in seeking after them, that if one be taken, many more go along with it; like many links in a chain that are closed into each other. The means and the end must not be severed.

Where there is such a connexion of duties, graces, and blessings the matters may be sometimes expressed in a conditional form, with an *if,* as, Rom. x. 9. *If thou shalt confess with thy mouth the Lord Jesus, and shalt believe in thy heart, thou shalt be saved,* Such *ifs* note the verity of such propositions in their connexion; they affirm this or that to be a certain truth, as that, he which believes shall undoubtedly be saved, yet that grace is not properly the condition of salvation; for, even believing is absolutely promised, so as nothing shall intervene to hinder it, Isa. liii. 10, 11. Heb. viii. 10. In that improper sense, some scriptures seem to speak of conditions, *viz.* they intimate a connexion between covenant blessings; some are conjoined as means and end, yet the promises are really absolute for their performance.

There is a vast difference between the way of the Lord in the dispensation of covenant blessings, and the tenor of the covenant. Or, between the new covenant itself, and the means which the Lord uses for its execution and accomplishment.

The covenant itself is an absolute grant, not only to Jesus Christ, but in him to the house of Israel and Judah, Heb. viii. Yet what the Lord has absolutely promised, and is determined and resolved upon to guarantee to them, may be conditionally propounded as a quickening means to souls seeking a participation of it. As, it was absolutely determined, yea, and declared by the Lord, that those very persons which were in the ship should be preserved, Acts xxvii. 22. *There shall not be a loss of any man's life,* and verse 25. *I believe God, that it shall be even as it was told me.* Yet, as a means to their preservation, he speaks to them conditionally, verse 31. *Except these abide in the ship, ye cannot be saved.* So although the salvation of all the elect, and also the causing them to believe, is absolutely intended; yet, as a means that he may urge the duty upon souls with greater vehemence and earnestness, the Lord may speak in a conditional way, *if ye believe ye shall be saved,* when it is certain they shall believe.

Answer. 2. There is no such condition of the new covenant to us, as there was in the old to Israel. For, the

The Covenant of Grace 179

apostle is comparing them together; and, in opposition to the old, he gives the new altogether in absolute promises, and that to Israel, Heb. viii.; and, showing that the new is not according to the old, he discovers wherein the difference lay, verse 9. *Because they continued not in my covenant, and I regarded them not; saith the Lord;* and, Jer. xxxi. 32. *which covenant they brake,* &c.

This argues that the condition of the old was such as the performance of it did give them assurance of the temporal mercies promised, and a right to them, and such as failed in, left them at uncertainties whether they should enjoy them or not; so as it was not only in itself and its own nature uncertain, but even as to the event, *I regarded them not, saith the Lord.*

If their performing the condition had been as absolutely promised, as the blessings of the new covenant are, then Israel would have continued in it (which they did not), and could not have forfeited what was promised thereupon, as diverse times they did, and were excluded out of Canaan upon that account.—Jurists say, a condition is a rate, manner, or law, annexed to men's acts, staying or suspending the same, and making them uncertain, whether they shall take effect or not.* And thus condition is opposed to absolute.

That there is no such condition in the new covenant to be performed by us, giving right and title to the blessings of it, and leaving at uncertainties and liability to missing of them, as there was in the old to be fulfilled by Israel, may appear,

1. If there be any, it must either be an antecedent or a subsequent condition; but neither.† There can be no such antecedent condition, by the performance of which we get

---

* Cowell, out of West. part 1. Symb. 2. sect. 156.

† L. Coke upon Littleton says, of one precedent, *Conditio adimpleri debet priusquam sequatur effectus.*

and gain entrance or admittance into covenant; for, till we be in it, no act put forth by us can find any acceptation with God, Heb. xi. 6. *Without faith, it is impossible to please God.* And our being, in covenant is, in order of nature, (though not of time,) before faith: because it is a privilege or benefit of the covenant, a part of the new heart, a fruit of the spirit; and so the spirit (which is the worker of it, and another blessing of the covenant,) is given first in order before it. Jesus Christ is *the first saving gift,* Rom. viii. 32., and with him he *freely giveth all things.* Men ought to be in the use of means; but it is the act of God that gives admission into the covenant, Ezek. xvi. 8. *I entered into covenant with thee, saith the Lord God, and thou becamest mine.* Immediately before, they were polluted in their blood, verse 6.; in an utter incapacity for acting in any pleasing way, so as to get into covenant. Neither is there any subsequent condition to be fulfilled by us: the use of that is, for the continuation of a right, and upon failing thereof, all is forfeited, as in the case of Adam.—Whereas there is no act of ours whereby our right to covenant blessings is continued unto us, upon failing whereof they may be forfeited. Our right, and the ground of our, claim, is upon a higher account than any act of our own; it is even the purchase of Jesus Christ; and they are *the sure mercies of David,* Isa. lv. 3. *Sure to all the seed,* Rom. iv. 16. And when they are become believers, eternal life is absolutely promised, John iii. 16, 36. 1 John v. 10, 11, 12., and it is a contradiction to say, that it is absolutely, and yet but conditionally, promised to them.

2. The Lord has given assurance that there shall never be an utter violation of the new covenant, and therefore it has no such condition as was annexed to the old; for, the Lord declares that *they had broken* his covenant, Jer. xi. 3, 4, 10. Jer. xxxi. 32.* But the new covenant is secured

---

* Littleton, speaking of an estate upon condition in deed by feofment, says, it is called estate upon condition; for that the

THE COVENANT OF GRACE 181

from such a violation: it cannot be disannulled so as the persons interested in it should be deprived of the great blessings promised therein, Jer. xxxii. 40. *I will make an everlasting covenant with them.* But may there not be such a condition of it as they may come short of all its blessings? No: *I will not turn away from them to do them good, but I will put my fear in their hearts, that they shall not depart from me.* If there were any danger of forfeiting and losing these, it must be either on God's part, by his leaving of them, or on their part, by their departing from him; and here the Lord has undertaken to secure against both these, and so the matter is out of question; it was not thus in the old covenant.

Indeed what the Lord hath absolutely promised, yet he has appointed means in order to the attaining of it, internal as faith, and external as ordinances; and commands utmost attendance upon him ordinarily in the use thereof; this is necessary as a duty, and sin arises upon the neglect of it. Thus the Lord is unalterably determined to guarantee a frame of obedience, Ezek. xxxvi. 25-30. Yet obedience is to be performed by us; we are to be the agents, and we may sin about the means in the way to the enjoyment of such mercy, as is laid up in absolute promises.—Faith is to be exercised in these, (else what use are they of?) and we may be faulty in not attending to it.

3. If there be any such condition of the new covenant, it were most like to be precious faith; but that is not. A condition properly taken, is influential into right: if performed, it gives right to the benefit promised; if not performed, there is no right, and therefore is a cause; it gives *jus ad rem,* which a man may have, and yet be forced after to sue for possession. If it be only in a mode or

---

estate of the feofee is defeasible, if the condition be not performed. Ten. lib. 3. cap. 4.

accident, it is thus: as if a great estate be granted upon paying a white lily, if a person brings a yellow lily, and not a white, he hath no right, all is null and void. Upon such a tickle* point are they who stand upon such conditions for eternal mercies.

Now faith gives no right, John i. 12. *To as many as received him, gave he power to become the sons of God, even to them that believe on his name.* Jesus Christ is offered in the free promise of the gospel; faith, that consents or receives him, and a right and title in him; to the blessings of the covenant, it does not give one.

The Father offers righteousness in a way of gift, Rom. v. 17. Faith accepts the offer, receives Jesus Christ for righteousness, and so conduces to justification, Rom. iv. 3. Abraham believed God, and it was counted to him for righteousness, *i.e.* it was reckoned a means unto righteousness; so verse 5. Not that faith itself was reckoned the least of that righteousness whereby we are justified, but a means for the applying of Jesus Christ, who is our righteousness. The covenant, as to that privilege of it, justification, is not so absolute as to be without all means; yet may be absolute, without any condition, properly so called. As condemnation (without any new act of receiving) results from the law upon disobedience, to all under the covenant of works; so justification is the result of a divine promise, upon the obedience of Jesus Christ, to all those that are under the new covenant. That unbelievers are not justified by it, is because they are not actually under it. Not because they have not fulfilled the condition of it, but because they are not interested in the obediential righteousness of Jesus Christ, which is the condition of it, Rom. x. 10. The act of God in justifying is to be answered by the act of faith, consenting to the offer of the gospel. As the death and satisfaction of Jesus Christ is enough to

---

* minute, tiny.

THE COVENANT OF GRACE 183

answer, if the accusation be, that we are sinners, and deserve eternal wrath; so, if the accusation be, that we have no interest or portion in this satisfaction, any thing that can evidence our interest in Christ, is a sufficient plea to answer that; be it faith or other graces, they may be pleaded as evidences, but not as titles; as fruits and effects of a right given, but not as causes, and conditions fulfilled by us, giving us that right. It is a great mistake to think, that there is no plea in this case, but from the performance of a condition; for, an evidence may be from the effects, as well as from causes: even in civil matters, a mere witness may carry it in such a charge, when he can testify, I saw the person put into peaceable possession of such an estate. Besides, if this charge be drawn up against those out of Christ, many things may make it good; if against those that are in Christ, then who draws this up? Not God, for he it is that justifies, and therefore he will not condemn, Rom. viii. 33, 34.; if Satan or their own hearts, then as gracious effects are enough to answer, so, by direct acts of faith, there ought to be a steadfast resisting and withstanding of Satan, and he will flee from them, 1 Pet. v. 9. Jam. iv. 7. No necessity of pleading the performance of a condition to help against this.

4. Our obedience, though evangelical, is no such condition of the new covenant, as there was of the old unto Israel. For, the Lord hath undertaken that his people shall obey, Ezek. xxxvi. 25-30. *I will put my spirit within you, and cause you to walk in my ways:* Heb. viii. 10. Obedience is as absolutely promised as any other blessings in the new, and therefore it cannot be the condition thereof. The apostle having asserted and largely proved, Rom. iii., that justification is by faith, not by the works of the law, he further clears it from the instances of Abraham and David, Rom. iv. 3. Abraham believed, &c. and verse 4. *Now to him that worketh the reward is not reckoned of grace, but of debt.* This strongly implies, that the reward must be reckoned

of grace, and not of debt. The emphasis is upon this; so as if it were otherwise, the whole force of his argument were taken away, and the stress is not upon the word *reckoned;* yet, if it were, the same word λογιζομαι (being applied to both) must signify a true judgment and just estimation (as Rom. viii. 18. and ix. 8. 1 Cor. iv. 1.); for, really and in true account the reward is of grace; and it is as firmly asserted, that if it were of works, it were (in the same account) of debt. Say some, only meritorious works would make it so: But let it be considered, that works can be meritorious only one of these two ways: either,

1. By being of such value and worth, as that in justice such a recompense is deserved by them, indeed, though there were no contract that way. And dare any say, that any works of men, even in innocence, could thus merit at the hands of God? Is not all obedience due to God, so as when we have done all, we are unprofitable servants? Luke xvii. 10. Job xxii. 3. and xxxv. 7. *If thou be righteous, what givest thou him?* Rom. xi. 35. *Who hath first given to him, and it shall be recompensed to him again?**—Or else,

2. They merit, ex pacto, by some contract or covenant; that though the works be inconsiderable in value to the reward, yet the Lord has promised such a reward to them. Thus only, and no otherwise, could the obedience of Adam, in a state of innocence, be meritorious; for he did owe all as duty to God, even by right of creation. He might have required all, without engaging himself to give any reward; and finite services could not merit in worth and value an infinite reward; but the Lord promised it to his perfect unsinning works. No otherwise did any among the Romans or Galatians expect justification or eternal life in a way of works; but only falsely imagining, that the Lord had made a promise of salvation unto these.

---

* Credendum est firmiter dari nihil ab hominibus per modum indebiti, vel accipi a Deo per modum lucri. Tract. Sacr.

Thus a reward may be of merit and of debt, and yet of grace, in some sense (though not of special gospel grace); for all good promised or given by the Lord to his creature is of grace, seeing God owes nothing to any. Thus the making of a promise to Adam in a state of innocence, for the rewarding of his works, was of grace; yet the promise being made, if he had continued in that state, the reward would have been of debt: And therefore, upon the same ground, if the reward were now promised to us upon evangelical obedience, then that were as truly meritorious (though the condition were more favourable), and life as really of debt, as it would have been to Adam upon his sinless obedience; for, only the promise must have made it so there, and the same is found here. The text in hand must refer either to the works of the law; which cannot properly merit, because due even by the law of nature, or else to those performed by Abraham after believing; and then he concludes, that if the reward were of these, it were reckoned of debt. Neither of these could render it so, but only by a divine promise, assuring such a reward upon the performing such works as the condition thereof; and, therefore, seeing he concludes it not of debt, hence no obedience of our own can be such a condition of the new covenant; It is difficult to understand how the reward can be a debt legally and in justice due, and yet God not a debtor, when it is only his compact or covenant that it becomes debt. If that may be our due which another possesses, though he be not bound to us, yet where it becomes due only by promise (as the case in hand), and that upon an act of ours, as the (supposed) condition, it seems that the promiser is a debtor, though considered antecedently to his promise, he was free; and, in Rom. iv. 4., not only is God denied to be a debtor, but the reward is denied to be a debt. Therefore, there is no promise of it upon such a condition as our works, which would make it a debt; in opposition to that, it is said to be of grace, that is, of gospel grace.

It is true, there are divine promises of the reward upon Christ's works; but they are not made immediately to us; either upon our believing or obeying, but mediately and at second hand; so as the ground of our claim is not our performing any gospel condition upon which it is promised (for then it were as really of debt as Adam's), but all the promises are immediately made to Jesus Christ upon his righteousness and meritorious obedience; on which account, all become debt to him. And thus God is not a debtor to us, but to himself, to his own goodness and faithfulness and to his Son, and not our works; but faith is the means unto our being counted righteous in his righteousness, which only merited our eternal reward, 2 Cor. i. 20. All the promises in him are yea, and in him amen, &c. We cannot claim any one promise in our own name, upon performing any gospel condition ourselves, though by the help of grace (for then, though it were never so small, it were of debt to us), but our only claim is in him, in the right of our elder brother, Jesus Christ; and thus it is of debt to him, but only of grace to us. Says Augustine, in Psal. lxxxiii. we can plead for nothing promised, but upon the account of divine faithfulness.*
Whereas, if any act of ours (though never so small) were the condition of any promise, then being performed, we might plead for what is promised in a way of justice, whose formal reason, Aquinas teaches, is, ut sit ad alterum: justice consists in giving to another what is his due, *viz.* by contract, promise, or otherwise. If divine promises pass into a debt, it is to none but himself, says Dr. Arrowsmith in his Tract.†

---

* Debitorem Dominus ipse fecit se, non accipiendo sed promittendo.

† Sacr. Ipsi etiam Deo competit duplex debitum, condecentiæ unum, fidelitatis alterum. And a little after, out of August. Deus sibi debitor est, ut agat condecenter & prout congruit bonitati suæ, uti seipsum negare non potest, ita non debet aliquid se

If either faith or obedience were a condition, then there were a suspending acts of God upon some acting of the creature, which cannot be without subjecting eternity to time, the first cause to the second, the Creator to the creature;* yea, then by our performing of it, the Lord were laid under an obligation to afford mercy promised, even life and salvation to us, and we might claim these upon our own act.

In short, therefore, we may have the recompense of reward in our eye as an encouragement to duty, 1 Cor. xv. last. Heb. xi. 26. and xii. 2; Yea, we may exercise faith as a means to the fruition of life and salvation; and yield evangelical obedience, that we may show forth the praises, or may honour him that hath called us, by such choice fruits and effects thereof, and as evidences of interest therein. Thus we may (in the strength of Christ) *strive to enter in at the strait gate, conflict with and overcome spiritual enemies, and work out salvation,* 1 Cor. ix. 24, 25. Rev. ii. 7. 11, 17, 26. Phil. ii. 12. We may pray, read, hear, believe, repent, as ways or means to the obtaining thereof; seeking the right thereunto only in Jesus Christ. But we may not believe or obey as a condition; for then, upon the performance thereof; we have right and title to the promised blessings, even to eternal salvation. Some act of ours, then, should give the title to life, and we might claim it upon our own act; but such doing for life is disclaimed and condemned in the gospel, whatever the act be, Rom. iv. 4. Eph. ii. 8, 9. 2 Tim. i. 9.

Faith itself receives but a right, does not give one. It is not upon any act of ours that the Lord is engaged to make good his promise, and that we lay claim to it. If a

---

indignum facere. And a little after, out of Davenant, Cum Deus dat vitam æternam Petro aut Paulo, Divina voluntas non solvit debitum creaturæ, sed sibi ipsi. See more, ib. p. 335.

* Dr. Owen of Perseverance, p.53.

malefactor had not petitioned to the prince, he had died, though no promise of life was made to him upon it; and so his petitioning was only a way or means to his being spared. Had it been a condition thereof, then the prince had been unfaithful, yea, unjust, if he had not granted it.

In the most absolute grants, or where there is no condition making an estate liable to forfeiture by the non-performance, yet there may be parties and stipulation.

It is the excellence and glory of the new covenant, that it runs upon absolute promises: it does not leave at uncertainties, no liability to a forfeiture of its special privileges; and these, with the admirable freeness of it, afford matter of great encouragement and everlasting consolation to all under it. See more for this, in the last question, concerning the use of those called conditional promises.

The new covenant brings in a real, plenary, and perfect remission of sins, and so is better than the old, which left short of it. Some sins had no sacrifice provided for them in the old, and were not forgiven so as they might enjoy temporal blessings promised. Some must be cut off, as they that did aught presumptuously were to be cut off from among the people, Numb. xv. 28, 30.; yet believers in that day might be forgiven those very sins, and enjoy eternal salvation, through the free promise in Jesus Christ; and, Acts xiii, 38, 39. *By him (i.e.* by Jesus Christ) *those that believe are justified from all things from which they could not be justified by the law of Moses.* The typical remission did not reach to all sins, as Christ's does, except to that against the Holy Spirit, Mat. xii. 31. 1 John i. 7.

The great design of the epistle to the Hebrews is, to show the excellence of Jesus Christ and his sacrifice above the Levitical; and how much better the new covenant is than the old, in the point of the remission of sins. There was imperfection in the legal sacrifices: the forgiveness there was only so far as temporal judgments were averted, and temporal mercies afforded; they could not really take away sin, did not purge the conscience, or make the comers thereunto perfect, Heb. ix. 9. Heb. x. 1, 2, 3, 4. But, in opposition hereunto, it is the glory of Jesus Christ, verses 12. 14. *By one offering, he hath perfected for ever those that are sanctified;* i.e. the people of God, those in covenant. This he clears, from the new covenant, verse 15. to 19. which says, *their sins and iniquities will I remember no more.* Says Calvin, from this we gather, that sins are now pardoned in another manner than they were in old time; but this diversity consists neither in the word nor in faith, but in the ransom of the remission; thus he. In the old, there was a repetition and iteration of their sacrifices: the typical pardon of new sins was stayed and suspended till they had offered new sacrifices, and there was *a yearly remembrance of their old sins,* verse 3.; but in opposition to that, it is the perfection of the new covenant, that, as there will be no more offering for sin, so there will be a remembrance of the sins of believers no more; that is, they will not any more come one moment under the curse or obligation of the law to eternal punishment for them. The declared discharge from this (which is that in which the pardon of sin properly consists, as it is God's act) is not suspended, till the putting forth new acts of faith or repentance (although these ought to follow), but is afforded to the believer, the very moment of his sinning, whether he then takes notice of it or not.

I confess there is difficulty here on either hand; for, if believers be under the law's curse and obligation by new sins, then they are unjustified as often as they sin (which may not be admitted); and if they be not under it, then it seems they are not daily pardoned, seeing pardon consists in a declared discharge from that obligation. This will be answered in a following objection. It is actual pardon that is here inquired after; for it will be granted, that at our first justification, all sins past, present, and to come, are virtually pardoned.

That the actual remission, pardon, or forgiveness of their sins, who are in covenant, and already justified, is the very instant wherein the sins are committed; so as believers remain not one moment under the obligation of the law to eternal punishment; or the immediateness of pardon may appear thus:

1. Believers have always an actual interest in Jesus Christ, his righteousness, and the satisfaction made by him; and therefore are not one moment so unpardoned after the commission of new sins, Eph. i. 7. *In whom we have redemption through his blood, the forgiveness of sins.* It is a glorious mystery of the gospel, that sin is removed upon a full satisfaction, and yet in a way of forgiveness. It was in a way of redemption to Jesus Christ, and yet in a way of pardon and free grace to us: it cost Christ dear, even his precious blood; it cost us nothing. The elect, whilst unconverted, are not interested in that redemption, in their own persons, and so are unpardoned; but (we) believers, not only shall have it hereafter, but have it already, and therein the remission of sins. They cannot one minute be without that; for, there is an inseparable connexion between these: they that have the one, have the other also; Christ is theirs, in whom they have redemption. There will never be an interruption of believers' union with him; and Christ being theirs, his satisfaction is theirs, which answers and discharges the obligation of the law; and so they are always in a state of freedom from that. Jesus Christ being theirs, they are always interested in his righteousness; and the law cannot actually oblige or curse any that are interested in its righteousness, but only those that want it. Righteousness and pardon are in such connexion, that the apostle argues from one to the other, Rom. iv. 6, 7, 8. He proves the blessedness of men in imputed righteousness, from David's saying, verse 7. *Blessed are they whose iniquities are forgiven.* Therefore, unless believers could be disrobed

of that righteousness, and for some space lose that blessedness, they cannot be the smallest season unpardoned. If souls were actually under the law guilt of any sin one moment, they were then not perfectly righteous; for, these are inconsistent, to be completely righteous, and yet to be under the law guilt of any sin at the same time. See 2 Cor. v. 21. Rom. iii. 23, 25.

Yea, further, Jesus Christ suffered not the tautundem, something in lieu or stead of what we should have suffered, but the idem, the very same punishment of the law that was due to us; and, therefore, continual interest in that must needs render at all times disobliged or pardoned, Gen. ii. 17. *In the day thou eatest, dying thou shalt die.* Death then was the utmost penalty that was exacted; nothing more was required of us by the law of works, and nothing less was suffered by Jesus Christ in our stead, Heb. ii. 9. *That he by the grace of God should taste death for every man.*

The very thing that was threatened was undergone by him for us. As to the eternity of the death, and such circumstances that we are liable to, these arise from the incapacity of our persons, that cannot bear infinite sufferings in a short time, as Jesus Christ did for us. Or, as Mr B. observes, that despair and death in sin proceed not from the threatening in itself considered, but from the condition and disposition of the persons upon whom the execution of the curse falls: punishment, properly, is satisfaction for injury done, but sin is a continuing of the injury.*

Gal. iii. 13. *Made a curse for us.* The very thing, all that the law threatened, was the curse; and Jesus Christ did not undergo something in the room of it, but the very curse of the same law that we were under, and therefore the idem. Jesus Christ having undertaken the office of a great high-priest, Isa. liii. 6. *The Lord hath laid on him the iniquity*

---

* See *Christ in Travel*, p. 71.

of us all. I cannot understand how iniquity itself could be transacted upon the Lord Jesus; it is a non ens, a privation of good, if it could pass from one subject to another; yet it could not fall upon any, without the pollution of the subject where it rests, for it is altogether evil. Any thing short of this is not sin; deny pollution, and you deny sin itself to be upon any subject. Jesus Christ was so infinitely pure, as he could not suffer the least tincture of defilement; therefore, by iniquity, must be understood the guilt of sin, or its obligation to punishment; not a tantundem; that had not indeed been our iniquity; but it was our very guilt: whatsoever the Lord threatened against us, and might exact from us on the account of our sin, it is expressed by his being *wounded for our transgression,* verse 5., by his *being made an offering for sin,* verse 10., by his *bearing iniquity,* verse 11. Whatsoever burden, therefore, was to be undergone, or man was liable to bear, for his iniquity, this was laid upon Jesus Christ, and that by the Father's hand, the Lord laid it there. O what grace was here to us! It was the Lord that was offended, provoked, dishonoured, by sin; and yet how desirous was he that we should be discharged from it, in that he would with his own hand lay it upon his beloved Son, Jesus Christ. And it is the iniquity of us all; it was not at an uncertainty: the persons were determined, by tale, by number, by name, in whose stead he underwent all this. He was *wounded for our transgressions, and bruised for our sin, and the chastisement of our peace was upon him,* verses 5, 6. 2 Cor. v. 21. Now, seeing Jesus, Christ underwent the idem, the very same penalty that was threatened by the law, and for the very persons, and believers are always interested therein; hence they cannot one minute of time be unpardoned.

2. Believers are at all times actually interested in the general acquittal obtained by Jesus Christ; and, therefore, are not without the actual pardon of particular sins one

THE COVENANT OF GRACE 193

moment after the commission of them; for that acquittal is our general pardon.

As he was charged with our sin, so he was discharged by the Father from it, Isa. 1. 8. *He is near that justifieth me,* &c. It is spoken of Jesus Christ, as appears, verse 6. He had justification not for himself (he needed none), but for us; our sin or guilt being laid upon him, and all demands of divine justice being fully answered, he was justified, obtained a general acquittal for the whole body of his seed; hence it is not only said, he was delivered for our offences, Rom. iv. 25. *i.e.* suffered death, the wages due to us for sin, but also *was raised again for our justification.* If he had not made full satisfaction for us, death would have held him still; in that it could not hold him any longer, this argues that it had no dominion over him, but he had a complete victory over that last enemy; and his resurrection was his general acquittal for all the elect. And thus it was for their justification.

Believers have ground to say, as Rom. viii. 34. *It is Christ that died, yea, rather that is risen again.*—They have then not only a continued interest in his death, but also in his resurrection; and they are put upon triumphing in faith on this account, verse 33. *Who shall lay any thing to the charge of God's elect? it is God that justifieth,* &c. It is the standing privilege of all that are in a justified state, that nothing can be justly laid to their charge; and therefore none of their sins are one moment actually unpardoned as to law guilt, for then they might be laid to their charge, Col. ii. 12, 13. *Quickened together with him.* He stood as a common person, and virtually his seed might be said to die and rise at the death and resurrection of Christ himself in their room and stead. But some actual sharing with him is here intended; for, he says, you are risen with him, through the faith of the operation of God. This privilege is not enjoyed till they attain a work of faith with power; and then the whole advantage of his resurrection becomes theirs—in Jesus Christ they have a general acquittal and discharge. Believers are risen with him: it is reckoned unto them as if they had died and risen again in their own persons. Neither is this suspended until daily acts of faith (although these are not to be neglected); but it is at their first conversion, at their first faith and recovery, out of a spiritual dead condition—*you being dead in your sins, hath he quickened together with him.* That general justification at his rising becomes theirs at first believing, which will secure from all law guilt, that it will seize upon them no more, as it follows, having forgiven you not only some, but all trespasses. They have, then, in their rising with Jesus Christ; a general discharge in hand, not only for sins past and present actually, but for all, even those to come virtually. This general pardon will be ever ready; that, as soon as there is an actual commission of particular sins, by that they will be immediately disobliged from them. The actual pardon will he as early as the actuality of the sin, and hence he speaks as if all were actually forgiven already.

3. Believers are always under justification unto life; and, therefore, cannot at any time be actually under the obligation of the law unto eternal death. It is nothing less than a sentence of death and condemnation, a dreadful curse that the law denounces against sinners, Gen. ii. 7. Gal. iii. 10. *Cursed is every one that continueth not in all,* &c. So that if believers were one day or moment laid under the obligation of the law by new acts of sin, then so long they must be unjustified again, there must be an intermission of their justification; for, condemnation is opposed to, and utterly inconsistent with present justification, Rom. v. 16, 18. Rom. viii. 33, 34. Whereas, it is expressly said, Rom. viii. 1. *There is no condemnation to them which are in Christ Jesus.* There is not a bare suspension of the curse; but they are distinguished in respect of their state from others which are out of Christ: after union with him, indeed, after the fullest pardon, yet

every sin deserves condemnation. Pardon does not remove the desert of sin; but the legal obligation, which is to condemnation, that is taken off, verses 33, 34. John v. 24. *He that believeth hath everlasting life, and shall not come into condemnation.* By daily pardons, there is a continuation of a person's justification, and some faith he has; but, although the new acts of faith may not always be put forth the same moment that he sins, yet he is secured from condemnation, even at first believing, or passing from death to life.

The same might be evinced from the declared freedom from the law and its curse, Rom. vi. 14. Gal. iii. 10. 13. *As many as are of the works of the law are under the curse.* This strongly implies that others, *viz.* believers, are not under the curse, so verse 13. And though materially the afflictions of the elect, before conversion, be the same with others under the curse, yet the least atom of that does not formally light upon them; for, Jesus Christ underwent the whole of it on their behalf. They were sententially by the law under the curse before believing, but not executively then; much less after, being united to Jesus Christ.

4. Believers are continually under the new covenant: and, therefore, the very instant wherein their sins are committed, they are remitted; or, the persons are disobliged from the law curse, and so actually pardoned. For, unto this there is requisite only interest in the satisfaction of Jesus Christ (which they have in union with him), and the Lord's declaring their discharge thereupon; and this is by the new testament, which was *established by his blood for the remission of sins,* Mat. xxvi. 28. All pardoning mercy is treasured up there; this is the very act of pardon.

Believers are always within the new covenant, and therefore have an actual right to the pardon of all sins, not only past and present, but also to come; they have it beforehand in the promise, though not actually in possession. They have a ground of claiming after-pardons, may urge the faithfulness of God in his promise for the affording of them; also the instant wherein their sin is committed, the new testament declares it remitted, for that is a standing pardon, ever speaking on this wise to all under it, *Your sins and iniquities will I remember no more,* Jer. xxxi. 31. 34., Heb. viii. 12., so as they cannot be under the law's obligation to punishment any more. Believers are under the promise of a new heart, and writing the law there, which assures that they shall further repent, believe, &c. Yet such spiritual frames may not immediately be afforded, seeing these are gradually attained by a real change; but remission of sin is a relative change, made in an instant by the promise upon all under it when they want it.

And here let it be observed, that pardon, or forgiveness of sin, is a divine grant by the law of grace, the new covenant, that is his act of oblivion, Heb. viii. 12., Heb. x. 16, 17., Rom. xi. 27. On which account we read of the law of works, and the law of faith, Rom. iii. 27., and this latter in reference to justification and remission of sin. As, present condemnation is by a law, even by the divine law of works, that passes sentence upon sinners; the seed of the first Adam, who are under it, the very instant of their sinning, whether they be aware of it or not: so, answerably, present justification and remission of sin is by the law of grace, the new covenant, that passes a sentence upon all the seed of Jesus Christ, the second Adam, who are under it, the very instant of their sinning, when often at the very time they do not discern it. And so among men, one may have his offences pardoned by an act of oblivion, which he is under, though no accusation be drawn up against him to put his case upon trial before a judge, that may come afterward. Thus it is not by a judicial act, by an act of God as a Judge, but as a Lawgiver, that he gives present justification, and pardons; they are the sentence of his law, the new testament, which believers are always under. Accusations from Satan or their own consciences may come afterward, and a trial before the Judge in the great day.

The failure to understand this, has led to many mistakes: some asserting justification to be from eternity. Whereas they might easily understand that the elect may, indeed, must be under a sentence of the law of works, (without the least execution of the curse upon them by the Lord as a Judge), till, by coming under the sentence of another law, even the new testament, they be discharged from it.

Others talk of pleading to a charge, and upon a plea being discharged as their justification. Whereas that is only the sentence of one law declaring a discharge from the sentence or curse of another law, upon their interest in the righteousness of Jesus Christ, by union with him. The Lord is not dealing as a Judge there. Often the Lord is mentioning judgment as a future thing: Paul reasoned *of judgment to come*—Acts xxiv. 25. Mat. xi. 22. 24. and xii. 36. 2 Pet. ii. 9. John xii. 47, 48. *The word will judge you at the last day.*

The present work of Jesus Christ is not to judge the world, but to save it. Now he cometh in a dispensation full of grace, with entreaties and beseechings, that he may win over souls to a subjection to the law of faith, which is a ministration of righteousness and life exceeding glorious, 2 Cor. iii.

But he will deal in another way when he comes forth as a Judge: then he will come clothed with terror, and we must all appear before his judgment-seat, 2 Cor. v. 10. When the times of refreshing shall come, then will *their sins be blotted out,* Acts iii. 19. Not as if they wanted a complete pardon till the day of judgment; they are now as fully and perfectly justified and pardoned, as they were condemned. It was by a law against them that they were under condemnation; and so it is by a law grant, *viz.* the new covenant, that they are justified and have the remission of sin. Some call it a sentential justification: there will be a repetition of its sentence, so as they will be judicially acquitted before all the world in the great day. In what court, or by what judge, are any so pardoned here? If the bar or tribunal of this judgment be a man's own conscience, that can hardly pass sentence, without discerning and knowing itself within the new covenant, and pleading that against the accusation of Satan; whereas a soul may have the righteousness of Jesus Christ, and justifying faith, before he knows it, or be able to discern it; and, therefore, justification and pardon may be before any judicial act of conscience.

Objection. If believers be not actually under the obligation to punishment (which is guilt), then asking the removal of it, or praying for daily pardon of sin, is unnecessary. If they be not obliged, they cannot be disobliged, and so not pardoned; therefore, it seems that the curse of the law must be in force against them for some space before the new pardon comes.

Answer. 1. Believers, in their daily pardons, are declared to be discharged from the very obligation and curse of the law itself, but not from a personal obligation to it. There is an obligation to punishment residing in the law; but it does not actually pass upon the persons of believers one moment.

It must be remembered, that present pardon is not a judicial act, but it is a sentence of a law of grace, which declares all under it to be discharged from the penalty of another law. Observe, when a violated law hath already passed sentence upon an offender, an act of pardon coming afterward in force to him, there it dissolves or takes off an obligation to punishment, which is already passed upon the person; and this is the case of the elect at first conversion.—But where an act or law of pardon is in force to any persons, and reaches to offences yet to come, or not yet committed, there the obligation to the penalty never passes one moment upon the persons; and yet they have as much forgiven (even the whole penalty of the law) as the other, and more grace in it; for, it prevents the passing of the sentence upon them.

Now, this is the case: believers are always under the new covenant, which is a divine act of pardon. This law is in force to them before their commission of new acts of sin; and declares their discharge from the penalty of the law of works, that the instant wherein the sins are committed, they are remitted thereby. The commanding law is not repealed (for then they were no offences); but yet the curse of it rests not upon their persons one moment, 1 John ii. 2, 3. *If anyone sin, we have an Advocate with the Father, Jesus Christ the righteous, and he is a propitiation for our sins.*

1. Pardons afforded to sinners are from Jesus Christ, as an offering priest, making satisfaction for sin; but if one of those who have fellowship with God, if believers sin, their succour and relief is also by the standing advocateship of Jesus Christ. Now, an advocate, or attorney, pleads a law in force, whereby his client is discharged; so Jesus Christ pleads, believers being already under the new testament, whereby they have a right to indemnity; that, though the cursing law remains in force still to unbelievers, yet this new act of grace grants a pardon to the saints for all transgressions committed against it.

2. It is yet unquestionably the duty of believers to be daily praying for pardoning mercy. Those who are taught to cry unto God, *Our Father,* Luke xi. 2., yet are to say, verse 4. *Forgive us our sins.* Those then which have the spirit of adoption, yet are to be praying daily for the pardon of sin. There is reatus simplex, as well as reatus redundans in personam.—Though believers are not to confess themselves to be personally, *i.e.* in their persons to be under the obligation or curse of the law (there is cause for highest thankful acknowledgment of grace in

their freedom from that), yet there is room for the deepest acknowledgment of their own sin, and guiltiness in deserving of it; and here is enough for their humiliation.— Though the person, by grace, is acquitted or pardoned, yet there is a dueness of such a penalty to such an offence, according to the divine law: and this may be owned even under the clearest evidences of pardon; for that does not remove the desert of sin, but frees from what is deserved thereby. Yea, there is a great deal of work for faith in prayer, upon this account.

Believers are to pray for the continuation of the pardon, which they do already enjoy, and for the remission of those sins which shall hereafter be committed by them. The new covenant contains in it a promise of future pardons; and, therefore, faith may act upon the Lord in it, and that although they know they shall be forgiven. The promise-assurance of a mercy does not exempt us from praying for it. Jesus Christ had assurance that he should be glorified, and yet he prays, John xvii. 5. *Father, glorify thou me;* he knew that he should be kept, and yet he prays for it, verse 11. David had an absolute promise of establishing his house and kingdom for ever, 2 Sam. vii. 14-16., and yet he the rather prays for it; and upon that ground, even the promise of it. So we may ask future pardons, though we certainly know we shall have them. Also, we are to ask clearer manifestations of our interest in pardoning mercy.

But further, believers, in praying for pardon of sin, are,

1. To ask a fresh application of the blood of Jesus Christ in the promise of pardon: he is said to be to that very end a propitiation through faith in his blood, Rom. iii. 25. Not only is a manifestation of pardon to be sought after, but faith is to be exercised in an application of the blood of Jesus Christ, as that which has purchased and procured the pardon; that is to be eyed as the price of redemption, as that which ratifies the new testament for the remission of sins, Mat. xxvi. 28. it

is that blood which cleanses those that have fellowship with God *from all sin,* 1 John i. 3, 7, 9. *He is faithful and just to forgive us our sins.* It must be by a word or promise that the faithfulness of God is engaged this way; and it is the work of faith to own that, and the grace of God that shines forth therein, Acts x. 43. *Whosoever believeth on him shall receive the remission of sins.* The Lord's giving it is in order of nature first, but to be followed with men's receiving it through faith. God's act of pardoning disobliging believers, the instant of their sinning, is to be answered with a renewed act of faith applying this to themselves, setting their seal to what God has done; in fact, renewed acts of repentance also are to follow. Under the old covenant, *it was not possible that the blood of bulls and goats should take away sins,* Heb. x. 4. But the new testament is better; for in it, through the blessed Mediator, believers obtain *real remission,* Heb. ix. 15.

2. To ask impunity, or immunity and freedom from the execution of the curse, and from other tokens of divine displeasure; if they know they shall have it, yet they are to ask it, as I before evidenced. Though believers know that God is a Father, and that the eternal curse will never seize upon them, yet they are to pray for a freedom from it; and the rather be encouraged and provoked to it, because the Lord hath promised it. Although by the new covenant, justification is continued; yet by gross acts of sin, the Lord may be provoked, so as many sweet effects of their being justified may be suspended. David, who was in a state of grace, when he had notoriously sinned, before renewed acts of faith and repentance, before confessing his sin, *his bones waxed old through his roaring all the day long,* Psal. xxxii. 3, 4. Day and night the hand of God was heavy upon him. By this it is evident, that although, at the instant of sinning, believers are declared really disobliged from the eternal curse of the law, yet they may not be sensibly freed from that, nor from temporal evils, till afterward. They are exempted from vindictive justice,

in order to the making satisfaction for sin; but not from paternal corrective dispensations, to the humbling for, and deterring from sin, Psal. li. 2, 7. *Wash me thoroughly from my sin,* &c. *Purge me with hyssop,* &c. He was deeply sensible of his pollution, defilement, and uncleanness, by reason of iniquity, makes confession, and seeks the removal of it, verse 4. *That he might justify God,* whom he had greatly dishonoured, and give glory to him by acknowledging his righteousness in all his judgments. He cries out, verse 9. *Hide thy face from my sins:* they were not only ever before him, but seemed to be so before the Lord also; as if he were always looking on them. Though he had not lost his salvation, yet he wanted much of the joy of it, verses 11, 12. Nathan told him God had *pardoned him his sin,* 2 Sam. xii. 13, 14.; only some tokens of divine displeasure must be expected. And I think he penned this penitential psalm after; for, the title shows that this confession was directed to the chief musician; it was for the use of the temple. He had confessed privately before to Nathan, now he does it more publicly, after he had told him of pardon, and also of judgments, verse 4.

So that, after souls are really disobliged, and have pardon itself, yet they may want the sense of it, till there be a fresh application of the blood of Jesus Christ, by the spirit, to them; so as they may cry out for it, as he, verse 9. *Blot out all my iniquities.* There may be inward cloudings and darkness; sin and guilt may lie heavy upon the conscience; there may be throbbing there, and a dreadful sense of it, which may be enough to deter from sin. He will *visit transgressions with a rod, though his loving kindness he will not utterly take from them,* Psal. lxxxix. 32, 33. And who is willing to see the frowning face of God, a tender Father; and to have such smart rebukes, not only by outward corporal afflictions, but by the withdrawing the light of his countenance, which is better than life?

The old covenant did not purge the conscience, but the new is a better testament; for, having mentioned the remission of sins afforded thereby, Heb. x. 16, 17., he adds, *Let us draw near with a true heart, in full assurance of faith, having our hearts sprinkled from an evil conscience,* so Heb. ix. 15. In the way of a fresh exercise of faith, they may have freedom not only from other fatherly corrections, but from those accusations of an evil conscience, which are the usual fruits of heinous sins, till renewed acts of faith and repentance.

5. The new covenant raises a choice spirit of filial love, and so is better than the old, which leaves under a spirit of servile fear. The new, being made up all of promises, must, needs have a tendency to raise into the sweetest spirit, Rom. viii. 15. *For ye have not received the spirit of bondage again to fear, but ye have received the spirit of adoption, whereby we cry, Abba, Father.* There is an excellence in the evangelical spirit, then, above the other. I understand that text of different states of the church, or people of God: seeing in the former and following chapters, he evidently speaks of believers' freedom from the law by the Lord Jesus; and the particle again intimates, that once they were under that fearing spirit, *viz.* under the old Mosaic dispensation, but now, in the times of the new testament, were freed from it. Some, by the spirit of bondage, understand operations of the spirit, in fear and terror in order to conversion. I cannot find that he is treating of that, and it is more suitable to understand it of the state under the old testament; and the rather, because it is brought in as a proof of their sonship, as the particle, *for,* intimates. It was, therefore, no desirable frame to be sought after; but a misery to be under it, and a mercy to be freed from it. The old covenant carried with it more of the spirit of a servant, as the word signifies; and, although serving the Lord chiefly, or only for reward, savours of a legal spirit, and is one difference between

the spirit of a servant, and the spirit of a son; yet here another difference is aimed at, for it is said, ye have not received it again to fear. The Sinai covenant put them on to duty by dreadful threats, presented curses before them, (and that not actually undergone for them by Jesus Christ), as arguments or enforcements thereunto; which terrify and fill with such fear as is found in servants by the severe threats of their masters. Israel was filled with fear and astonishment at the first promulgation of the law. And whether this was the proper effect of the Sinai law, to work into servile fear and bondage, so as to make that duty then, which now is not so; and whether it were the approved effect of it in that day or not, yet it intimates, that through the frailty of sinful man, this would certainly be the issue of it, and was even unavoidable; hearing the law from the mouth of an all-powerful God, as a consuming fire. And there was not enough in those conditional promises to free from this servile fear, and so it left them under it; and comparatively with the new covenant, which has more evangelical enforcements unto duty by Grace, and the free promise. The Sinai law hath a tendency to work into the fear of a servant towards his master; and so (as the apostle says) gives birth to bondage, rather than to the fear or love of a son, which is the issue of gospel revelations.

Christians now are to act upon more evangelical accounts, from more love, and more faith, having received the spirit of adoption, whereby we cry, Abba, Father. It is by this believing spirit that souls have liberty of access to God, with that freedom that children use to have in going to a tender father. The fearing spirit kept them at a distance from the Lord, like a servant, that does not dare come near an austere master; but, by this they may, with a holy boldness and firm assurance, go to him, *and cry, Abba, Father.*

This will appear more clearly, if we compare it with that parallel place, Gal. iv. 1, 2. &c. *The heir, so long as he is a child, differeth nothing from a servant,* &c. *Even so we, when we were children, were in bondage, under the elements of the world,* &c. Here, the state under the old Sinai covenant, plainly is expressed by bondage; not absolutely that of bond-slaves, they were not in pure slavery, nor so in the condition of servants; but as under tutors and governors, and in a state of subjection; that they differed little in outward appearance to themselves or others from servants; they seemed to have more of that spirit (being acted by fear), than of the spirit of sons. But, since the dispensation of the new covenant, they are freed from the servile state, redeemed by Jesus Christ from the rigour of the law, and have much of the spirit of adoption, verses 5, 6.; there is such an alteration for the better, as if their sonship now began, verse 7., that is, comparatively with the other. Therefore, Christians now are to act in a different way from what they did of old; more in a free spirit of adoption. Thus bondage and freedom are opposed, verses 24, 25, 26, 31.; not as taken for simple slavery, but for a state of less freedom, though in the same family and house, as Hagar and Sarah were; the one expressly intending the state under the mount Sinai covenant, the other under the free promise: so Gal. iii. 24. *The law was our schoolmaster until Christ;* so it is in the original, we have not there those words, *to bring us.* This text doth not speak of a work of the law still continuing in order to conversion, before closing with Jesus Christ, for the bringing souls unto him; but tells us of the rigorous discipline of the law of old to Israel, the people of God; like a schoolmaster with a rod compelling to duty, *until Christ, i.e.* until his incarnation, until his satisfaction. It speaks of such a use thereof which is now at an end in gospel times, as appears by the antithesis, verse 25. *But after faith is come, we are no longer under a schoolmaster,* &c.; that is, after Christ, the object of faith, is come in the flesh, and hath satisfied the law, has purchased redemption for us, now we are no longer under the menaces and severities of the law as a schoolmaster: As Christ is said to be our hope, so he is our faith, that is, the object of it, the thing believed. That which is held forth here by the coming of faith, is expressed by *the coming of the seed,* verse 19., which is Jesus Christ; and our present freedom from the law, as a severe schoolmaster, speaks the betterness of our state, and so of the new covenant.

6. The new covenant is established upon spiritual promises, and so is better than the old Sinai covenant, which did run upon temporal promises to Israel.—Now I speak of it as an administration to them: All the promises of the new are of a spiritual nature, that promises *to give the law into their heart, that God will be their God, their sins shall be pardoned,* Heb. viii. These spirituals are firstly promised, and temporal things are comprised in these: godliness hath the promise of this life; but spirituals are mentioned here, that we might be taken up mostly with spiritual enjoyments, *grace, peace, communion with God,* &c. I have wondered why the new should be made up of such promises, as if only real Christians could be interested therein; but I consider he speaks of it not to exclude all from visible interest, which elsewhere is witnessed to, (Acts viii. 12.) even when the real was wanted; but, in opposition to the old, to discover how these promises are better than those of the old covenant, which run upon temporal things to Israel, as, long life, the land of Canaan, &c. Deut. v. and xi. Lev. xxvi. These were most obvious there, and better things represented by these; whereas the new puts on to duty rather by spiritual promises and blessings, than by temporal, and so is a better covenant.

7. The new covenant itself ushers in spiritual blessings, and in a more immediate way than under the Sinai covenant, and so is established on better promises. The more immediate mercies of God the better; the more new,

pure, and fresh from the fountain of divine love. Immediate visions of God in heaven, will render them surpassingly excellent; and in this world, those that are not without all means, but comparatively immediate, are the best mercies, as the more immediate judgments are the worst of these.

The old covenant did not itself dispense out spiritual and eternal blessings, but provoked to have recourse unto the Abrahamic covenant for these; they must fetch a greater compass in travelling to those enjoyments than under the new: they must look from the old for remission of sin (which was, typified there), and so for such other mercies, unto the free promise. In the new covenant, mercies are absolutely promised, Heb. viii.; and therefore the application of them is more immediate than under the old. They may forthwith, by an eye of faith, look to Jesus Christ for a fruition of them; there is not such a veil of typical institutions to intervene, that is a better way to the obtaining of those blessings, John i. 17. Yea, the dispensation is also better: the apostle says, Heb. i. 1, 2. *That God in the last days hath spoken to us by his Son.* This is the excellence of gospel discoveries above visions, dreams, and such like; afforded in old testament times; that now Jesus Christ himself speaks to us with his own mouth, we have more immediate manifestations; and, on that account, there is infinite danger in non-attendance to what is spoken, Heb. xii. 25. As the gospel is more extensive, it reaches not to Jews only, but to Gentiles also, as equal sharers in the blessings by faith, the partition-wall being broken down— Eph. i. 12, 14. Rom. iii. 22.

So there is a more open door of access to God, Heb. ix. 8. Under the old, the way was not yet opened into the holiest; which implies, that since the way is open, there is a greater freedom, (Eph. ii. 18. Heb. x. 19, 22.) and better encouragements: the price is already paid, and now Christians ask mercy as already purchased. Of old, the people must not come near to the holiest, but only the priests; now, believers have become priests unto God, Rev. i. and may have more immediate communication with him than before. All which argues this to be a better covenant.

8. The new covenant is full of efficacy, and so is better than the old. In the new, all is undertaken by an omnipotent God, Heb. viii. 10, 11, 12.; and, therefore, whatever difficulty or opposition lies in the way, yet this word of power is enough towards the accomplishment of it. Whereas, in the old covenant, much is required of Israel; but no such absolute promises assuring effectually of their accomplishment. There is such a difference between the old and the new, as between *the letter and the spirit,* 2 Cor. iii. 6. The ministers of the new testament are not of the letter, but of the spirit; *for the letter killeth, the spirit giveth life.* The Lord not only uttered the law by a lively voice, but wrote it with his own fingers in those lasting monuments, tables of stone; and the Jews, grossly mistaking, did too much take up in the letter, in external literal obedience, the chief efficacy and impression they felt thereby was in the threatening part, *the letter killeth;* the divine curse was a killing thing, struck into the fear of death. But the new hath more efficacious vivifying operations, verses 6, 8., *the spirit giveth life;* and so that is a ministration transcendently glorious: that is a powerful means for recovering the heart out of the greatest spiritual deadness, indisposition, disconsolation; it is full of quickening, life-giving influences. Abundance of the spirit in the gifts and graces of it may be found there; and so it is a better covenant.

Lastly, The new covenant is more durable and lasting, not liable to such violations as the old; and so is a better covenant. The Lord, in promising to make a new covenant, adds, Jer. xxxi. 32. *Not according to the covenant made with their fathers,* &c. *which covenant they brake,* &c. So Jer. xi. 4, 6, 10. Heb. viii. 9. Yea, the old covenant itself is said to be *vanishing,* verse 13., which imports, that this is a grand difference between them, that the new should not be subject to be broken as the old was. If those that are only externally, and by visible profession, within the new, may totally, and others who are internally and really in it, may partially break it; yet not totally, so as to cast themselves altogether out of it, nor comparatively with those within the old. The vital principles and impressions of divine love in gospel times shall be so strong, and the divine law imprinted and engraven in such lively characters upon the hearts of men, as shall wonderfully secure those that are really in the new from the violation of it; far above the other; and unsteadiness of spirit, or want of establishment, is an argument that souls have but a slender participation of its blessings. And the new shall never be antiquated: there is none to succeed that, both the Mediator and the privileges of it are eternal—the blood of Christ is the *blood of the everlasting covenant,* Heb. xiii. 20, 21.; and therefore it is a better covenant than the old.

CHAPTER XI.

Of the Time of First coming into Covenant.

IT may be asked, When is it that any are actually and personally interested in the spiritual benefits or blessings of the new and better covenant?

It is not a virtual, but an actual interest, that is here inquired after; and not, when they were representatively in covenant in their common person, but when personally, by an application of its blessings to their own persons. And indeed the new covenant is for application, and is the sum of all that is to be applied, though it be not the whole covenant of grace, which takes in all articles between God the Father, and Jesus Christ the Son, in order to our restoration. And it is to be noted, that some are visibly, others are really under the covenant.

Some, who are branches in Jesus Christ, yet may *be broken off,* John xv. 2, 6.; Rom. xi., and therefore were but visibly in him. Some are *sanctified with the blood of the covenant,* and yet afterward may *count it an unholy thing,* Heb. x. 23., and so are but visibly under it, by an outward separation to, or profession of the name and faith of Jesus Christ, so as to partake of common privileges belonging to its external dispensation. Persons thus in covenant, and under the sign of it, may be in a perishing condition still, Acts viii. 13, 25. Outward profession of faith is not that which entitles to the external administrations of it, but only is a character or mark of persons fit for them, as showing a visible interest in the promise by a possession of the things promised; and their seed have as sure a mark of their being visibly under the promise, by the Lord's declaring them interested therein with their parents, Gen. xvii. 7, 9.; Acts ii. 38.; and this not by the old covenant (as some would have it), which is disannulled, but by that with Abraham, which is yet in force, Gal. iii. 17. And besides, the same that are the subjects of the new covenant, were the subjects of the old, even *the house of Israel and Judah,* Jer. xxxi. 31, 32. Heb. viii.

As the faith of Abraham was to be exercised in the promise (which was made to him) for his seed, so may other parents' faith be acting for theirs. It is true, all of them may not be saved—the same is to be said of adult professors; and therefore the promise unto either (as to real interest) is to be understood indefinitely, not universally: even as promises attending family instruction, yea, and the public preaching of the word. Christ is with his ministers to the end of the world, though all that hear be not converted; they are the means usually blessed to such ends. But there is a real interest in the new covenant, such as is certainly attended with salvation, when the special blessings of it be theirs, Heb. viii. 10. 1 Pet. iii. 9. 1 Pet. i. 23. This is it that I would chiefly inquire after here, when it is afforded?

Real actual and personal interest in the new and better covenant, is afforded unto souls when they attain unto union with Jesus Christ, and the gift of faith, not one moment of time before.

Abstractedly from Christ, or till in him, not one promise is yours; for, *all the promises of God in him are yea, and in him amen,* 2 Cor. i. 20.; Ephes. iii. 6., all made, treasured up, and fulfilled or accomplished in him; if Christless, then promiseless, Ephes. ii. 12. Rom. viii. 32. Jesus Christ is the first saving gift of God; Christ and the promises go together. There are special marks of distinction whereby persons in covenant are differenced from the world, which agree to none that are *out of Christ,* Heb. ix. 15.; they are called ones that receive the promise. Abraham, that

THE COVENANT OF GRACE 213

famous covenanter, was not actually so, till the time of his effectual calling: from thence the four hundred and thirty years do commence, which give the first date to the covenant or promise, as made with him, Gen. xii.; Gal. iii. 17.; not from the day of his nativity, much less from eternity, although then he was an elect vessel. By becoming Christ's, men become Abraham's seed, and heirs of promise—verses 9, 14, 26, 29.

So the new covenant runs to the house of Israel and Judah, Heb. viii. 13. and none are the spiritual Israel for life and salvation till in him, Rom. ii. 28, 29. Till then, they are so far from a covenant state, which is of *life, peace, mercy, salvation,* Mal. xxv.; Isa. liv. 10. and lv. 3.; Luke i. 71, 72.; Rom. xi. 26, 27., that they are declared to be in an opposite state, they are *at enmity, dead in trespasses and sins,* and *children of wrath,* as well as others, Eph. ii. 1-3, 5, 8, 15-16.; Col. i. 21.

This may appear further, by an enumeration of the principal blessings of the new covenant: It is promised there, that he will write his law in their hearts, and be to them a God, Heb. viii. 10.; but, till in Christ, they are *without God in the world,* Eph. ii. 12. The greatest difficulty is, as to the great privilege of pardon or remission of sin, under which the whole of justification is signified, Heb. viii. 10, 12;. Rom. xi. 27. Some think, that we are justified from eternity, others at the death of Christ; but actual personal justification of a sinner before God, is at his union with Jesus Christ, and the gift of faith, not before. For,

1. None are actually interested in the righteousness of Jesus Christ, before union with him and the gift of faith: it is he that is *made unto us righteousness,* 1 Cor. i. 30.; 2 Cor. v. 21. If without Christ, then without his righteousness, Rom. v. 18. *By the righteousness of one upon all unto justification of life.* None, therefore, ever attain justification without a righteousness; for, it consists in a divine declaration of a person's being righteous; and if he were

not so, it were a false sentence, which is incompatible to the true God.

Neither will a righteousness of his own working out (though by the help of grace), serve for this end of justification, but of that one, Jesus Christ: hence verse 19. *By the obedience of one, many are made righteous?* As, his suffering and death did make satisfaction for sin, so his obedience is a righteousness meriting blessings, even eternal life, verse 21., and it is called *the righteousness of faith,* Phil. iii. 9.; that being a means for our application of that righteousness which is given, Rom. iii. 22. 25, 26. Not that faith is the meritorious, procuring cause of our justification; it hath not the same causality therein, that Jesus Christ hath. No more is required to the release of our obligation itself; than what the law (by which we are obliged) doth exact, which is satisfaction as to duty and penalty. The solution thereof was by Jesus Christ alone; but more is required, partly to make way for this, *viz.* a compact, or new covenant, concerning it: without which, all sufferings by another had been of no advantage to us; partly as a means of application, *viz.* faith, Rom. x. 10. *With the heart man believeth unto (i.e.* as a means unto) *righteousness:* and hence justification is often said to be by faith, Rom. iii. 28.; Rom. v. 1. And the question, then, was not, how are men manifested and declared in their own consciences to be justified; but, how are they justified before God and in his sight? and that is, not before, but by faith, Gal. iii. 11.

The scope of the apostle, Rom. iv. is, to prove that we are *justified by faith and the righteousness thereof, and not by works of the law,* without cause of glorying, verse 2. from the instances of Abraham and David, verse 3. for what says the scripture, *Abraham believed God, and it was counted unto him for righteousness;* and, verse 6. David describes the blessedness of the man unto whom God imputes righteousness without works: And here note,

THE COVENANT OF GRACE 215

pardon of sin is not the whole of justification; there is also necessary unto that end, a righteousness. If it were of our own working out, then we were justified and saved by our own works (which the scripture generally denies); this were to confound justification and sanctification: As if Jesus Christ only satisfied for the sins and defects of a righteousness which we perform, so as that is accepted unto life; whereas, it is by a righteousness of faith, which is not of our own working out, but wrought out for us by Jesus Christ. The false prophets themselves from among the Jews, that urged these works of the law upon the Romans and Galatians, insisted much upon the ceremonials, which plainly implies an acknowledgment of sin; and argues, that they did not expect justification without pardon, but carnally looked for pardon in the way of their own works. And the apostle, in opposition to them, excludes out of justification not only works wrought by their own natural power, but even those which were by sanctifying grace; for the works of Abraham and David (who were believers) are here excluded.

Some think the righteousness of Jesus Christ, or his active obedience in our stead, needless; unless as a part of his satisfaction for sin; because, say they, the law requires not of us both suffering and obedience.

I answer, The law, as a covenant of works, required suffering in satisfaction for sin; and, as it belongs to the covenant of grace, so it requires perfect obedience (to be fulfilled by Jesus Christ) as the condition of the justification and life of sinners; and new obedience (which refers to sanctification) is to be performed by Christians as the fruit and effect of their spiritual life. Rather it was needless that Jesus Christ should fulfil righteousness, or yield active obedience to the law, as part of a satisfaction for sin, when, by his passive obedience, he underwent death, which was the very same, and all that the law threatened against the sinner.

If man had never violated or broken the covenant of works, or had never sinned, then the law would have required only righteousness of him, for life; the tenor of it being, *Do and live.*

When man had sinned, then the law (as a covenant of works) required only suffering, and *threatened death,* Gen. ii. 17., but ceased in its *promise of life;* that immediately became null and void. It is true, the law, as a natural rule of righteousness, required still perfect obedience; that was due to God by right of creation, and his sinning could not free him from the obligation of it. It promised nothing to a sinner; it would imply a contradiction that it should promise life to him still upon perfect unsinning obedience, when he was already a sinner under the threat of death. Indeed, if immediately after Adam's sinning, satisfaction had been made, and he pardoned, yet he had been but in *statu quo prius,* in his former state. If the covenant of works had been in force again, as at the first, he must afterward have yielded perfect obedience, else no promise of life; and, therefore, there is no incongruity in saying, that, man sinning, the law required satisfaction for sin, and yet also required righteousness unto life; much more in our case: for, there is another covenant, *viz.* of grace, made with Jesus Christ, the second Adam, wherein he hath undertaken, by suffering, to make satisfaction for our sin; without which, we could never have been freed from the threatened death—there was no other way to it. The Lord might have refused a substitute; and; therefore, might (without any show of injustice) put in what terms he pleased for our restoration unto life.

If freedom from threatened death were obtained, still the Lord might have annihilated us: we had no promise of eternal life, that in the covenant of works being null and void, upon the transgression of the first Adam. Behold, therefore, the Lord agrees to stand to the first terms: the second Adam undertaking to do what the first should have done, to fulfil the same righteousness, the Lord thereupon promises life again. Thus the law is drawn into the covenant of grace, and requires the same perfect righteousness as before, to be fulfilled not by ourselves for life, but by Jesus Christ, the second Adam, as the aforementioned scriptures do witness; which assert not only suffering, but also the righteousness of that one Jesus Christ to be necessary unto *justification and life,* as Rom. v. 18, 19. &c. And hence the Sinai covenant (which he fulfilled) ran in the first form of *Do and live.*

The ground of this mistake is a false supposition, *viz.* that no more is needful unto life, but satisfaction for our sin and disobedience; as if life would naturally follow upon that, which is to say, either that we have life without any righteousness (whereas there is no promise of it to Adam, or, to any since, that run that way), or else that we have it by a righteousness of our own working out, Christ satisfying for our sins and defects therein; and this is to affirm that we have life still by the covenant of works, and in the way thereof, which to affirm is very anti-evangelical and unscriptural: For, there are many testimonies that unto the pardon of sin there is needful a new covenant, Rev. viii. 12.; and that life is by that, and the righteousness required to it, wrought out not by ourselves, but by another for us, even Jesus Christ.

And thus the death of Jesus Christ was needful to our freedom from death, although we obeyed in him, or he obeyed in our stead, to merit for us eternal life, which is promised thereupon, not now by the old covenant of works, but by the new covenant of grace. And thus, although Christ fulfilled the law for us, so as it is imputed to us, and we *made the righteousness of God in him,* 2 Cor. v. 21., yet it doth not follow that we should be freed altogether from the obligation of the law unto obedience: For, the righteousness of Jesus Christ, his obeying and fulfilling the law for us, was as the condition of life, or that upon which the Lord hath promised justification unto life. But we may be (and are) obliged to obedience, not for that, but for other ends: not in the least for our justification and title to life, but as a part of our sanctification; and we sin in not obeying, that we may glorify God by those fruits of our being spiritually alive.—Christ's obedience was for one end, ours is for another—as his sufferings were for one end, our afflictions for another; and neither of them unnecessary.

2. No actual interest in the promises of the new and better covenant, before union with Jesus Christ and faith. Even the elect of God, so long as unconverted and without Christ, are without promises, as I have manifested, Eph. ii. 12.; 2 Cor. i. 20.; Gal. iii. 22.; they were not from eternity the seed of Abraham, verse 29., he had no seed so early.

If the sinner himself had satisfied, then it had been no pardon; for he is not pardoned that pays his whole debt himself. But Jesus Christ interposed, he underwent the curse; and the new covenant, or free promise, is God's grant or act of pardon, Heb. viii. 11. and x. 16-17. *This is my covenant—their sins and iniquities will I remember no more.* Remission of sin, then, is a glorious fruit and benefit of the new covenant, not only manifested, but conferred thereby. *God justifieth,* Rom. viii. 33., and this is his pardoning act. Not faith itself or any grace within us, is that which gives the pardon; faith only receives the remission of sins, Acts x. 43: and the divine gift of it is by an immutable thing, even by the promise of the new covenant. And hence, if any object, that Jesus Christ, as a surety, had the obligation of the elect transferred upon him, and made full satisfaction to the law for them, and so disabled it for holding them obliged, because they cannot eventually be damned.

It is answered, as our obligation and condemnation was by the covenant of works, so our declared freedom from its obligation, and our justification, must be by the new covenant; that is the way laid out for the giving of it forth. And though our sin was transferred upon him, and an act passed which rendered it certain that we should be justified (yea, and sanctified too) in due season; yet not so as that we were immediately disobliged, but in the way laid out by divine appointment for that end.

The covenant of works being violated, though satisfaction must be given to that, yet that contained no promise of life to a sinner upon another's undergoing the very penalty threatened therein; and therefore was so far from giving *ipso facto* deliverance, that it would have availed nothing towards it; without a new covenant, because payment by a surety was a satisfaction able to be refused: the Lord (without any appearance of injustice) might have said, the soul that sinned, it shall die. Therefore, the sentence of the law lies against us, till by the covenant of grace we be discharged from it, in the way and time therein appointed, which is at union with the Lord Jesus Christ.

3. None are actually and personally the seed of Jesus Christ, as the second Adam, before union with him, and faith: therefore, none are actually and personally justified till then.

They are only his seed, such as he redeemed that he justifies, Isa. liii. 10, 11.; Rom. iii.. 24, 25. The two Adams are paralleled, Rom. v. 6. to the end. The day that the first Adam sinned, the law passed a sentence of death upon all his seed, verse 12.; virtually they all sinned and died there, but not actually, till they exist or have a being. And as none are the seed of the first Adam, actually under his sin and condemnation, till they be naturally born of him into the world of sinners; so none are the seed of Jesus Christ, the second Adam, actually under his righteousness to justification of life, till they be spiritually born of him into the world of saints, verses 16, 18, 19.; John i. 12.; Gal. iii. 16. The one seed Christ, to whom the promise is made, is not exclusive of infant seed, as to ordinances; but of an adult seed, which sought justification and eternal life, by the works of the law. Thus the one seed is that of faith, ver. 26. *For ye are the children of God by faith in Jesus Christ.*

Indeed, representatively, we were not only justified, but also sanctified and glorified at the death, resurrection, and ascension of Jesus Christ, Eph. ii. 5, 6. *He hath quickened us together with Christ, and hath raised us up together, and made us sit together in heavenly places in Christ Jesus.* Not that we were the principal actors by him, and he merely our delegate; for, then we were self-redeemers, self-saviours—it were more properly our act than his. Jesus Christ so represented us, as he was the principal actor, and owner of all still; the redeeming act was his, not ours, Gal. iii. 13.; Rev. v. 9.; Gal. iv. 5.; Rom. iii. 24, 25., the righteousness his, Rom. v. 18, 19, 21. It is his subjectively, he is the subject of it; objectively ours, we the objects: indeed, he so represented us, as all was federally ours in him; it was agreed that afterward we should have it. All was for us in the covenant; but we are not actually his seed one moment of time before faith, Rom. v. 1.

To say, therefore, that we are justified, not in our persons, but to our persons, in Christ, is to grant what is desired. For, men cannot be actually justified but in their own persons, and that cannot be till they actually exist, and have personality: and seeing, after their nativity, their persons are unjustified, they cannot at the same time be said to be justified.

Indeed the persons were determined; Jesus Christ had full assurance that he should not die at uncertainties, Isa. liii. 11. But that does not argue the immediateness of their justification, that is in the appointed season. We must, therefore, carefully distinguish between justification itself in the abstract, (consisting in remission of sins and righteousness prepared), and our being justified.* Or, distinguish between justification actually procured, and it actually applied; the former is before faith, the latter not so. As to the former, see Rom. v. 8-10. Our being reconciled was at the death of his Son, not at the time of our conversion. Justification, in this sense, is the object of faith, and may be before the act: thus Heb. i. 3. *When he had by himself purged our sins, sat down on the right hand of the Majesty on high,* so Heb. ii. 17. Remission of sin, then, purging, and reconciliation itself; were complete at the death of Jesus Christ; then prepared for us, but not conferred upon us, till union with Jesus Christ and faith.

4. All are in a state of condemnation till union with Jesus Christ by faith, and so have no actual justification till then; for these are opposite, Rom. viii. 33, 34. *It is God that justifieth, who is he that condemeth?* The same persons then cannot, at the same time, be both justified and condemned; for, he proves immunity from condemnation by their being justified; and they are persons in Christ Jesus that only have this immunity, verse 1; None out of Christ actually enjoy it, and no union with him one moment of time before regeneration and faith; for, *if any man be in Christ he is a new creature,* 2 Cor. v. 17. All unbelievers are condemned already, John iii. 18. *The wrath of God abideth on them,* verse 36. *Are children of wrath,* Eph. ii. 3. Even elect vessels, before faith, are here said to be in that state, under a sentence of wrath and condemnation; not only naturally, *dejure & quoad meritum,* as to desert, for so are all; the sinful actings of saints deserve wrath. Whereas, here, such wrath is intended as differenced their state in time past, from what it was since they believed; it was inconsistent with present justification unto life. Though Jesus Christ alone made satisfaction to justice for their sin, and was made a curse for them, so

---

* Mr Norton saith, Orthod. Evang. p. 314.

as not the least atom of the curse formally, that is, of vindictive wrath, shall fall upon them in execution; yet not only materially they are under it, but the law's sentence of condemnation is against them. And they are obnoxious to many tokens of wrath, not only in their bodies, in many sicknesses, infirmities, and painful diseases, but in their souls, by ignorance, darkness, with many other sinful dispositions and inclinations; and in their whole man by subjection and thraldom to Satan, (Col. i. 13.; Acts xxvi. 18.; 2 Tim. ii. 26.) and deprivation of fellowship and communion with God, and liability to the terror of such a state. And all these not in the least to make satisfaction, but for other ends; as that grace may be the more admired in salvation out of such a miserable state, Eph. ii. 11, 12., to humble them, &c.

If it be objected, that our obligation being transferred upon Jesus Christ, and he having borne our sin and curse, justice and equity requires that the elect should, upon his death, be *ipso facto* actually discharged; their debt being paid, it cannot afterward be charged upon principal or surety.

It may be answered, More is to be considered in this case than a mere debt; for here, the person was firstly and principally under the obligation, as Dr. Owen observes, satisfaction by a Surety being accepted, the Father might put in what terms he pleased, without any show of injustice; and so there is no necessity that the discharge be *ipso facto* upon his death. Also, a debt may be charged upon the principal debtor, till he obtains an actual interest in the satisfaction of the surety: till then, though no further satisfaction will ever be exacted from Jesus Christ or the elect, yet the law's obligation unto wrath may lie against them for other ends; as, to quicken them to seek deliverance out of that deplorable condition they are in. The want of an immediate freedom is not from the defectiveness of the satisfaction made by Jesus Christ, but from a present incapacity in those who are to be the subjects of the freedom. As a full ransom may be paid for slaves, yet, by reason of the distance, an after-day may be set for their release; so the elect, whilst unborn, are incapable of being actually disobliged; for the subjects must exist before even a relative change can pass upon them: Also, after they are at a great distance from God, without making up of that, they are incapable of an actual possession of redemption. As a common person, Jesus Christ represented many that lived in several ages of the world; and therefore, of necessity, the actual discharge of particular persons must be at different times—not all at once, but when they become his seed.

Further, A debt may be charged upon the principal debtor by an old law, till a new law or covenant declares his discharge from the obligation. Thus the sentence of the violated covenant of works may stand against men, till they be declared to be discharged by the new covenant, Heb. x. 16, 17. For, observe, Jesus Christ, in suffering death for our redemption, stood as *Mediator of the new testament,* Heb. ix. 15. Though therein he satisfied for our breaking of the covenant with the first Adam, as this was drawn into the covenant of grace, as the condition thereof.

Once more, A debt may be charged upon the principal debtor, after a surety's satisfying the obligation, in case the surety's name was not at first in the same obligation, but is admitted afterward by voluntary contract, covenant, and consent. For there, the covenant is the only determining rule of all matters concerning the discharge. Why are they not sanctified and glorified immediately after their coming into the world (these being effects of the death of Christ), but because the covenant provides otherwise?

If the name of Jesus Christ (as a surety) had been originally or at first in Adam's obligation, then more might have been said for an immediate discharge upon his payment of our debt, and suffering death. But this was not the case; for, if it had, then his suffering death had been necessary and unavoidable, though no new testament had ever been made; yea, the making of it had been unnecessary, vain, and useless. Whereas, it was extremely necessary: there could have been no transferring of our guilt to him, without it; and his submitting to death was by a voluntary act, John x. 17, 18. And his name not being at first in our bond, hence his payment was a satisfaction capable of refusal.

It was by an act of free grace that he was admitted to undertake for us, and his payment accepted in our stead; and so, though he paid the *idem,* the same that we did owe, yet there was nothing contrary to justice or equity, if the Father added other terms than before, and so no need that we should be *ipso facto* discharged. And the law passes sentence not only upon sinful actions, but upon the persons for them, Gen. ii. 17. Gal. iii. 22. And therefore no justification, till delivered out of this state, which is at union with Jesus Christ and faith.

I might argue from the many absurdities that attend the asserting justification from eternity: It would sound harsh to deny that Adam was an elect vessel; and being elected, if eternal justification be admitted, then he must be actually both under the covenant of works, and the covenant of grace at once; and so was bound at the same time to seek life in two ways utterly inconsistent each with other, Gal. iii. 12. *viz. by works, and by Jesus Christ through faith.* Yea, then Adam was actually justified from sin, before he had any sin to be justified from, before sin entered into the world by his fall, Rom. v. 12., and did not become guilty by his falling, being disobliged from eternity.

Neither will this be evaded by saying, our sin was imputed to Jesus Christ before committed, and an actual existence of sin is no more requisite unto our disobligation, than unto our obligation unto the punishment thereof.

I answer, The sins of the elect were not actually upon Jesus Christ, till he came actually under the law, which

THE COVENANT OF GRACE 225

was their very obligation, Gal. iv. 4, 5. And thus all their sin by that law did meet upon him before committed; answerably, when persons do actually come under the new covenant, I grant they are justified; yes, even virtually from sins not yet committed. But the old law of works must needs be in force against them till a new discharges from it; and this is not till union with Jesus Christ and the gift of faith.

And O how miserable, then, are all they who are out of Christ! They are in an unjustified estate, seeing they have no word or promise to assure them that the Lord has dropped his lawsuit* against them. But great is the happiness of all in Christ; of all believers, in that they stand justified before the Lord, Rom. iv. 7. *Blessed are they whose iniquities are forgiven,* &c. It is sin alone that renders miserable; and now the apostle challenges even earth and hell for all such, Rom. viii. 33, 34. *It is God that justifteth, who shall condemn?* It was God that was injured by sin, and who has power to discharge from it; none can reverse or disannul God's act; who shall lay any thing to their charge? Sin, Satan, their own hearts, may draw up many charges, but will be able to make none good against them; why? it is God that justifies. It is very extensive; it reaches to all sins, Col. ii. 13. Jesus Christ is a propitiation for the sins that are past, Rom. iii. 25., that is, for sins committed before his incarnation; for it is spoken in opposition to those that sought to be justified by the works of the law, verses 20, 21. To draw off from this, he tells them (as Heb. ix. 15.) that the redemption of transgressions that were under the first testament, or their remission, was not by legal sacrifices and observances, but by the blood of Jesus Christ. It doth not deny his being a propitiation for sins to come; his faithfulness is engaged to afford the remission of these, 1 John i. 8, 9.;

---

* laid down his suite *[orig.]*

1 John ii. 1, 2. Even believers are daily sinning, and the Lord will be extending pardoning mercy unto them; indeed, he will all their life long be magnifying this title or part of his name, *The Lord God pardoning iniquity, transgression, and sin,* Exod. xxxiv. 7. It is his glory that he is *a sin-pardoning God,* Micah vii. 18. *Who is a God like unto thee, pardoning iniquity?* &c.

CHAPTER XII.

Of the Evidences of interest in the New Covenant.

IT may be questioned, How or by what means may a soul know its actual interest in, and title to, the new and better covenant, and the better promises thereof?

For the clearing of this, I shall not insist upon the testimony of the divine spirit, which is the primary evidence, Rom. viii. 16.; 1 John v. 8.; nor upon sanctification, as it stands in spiritual dispositions and inclinations for compliance with the divine will, either in causing an answerableness of heart, to what is commanded from us, (comprised under a writing the law there), or working into evangelical obedience in the life, or bringing up to a self-resignation to the Lord, as Isa. xliv. 5., in the covenant it is expressly promised—*They shall be my people.* These things are insisted upon elsewhere, indeed, frequently by others; therefore, I shall pass over them at present, and mention only one evidence.

Answer. By the operations and actings of precious faith, a soul may have a clear knowledge of its actual interest in the new and better covenant. That noble grace of faith has such a special relation to the covenant (which is made of promises), that the gospel is called *the word of faith,* Rom. x. 8. It is so expressive of the great matters of it, that faith often, and the law or old covenant, are the opposite terms of a distinction, Gal. iii. 2, 5, 12, 23. In verse 9., they that are of faith are blessed with faithful Abraham; they are sharers with him in the same covenant, and blessed therein. The very blessings of Abraham come on the Gentiles through Jesus Christ, verse 14. *That we might receive the promise of the spirit through faith.* Much is to be drawn out of the free promise, for our relief and succour in any condition; indeed, for the influencing of any other graces, by faith. By that, our intercourse with God here is kept up: not that the promise is made to believing as a grace in us, or as a gracious act put forth by us, but to the believer as in Christ. Faith is not magnified as a quality, but as in the office of receiving the promise, and of excellent use therein—verse 22. *That the promise through the faith of Jesus Christ might be given to them that believe.* Faith is not then properly the condition of the covenant, upon the performance of which they have a right and title to it; but a choice effect of it, and a singular means for the application of the promises, and fetching in of covenant blessings to the soul. By that, the promise, or what is in the promise, is given to it; and faith having thus to do with the promises, it must needs have an aptitude above other graces: above sanctification and evangelical obedience, to witness a soul's interest in the everlasting covenant, Heb. xi. 1. *It is an evidence of things not seen;* and, therefore, itself is not as inevident as those other things.

There are various acts of faith, that, by the concurrence of the divine spirit may evidence interest in the covenant.

1. By faith in the free promise such glorious discoveries of the grace and love of God in Jesus Christ unto sinners are afforded, as their hearts consent to the offer thereof. It is by the shining of gospel light through the free promise into the hearts of men, that *they are turned from darkness to light,* Acts xxvi. 18. The highest natural light will leave them short of a discovery of sin, in its exceeding sinfulness, and of the riches of grace in Jesus Christ for the recovery of lost sinners; they cannot see these aright till they be revealed by the divine spirit, Mat. xvi. 17. 1 Cor. ii. 10, 14. Titus ii. 11, 12. Unbelievers may have a notion of these things, but when they are seen by an eye of faith, they appear in another manner, Rom. i. 16, 17. *The gospel is*

the power of God to salvation, to every one that believeth. The heart stood immediately before at an infinite distance from the Lord Jesus, and was full of opposition against him; but when there is a work of faith upon it, then divine power is exerted by the word or promise of the gospel, for the drawing it off from all other objects to pitch it upon Jesus Christ alone for salvation in a way of free grace: then it accepts the blessed offer, when all arguments in the world before would not prevail with it. The heart that stood off from him is then brought over to him by the gospel, and why? *For therein is the righteousness of God revealed from faith to faith.* It is in a gospel-glass that a soul gains a right discovery of the excellence of Jesus Christ, and that righteousness of his, without which, no salvation. It is by faith that there is a learning of the Father, so as effectually to be drawn to the Son. This cordial consenting to the offer of the gospel, in submitting to the obediential righteousness of Jesus Christ alone for acceptation, unto life, this is faith unto justification, Rom. x. 3, 4, 6, 10., as the like consent to have him for our Lord to rule over us by his spirit dwelling in us, is faith unto sanctification, Acts xv. 9. Rom. viii. 9-16. Thus the soul looks1 to the blood of Jesus Christ for cleansing from all sin; and the first act of closing with Jesus Christ is by faith in a free promise: that is the first grace that lives in it; the first breathings of spiritual life are by this. Such powerful and admirable alterations are found at first acquaintance with Jesus Christ, by discoveries above sense, fetching in the heart unto him beyond all other means, that they must needs be evidencing of interest in the promise of covenant, from whence all these come. Such first things have a mark upon them, and often are most discernable; the state thereupon being so vastly different from what it was, how refined soever the nature was before.

---

*1 maketh out *[orig.]*

Thus some have had their interest cleared up in such a word as that, 1 Tim. i. 15. *This is a faithful saying and worthy of all acceptation, that Jesus Christ came into the world to save sinners, of whom I am chief.*

By the eye of faith, a soul gains such a prospect of matchless love and free grace, as it is won over to Jesus Christ thereby, through a powerful application of the spirit to itself, 1 John v. 10, 11. *He that believeth on the Son hath the witness in himself;* he being enabled by grace to entertain and cordially subscribe to the blessed record upon a divine testimony, *viz.* that God has given to us eternal life, and this life is in his Son. Thereby he sets to his seal that God is true in the word of his grace, that has a witnessing power, and the person has the witness within himself, even when he sometimes doesn't discern it.

2. By faith, the soul looks to Jesus Christ in the free promise, as he alone that gives it subsistence in spiritual life: oneness with Jesus Christ cannot be without interest in the covenant, 2 Pet. i. 4. *In whom are given to us exceeding great and precious promises,* &c. Eph. iii. 6. *Partakers of the promise in Christ,* verse 17. *That Christ may dwell in your heart by faith.* It is a promise-hold that we have of Jesus Christ here, his in-being and in-dwelling is by faith; so he even animates the souls of saints, Gal. ii. 20. *I live, yet not I, but Christ liveth in me;* how? *I live by the faith of the Son of God.* Others live by sense: they feed upon earthly comforts, but Christians live by faith; by what is laid up in divine promises, by these things they live. They know not how to subsist in any state or condition without a promise; they would count themselves dead creatures without that, whatever earthly enjoyments they had in possession. Neither will a promise alone satisfy; without Jesus Christ in it—*Christ liveth in me.* He is the very life of their lives: without him, nothing but spiritual swoonings, faintings, dyings, and all from the want and failings of faith. That fetches in all influences from Jesus Christ for the

supporting, and has the great hand and stroke in all the actings of spiritual life; all spiritual motions are managed thereby, Heb. xi. 6. *Without faith it is impossible to please God.* And, therefore, sanctification is but a secondary or after evidence. This is not discernable till first there be a discerning faith; which speaks justification. If faith be inevident, all other graces will be so also.

Faith may be showed unto others by works, Jam. ii. 18. A man may be declaratively justified by works; but if a man doubts his faith, he will as well doubt his works, whether they be from a gospel root or not. For, no love of the right stamp (and so no new obedience), but what is the fruit and issue of faith in the Lord Jesus; for, that *worketh by love,* Gal. v. 6. As first acts of faith do not consist in believing that our sins are pardoned, but in a receiving Jesus Christ and his righteousness as the way to pardon, John i. 12.; so, if Christians kept up in acts of faith by outgoings of heart to him; in the way of the promise, for all that is wanted, there would be not only sweet flowings of love and evangelical obedience issuing thence; but also they would be filled with *all joy and peace in believing,* Rom. xv. 13.

I have often thought, if Christians did give more attendance to such direct acts of faith, and spent less time in questioning their conditions, or giving way to doubts about them, they would find their interest in the covenant cleared up, and consolation also coming in as by the bye.

3. By faith souls are venturing upon the free grace and faithfulness of God in his covenant, in the greatest distresses, with good success. The new covenant is made up all of promises; and the gospel is called the word of faith, because it is the work of faith to draw out what is contained there, Heb. x. 38. *Now the just shall live by faith.* Not only as to justification, but as to expectation of mercy promised. Many would be acting faith, in the concluding interest in Christ and eternal life; but they should be acting it by a cordial owning or evangelical principles.

Indeed, Christians should lead their whole life in looking to the love and faithfulness of God in his promise, for all their relief and succour in any condition they come into here; even for eternal mercy, Heb. vi. 18. They are pursued by spiritual enemies, corruptions, and temptations, and are in great danger; but, by hope (which flows from faith, and can act no higher than faith does), they go, yes run, for refuge to the hope, to the heavenly glory that is set before them, so as they lie as at anchor in such stormy days: And here are two immutable things, the promise and the oath of God, that by these they might have strong consolation. By faith they realize the very things contained in the promise or covenant, and so their interest in it is experimentally witnessed to them. They can say, at such a time when we were in soul-distress, so as all the means in the world could contribute nothing towards inward ease, quiet, and consolation; then, we being enabled by grace to bear the weight of our souls, and our conditions upon the faithfulness of God in his covenant of free promise, we found relief and refreshment. It was not merely our own fancy and imagination, but we were delivered out of our distresses: by faith we were enabled to draw out of the promise the milk of consolation, which it was beyond the power of all creatures to afford us; and thus they find that the covenant or promise is their own.

4. By faith in the free promise, there is a standing; conquerors in Jesus Christ over all spiritual enemies. It is a great matter of the covenant, that the seed of the woman should break the serpent's head, Gen. iii. 15. And, therefore, there is (through grace) a vanquishing all the enemies of salvation, sin, and Satan, through the blessed seed, the Lord Jesus. The promises are accomplished within the soul; but the way is—Ephes. vi. 16. *Above all, take the shield of faith.*

That not only is best for discerning Satan in all his stratagems, but for the withstanding of him also, John v.

4. *This is the victory that overcometh the world, even our faith.* When the soul has combats, or spiritual conflicts, and reason is foiled, cannot bear up, then faith appears as victorious, not in its own strength, but in the strength of Christ and his conquest, which it makes use of in these encounters. And thus conquering acts of faith, as before venturing, relieving, and discovering acts, are useful for witnessing interest in the covenant.

I might show that faith has other acts: as, acts of assurance, drawing up conclusions; he has *loved me, and given himself for me,* Gal. ii. 20. But I have said enough to show that it giveth a knowledge of being within the new covenant.

CHAPTER XIII.

Of the Use of Absolute Promises.

THE question will now be, What use is there of absolute, better promises? When, or in what cases, are they to be made use of?

Answer 1. They are of use for the manifestation of the riches of divine grace and love to sinners. If there may be some grace in promising great blessings upon a very small condition, certainly there must be more grace and love in promising the same absolutely, without any condition, This magnifies the Lord in his owning Israel above all people, that he *loved because he would love,* Deut. vii. 6-8. Not because they were greater, or more lovely than others, or had any beauty or comeliness in them, but for his own sake, as is often intimated. Absolute promises are high expressions of divine love, as Heb. viii. 10-12. They proclaim *rich mercy and great love,* Eph. ii. 4, 5. That the Lord should break through all unworthiness and undeservings, this may work into the greatest self-emptiness and self-abasement. The Lord peremptorily promised the establishing of David's throne for ever, 2 Sam. vii. 13, 16.; and this grace melts his heart into a deep sense of his own nothingness, verses 18, 19. *Who am I, O Lord God; and what is my house?* &c. *Thou hast spoken also of thy servant's house for a great while to come; and is this the manner of man, O Lord God?*

So that absolute promises of divine grace are of great efficacy to render deeply humbled and abased; and he breaks forth into admiration of God on this account, verse 22. *Wherefore thou art great, O Lord, for there is none like* thee. And as the absoluteness of the promises sets forth the excellence of the new covenant above the old; and the gloriousness of this dispensation above any that was preceding: so it may help against that temptation to live in the spirit of the old covenant, and it is mentioned in the epistle to the Hebrews for this purpose.

2. They are of use in the impartation or communication of first grace unto the souls of men: their first interest therein, is by the efficacious operations of the spirit in absolute promises. These are called, by some, promises of grace, which presuppose a being without it, thus Heb. viii. 10-12. Immediately before writing the law in the heart, another law of sin was found in its power there. The moment before the Lord's becoming their God, they were without God in the world (Eph. ii. 12.) The instant before the remission of sin, the guilt of it was found there. All first grace is comprised under these promises; so that the bringing souls over to a first close with Jesus Christ, is by an absolute promise. Though they may have their eyes upon those called conditional promises in conversion, yet if ever they arrive at any drachm* of especial grace, it is in an absolute way; it is the fruit, the result, and issue of an absolute promise: for, as all first grace is contained therein, so, till that be accomplished upon them, no qualifications or conditions are wrought in their souls, altering their state, or which are acceptable and pleasing unto God. The instant before quickening, souls were *dead in trespasses and sins,* Eph. ii. 4. Immediately before reconciliation; they stood at enmity against the Lord, Col. i. 21. The moment before sanctification, they were under sin and pollution. It is groundlessly, therefore, that any souls stand off from Jesus Christ and the free promise, upon the account of a want of any qualifications; they

---

* A weight or measure formally used by apothecaries, one eighth of an ounce, thus a minute quantity.

THE COVENANT OF GRACE 237

should rather immediately close with him therein, as the way to gracious qualifications which are derived to them through the absolute promise. The Lord is a free agent, may work how he pleases; but has not warranted any souls to stay one moment before closing with Jesus Christ, upon the want of any qualification, or upon any account whatsoever. Indeed if he had, then he must testify his allowance of their persisting so long in unbelief; whereas that is hateful and abominable to him.

3. They are of use as a provocation to seek, and a direction where to find, all supplies of grace wanted. Other promises may refer to some particular state or condition; but there are absolute promises that are of general use, whatever the condition or complaint be, Heb. viii; 10-12. As first grace is promised there, so all after degrees of it, in that of writing the law in the heart. As first interest in God is promised, in that of his being their God, so all after communion with him is included in it. As first justification is promised, in his remembering sin no more, so all after remission of sin that is afforded to those in covenant with him. So that absolute promises are useful at all times; when souls are ready to say, what have we to do with other promises, there is enough in these to help and succour in all cases, when souls are at the greatest loss, and cannot find other promises mentioning their particular conditions. To be sure, they must either want some grace, or fellowship with God, or pardon of sin. And the absolute promises extend and reach to all these; that they are a standing relief, bread that will never fail, waters that are for ever sure; all is laid up here that souls can, on good grounds, desire at the hands of God. And, being absolute, they are free promises, no discouragement laid in the way of souls closing with them. Often men do ungroundedly take discouragement for meddling with other promises, because they cannot see that they have the qualifications which they are annexed to; but, to be sure, those that are

absolute, do not presuppose any such qualifications as necessarily antecedently to the closing with them; but they promise all gracious qualifications that souls have the deepest sense of the want of. Whatever grace or degree of it they want, it is here; they are directed to turn in hither. No ground to stand off from these one moment upon the account of a want of humiliation, &c. but the rather should they have recourse here for it, and for first grace when they seem to be without it, for evangelical sorrow, and all spiritual frames of heart desirable. When there is nothing discerned as the qualification but sinfulness, then they had the more need look to, and fasten upon, the Lord in absolute promises, that all desirable qualifications may be wrought within them. How should they obtain these, but by looking to the free promise? The absolute promises are theirs, so far as to make use of them, and venture upon the Lord in them, for the obtainment of grace wanted; though they cannot claim an interest so as to conclude a good estate thence, or that grace is enjoyed, before a powerful application of them.

4. They are useful for the strengthening against, and supporting under, all temptations that gracious souls can be attended with. If it be suggested that the promise is none of theirs, they have nothing to do to meddle with it. Here is enough to answer, possibly other promises may be theirs, though at present they cannot discern it: there are such cloudings, as all experiences, all qualifications may be out of sight; they may thus *sit in darkness and see no light,* and yet may be children of light, Isa. 1. 10. But, however, though they cannot claim any promise so as to conclude interest in salvation and eternal life thence, yet they may so far as to seek an interest therein. The absolute promise is theirs in the offer of it, if they should yet be without the special grace offered therein. All, where the gospel cometh, have so far a right and title to the absolute promise, as it is their duty to fasten upon it, for

the begetting all gracious qualifications that they seem to be or are without, else they could not be blamed, condemned, and punished for unbelief, as many are, Mark xvi. 16. John iii. 18. Rom. xi. 20.

If the temptation be, that it would be presumption to meddle with the promise, which is none of yours, it is answered, you are to look to the Lord in the absolute promise, that it may be yours, that grace may be yours, that God may be your God, that pardon of sin may be yours; though you cannot discern at present that these are yours.

Such a looking to the promise, as thence to take encouragement to indulge itself, or persist in sin, this indeed is presumption; but a cordial looking to the Lord in, and venturing to take hold of, the absolute promises, for the gaining a freedom from sin, and every gracious frame; this is duty, and the neglecting of it is presumption, as being a standing out against a divine call.

There is a ground for putting forth direct acts of faith upon the Lord in the absolute promise, for all grace wanted. When there is not a present discerning by a reflexive act, that gracious qualifications are enjoyed, yet there may be an out-going of heart in the promise to God in Jesus Christ for them, or that they may be afforded. It is a great mistake to think that we are to exercise faith upon the Lord in the promise, only upon a sight of a condition in ourselves; this were to ground our faith rather upon something of our own, than upon the Lord in his free promise; it were to subject the absolute promises, and make them depend upon those that are called conditional, as to their efficacy and usefulness, whereas the truth lies the contrary way: For, the new covenant is, as it were, the fountain of all the promises to us, and that runs altogether upon absolute promises; and, therefore, those which are called conditional promises, being streams flowing thence, and branches of that tree, they must be reducible to, and partake of, the nature of the new covenant, and so are really absolute in themselves; only, as a quickening means to our seeking after the blessings of them, they are represented sometimes as if they were dispensed out in a conditional way. But the Lord doth not confine himself to that way: for, when Israel was destitute of commendable qualifications, had failed in the worship of God, and wearied him with their sins, yet he turned their eye upon an absolute promise, Isa. xliii. 25. *I am he that blotteth out thy transgressions for my name's sake* .

5. They are of use for the evidencing interest in Jesus Christ, and clearing up how the case stands as to their eternal conditions. The Lord can make a saving change (*i.e.* such as has salvation and eternal life infallibly in connection with it) in the opening of any promise, but it is from absolute grace. The begetting of faith, or first grace in the souls of any, is by an absolute promise; for, what condition can there be, in any soul, before first grace, to have a promise annexed to it? It were to frustrate and make void the undertaking of Jesus Christ, to assert, that the Lord has promised eternal life to a work of nature; or that souls are in a state of salvation before union with Jesus Christ, which they must be, if they had any qualification which had salvation certainly promised to it. The Lord says, Ezek. xxxvi. 26. *A new heart also will I give you, and a new spirit will I put within you; and I will take away the stony heart out of your flesh, and I will give you an heart of flesh.* What precedent qualification was here, but stoniness and hardness of heart? and so uncleanness before the sprinkling, verse 25. Here, then, is a promise of first grace, and it is absolute; and the operations of the spirit herein are as supernatural and transcendently glorious as they are evidencing. The word of the gospel cometh in such power, for the accomplishing the very end which the promise is appointed to; and there are such sparklings of divine excellence in the impressions that are made upon the spirits of men thereby, that, without having recourse to any other promises, (which

are called conditional), they may read or see their personal interest in an absolute promise. By its efficacious application, or the fulfilling of it, by their actual enjoyment of what is promised, they may discern their sharing in it. And seeing all gracious qualifications are begotten or first wrought by an absolute promise, why should not that give evidence, as well as the after-sanctified frames?

Besides, the absolute promises are made to some persons, even *to the house of Israel and Judah,* Ezek. xxxvi. 21. to the end, Jer. xxxi. 31.; and, being expressions of the determinate will of God, hence they must needs be evidencing. For, the chief intendment of promises is, to give assurance how the heart of God stands towards persons under them; the Lord is ever speaking to them therein after this manner, *I will be your God, and your sins and iniquities will I remember no more,* Ezek. xxxvi. 28. Heb. viii. 12. This is the natural language of the covenant to them. And, though unbelievers (who are out of covenant) may fancy the same things, and delude themselves, yet this hinders not, but that the Lord may really speak thus to believers, who are undoubtedly under it. So, sometimes the state or condition of a soul is evidenced, by such words or promises as these, Isa. xli. 10. *Be not dismayed, for I am thy God,* Ezek. xxxiv. 31. *I am your God, saith the Lord God.* Isa. xliv. 22. *I have blotted out as a thick cloud thy transgressions, and as a cloud thy sins,* &c.

The divine spirit often makes such a powerful application of such promises, and makes such glorious discoveries of the loving kindness and free grace of God to the soul, as he gives it clearly to understand that God is speaking to it therein; and it is the voice of God, and not of man or of Satan; and thus it is evidencing.

The Lord is so shining upon his own graces, as then a soul usually can discern these; yet it is not merely a reflection upon faith or other graces, that now give the evidence; but faith receives it, as it were, upon a divine testimony.

6. They are of use for the filling souls with consolation in the saddest conditions, and under the most trying dispensations. Jeremiah was sent to prophesy of the Jewish captivity, procured by their sin, for the space of seventy years; yet to keep them from despair and utter despondency, and to comfort them against all their trials, he not only assures them of a return, but prophesies of the new covenant, and its being put into an absolute form, Jer. xxxi. 31. Therefore, the absolute promises are of comforting use against the saddest trials that sin itself may bring us under. The apostle turns their eyes upon those two immutable things, the promise and the oath of God, Heb. vi. 18., as those which the Lord appointed on purpose to usher in strong consolation.

Thus we see, that when the condition of sinners seems most despicable, and when the graces of saints are most out of sight; yet then they may have recourse to the absolute promises, and look unto the Lord therein, for all grace and supply that is wanted.

CHAPTER XIV.

Of those that are called Conditional Promises.

SOME may enquire, What use is there of those called conditional promises? Or, when and in what cases are they to be made use of?

Answer 1. Some of them are of discovering use what an extensiveness there is in divine grace, suitable to all the worst conditions that souls can come into. The conversion of a soul to God, ordinarily, is not without a special discovery of sin, and a lost undone condition by nature, in a gospel glass; yea, a work of evangelical repentance is experienced there. Also, there may be sometimes a common work, a legal conviction of sin, before and without a saving change; but that in the ordinary way of God's dispensation, there is a necessity hereof, on our part, so as if we do not find it, we must stay for it till we have it, may not be looking to Jesus Christ, or meddle with the promise; yes, as if it were presumption to attempt believing, that we may be (as many are) shy of Jesus Christ and the free promise, and stand off from them—this I see no rule yet for. I think the worst of sinners (even insensible ones) are immediately under the invitations and calls of the gospel; for they may be condemned for unbelief, as standing out against them—Mark xvi. 15, 16. Mat. xxii. 3, 4, 9, 10. Rev. iii. 17, 20.

Many scriptures, alleged for the necessity of such preparations before conversion, are mentioned as conditional promises: whereas those are not restrictive, do not restrain the promises to those that are so qualified; but rather declare, that large and suitable supplies are to be had in Jesus Christ, even in such conditions when it seems most unlikely. And of such use are these words, Isa. lv. 1-3. *Ho, everyone that thirsteth, come,* &c. Their thirsting was no desirable qualification; it was for that which did not satisfy, they laboured for that which *was not bread,* verse 2., and yet are invited immediately to come to him, as to one that hath a variety of supplies, water and wine to refresh, milk to nourish, and all offered freely, without money, and without price.

Thus, Mat. xi. 28. *Come unto me, all ye that are weary and heavy laden, and I will give you rest.* Many are ready to think that they should seek to be thus weary, and heavy laden, and till then they may not attempt to come unto Jesus Christ. Whereas it doth not appear that these were any desirable or commendable qualifications to be sought after; but rather are expressions of their sad conditions: and yet here is revealed suitable relief in Jesus Christ. If they be weary and heavy laden (not only by sin, but) with the yoke of the law, (though unduly imposed upon them by the Pharisees), yet coming to Jesus Christ, they might have rest; and so whatever other burden they had sinfully pulled upon themselves. And besides, the promise is not in this or the other text, annexed to thirsting or weariness, but to coming to Jesus Christ.

Thus Jesus Christ is said to be anointed to preach *glad tidings to the meek or the poor,* Isa. lxi. 1. Luke iv. 18., and to *heal the broken-hearted,* not only by a sense of sin, but broken by affliction, and distress, temptations, any way. His scope is not to restrain the promise, as if it did belong only to those that are thus qualified; but, to show that the grace of Jesus Christ reaches and is suitable to those in such deplorable conditions: These are not frames to be sought after, any more than those that follow, of being captives, blind, bruised; but consider men under whatever notion of misery you can, and here is declared, that there are those very supplies to be had in Jesus Christ that are suitable and relative thereunto: as rest for the weary, so sight for

THE COVENANT OF GRACE 245

the blind, deliverance for the captives; and these take in the worst, even insensible sinners—he, by discoveries of his grace, brings them into a due sense of sin.

Thus Mat. v. 3, 4.6. *Blessed are the poor in spirit, and those that mourn,* &c. Not, that these note conditions properly, upon coming up to which they have right to promised blessedness, else not; for, among others, persecution has the blessedness twice annexed to it, ver. 10, 11., and outward poverty is partly intended, Luke vi. 20, 21. as is evident by the antithesis or opposition, ver. 24, 25. *Woe to you rich,* &c. *and you that are full.* Yet, who will say that poverty or persecution are desirable, and to be sought, that we might enjoy the blessedness, by coming under the condition of it? Nor can one say, I am poor, therefore blessed, more than persecuted, therefore blessed. These are not qualifications giving right and title to the promise, and without which they have it not; but these things are spoken to the disciples, ver. 20.: the promises are annexed to discipleship, or to the person in Christ, rather than to his qualification of mourning, &c.; and whereas, they (who before had a right in Christ to all the promises) might be tempted to think themselves unhappy by these things, here is a discovery that the seeming sadness of these conditions, as poverty, persecution, &c. did not exclude from the promised blessedness—there is suitable relief for them in the promise still. Hence, in opposition to these, there are woes denounced against others in the opposite conditions, which, to outward appearance, seemed better, as against the rich, those that are full, &c.

And thus these seeming conditions, instead of being limitations of the promise, they are discoveries of the extensiveness thereof; holding forth supplies and succours for souls in Christ, under their saddest trials and temptations, and in all the various and worst conditions they can come into, though not upon the condition of their coming into them.

The following particulars are to be understood when something of special grace is mentioned, as if it were a condition.

2. Some, called conditional promises, are of declarative use what a high approbation the Lord has of the persons or things concerned in them. Thus, speaking promiscuously to professors, some of whom are sincere, others not, sometimes it is with an *if,* as Heb. iii. 6. *If we hold fast our confidence unto the end.* To note, that perseverance, in holding fast, is a character of sound believers, in opposition to others who do apostatize and fall away. Thus some scriptures contain a description of the persons who shall obtain those blessings of the covenant: they are such as are found believing, repenting, obeying, in opposition to those who are infidels, disobedient, &c. as Heb. v. 9. *He became the author of eternal salvation to them that obey him.* Those that are in a state of salvation, are characterized by such effects as obedience, such words conclude negatively; they that have not these in some degree, are not saved ones: but the promises are made rather to their persons in Christ, than to their qualifications (as believing, obeying), though these are necessary for the persons. As it was incumbent on the great high-priest, even Jesus Christ, (who had the promises made to him), to be holy, harmless, undefiled, yet they are not made to him upon the condition of his holiness, or undefiledness.

Yet I would add, that such promises do testify how acceptable these acts are to the Lord, as being duties commanded by him, though they be not properly conditions upon which covenant mercy is promised to us. Will any say, that nothing is acceptable unless it be performed under the notion of a condition upon which the Lord hath obliged himself to give out mercy? Thus many scriptures that seem to run in a conditional form, are to be understood—as, Col. i. 21-23.; Rom. ii. 7.; they declare his approbation of faith, hope, obedience, &c.

3. They are of exciting and encouraging use to the duty of seeking in an absolute promise those gracious qualifications which the other promises are annexed to. The seemingly conditional expressions are not intended as discouragements, but as powerful provocations and encouragements to that duty, or seeking that grace conjoined with the promise. Whatsoever mercy is mentioned anywhere, either with, or as a condition, is absolutely promised, in the new covenant, Heb. viii. Particularly, the remission of sin is promised there; yet it is said, Mat. vi. 14, 15. *If ye forgive men their trespasses, your heavenly Father will also forgive you,* &c.

Not as if divine pardons were suspended till we have forgiven others; that so long any were unpardoned, and so condemned who before were justified. This were to make divine acts have dependence on our actings; and so to subject (as one says) the Creator to the creature. Our forgiving others is not properly a condition, as if a performance of ours did engage the Lord or lay him under an obligation to forgive us; or, as if we had right and might lay claim to divine remission upon such an act of ours: but, it is expressed in a conditional form, as a pressing argument and a quickening spur to so necessary a duty as the forgiving others, although the Lord has absolute intentions to pardon us, and to cause us to forgive others. Thus many other scriptures are to be understood, as Mat. xviii. 31.; Mark xi. 26.; Luke vi. 37.; thus repenting and blotting out of sins are conjoined, Acts iii. 19. As a father, who is absolutely determined and resolved to afford some great favour to his son, yet may speak of it to him with an *if,* that he may lay an awe upon him towards some duty, which yet is not in the least the condition of his affording it.

4. They are of directive use unto the right way and means of seeking the mercies promised. The eternal decrees of God are not conditional, but absolute and unalterable; yet are not exclusive of all means in order to

their execution in time. So divine promises, which are absolute, without any conditions properly so called, yet are not fulfilled without any means. It is a gross mistake to think, that if there be no condition to be performed by us, then we need not take any care, or trouble ourselves about the matter. For we must know, there are divine commands putting upon the use of means in order to the execution of absolute promises; and those that are called conditional promises are of this use, to declare in what way, and by what means, those great favours shall be derived to us. And men, neglecting to seek mercy in the way of divine appointment; may miss of it; not because they have failed of performing a condition, but have neglected a duty, and, by sinning, provoked God to cut short, Jam. i. 6, 7. Psal. lxxviii. 21, 22.

The promises of first grace are generally granted to be absolute; for, if they did run upon any condition, that must be performed before union with Jesus Christ; yea, that must be seen in the soul before it had a ground to meddle with the promise; and so it should be ascertained of salvation whilst it is in a state of nature. If faith were supposed the condition, that then must be pre-existent in the soul, and discerned also, before it had a ground to believe in the promise that it were the condition of; whereas faith is a grace and is the fruit of a promise, as well as any other graces. Indeed, the promises of first grace (though absolute, yet) seem to be as conditionally propounded as any. Prov. ii. 3-5. Mark xvi. 16. John iii. 16. Herein is held forth the way and means to obtain salvation; for it is propounded and offered indefinitely, to all, elect and not elect; not particularly promised to any, but as it turns into an absolute form to those persons described as the subjects of it.

Thus the Lord gives forth a cluster of absolute promises, Ezek. xxxvi. 25-27, &c. *Then will I sprinkle clean water upon you, and you shall be clean; a new heart also will I give you*, &c.; and yet, ver. 37. *Thus saith the Lord God, I will yet for this be inquired of by the house of Israel to do it for them.* This inquiring is not mentioned properly as a condition, for all was before unalterably determined, but as the way and means to the fruition of what was absolutely promised; and thus, as a means to promised mercies, we may not only believe, but exercise ourselves in other duties, ordinances, and appointments of the Lord Jesus; as, pray that we may be pardoned, justified, saved, that the Lord would *give us a new heart, and put his spirit within us,* &c., though not as conditions giving right to salvation; for no act of ours lays the Lord under an obligation by promise to afford these to us—all is from mere grace and good pleasure. But yet, as a man may have purchased physic that would cure a disease which he labours under, he may have paid for it, and so performed the condition, and hath right to it; yet if he doth not make use of it, he may be uncured. So believers have a right to all, even to those that are called conditional promises, they being in covenant, all are theirs (2 Pet. i. 4. 2 Cor. i. 20.); yet if they do not make use of these, they may come short of mercies promised, not because they fail of a condition, but because they use not the means to the fruition thereof: like men that have a civil and absolute right to great estates, and yet are without the comfort thereof, because they make not use of them.

5. They are of some evidencing use, who the persons are that are interested in the promises. Though other promises are primary, yet these are secondary evidences: when these gracious qualifications can be discerned, they are useful for the confirmation of our interest in eternal mercies. They give a description of the persons, and are so far distinguishing, as, when they are seen, we may measure our estates and conditions by them.

Thus many scriptures speak of those qualifications, not as conditions, giving right; but as declarative evidences of a title to covenant blessings, even to salvation. So Rev. xxii. 14. *Blessed are they that do his commandments, that they may have right to the tree of life.* Not that their keeping of them did give a right and title unto life, for none can duly keep them before believing, and then they have it; but, that their right to it may be evidenced by such good effects. For, these were already in a state of grace, and were before interested in Jesus Christ unto eternal life; on which account, they are opposed to those that are without, ver. 15. *without are dogs,* &c. The use of the tree of life was the confirming in life, Gen. iii. 22, 23.; so, this keeping his commandments (of which believing is chief) is the way to a confirmation in a living state, or to give a further testimony of their right to life. So Jam. ii. 24. *By works a man is justified, and not by faith only.* Not that love or evangelical works come in the least into justification itself, as a cause or condition thereof; the epistles to the Romans and Galatians are full against this; but are the fruits and effects of it. They, as evidences, testify to a man's self, or to others, that he is justified; as, ver. 18. *I will shew thee my faith by my works.* We are, then, not properly, but only declaratively justified by works; they, as precious effects do argue a lively faith, which is a means unto imputed righteousness and justification, not a syllable that it is a condition thereof. So, 1 John i. 9. *If we confess our sins, he is faithful and just to forgive us our sins, and to cleanse us from all unrighteousness.* Not that our confession is properly a condition, engaging the faithfulness and justice of God to forgive, (I proved before, that is not suspended till our confessing); but a way and means to our gaining a sense, a fresh application, an evidence and manifestation of our interest in forgiving grace.

And as evidences, so they may promote comfort; only we are to take heed that we do not ground and bottom our consolation on the qualifications within, but on the promise itself (or the Lord therein) without. Many are drawing and fetching their comfort from their faith and other graces, and lay the stress of it there; and, accordingly, are up and down, ebbing and flowing therein, instead of fetching it from the Lord in the promise, an immutable thing, Heb. vi. 18., by the means of faith; and taking that and other graces only as evidences of interest in it. Some, because they are weary and heavy laden; thence take their rest and refreshment, whereas they are called out of themselves, to come for it to Jesus Christ, Mat. xi. 28. When qualifications lie most dark, or are most clearly discerned, yet we should not look so much to these, as to Jesus Christ in the promise, for consolation.

Thus I have endeavoured to open the nature of the old and new covenant.

As to the mediatorial office of Jesus Christ, it is largely handled by others, and so shall not be insisted upon by me at present. Only I would say thus much, when Jesus Christ was upon earth, he performed the office of a mediator, as to satisfaction; and now he is in heaven, he doth it still as to intercession, Heb. vii. 25. He presents his obedience continually to the Father for our obtaining what he has purchased. Would we have any fæderal blessings, the law written in our heart in more lively characters, the Lord witnessed more fully to be our God, or sin to be pardoned? Let our faith be acting upon him as one that mediates for our obtaining all; for he is the Mediator, not of the old, but of the new and better testament, which is established upon better promises.

THE END.

www.ingramcontent.com/pod-product-compliance
Lightning Source LLC
Chambersburg PA
CBHW071428150426
43191CB00008B/1081